30일만에 끝내는
토텝
영숙어
900

30일 만에 끝내는
토텝 영숙어 900

저 자 FL4U컨텐츠
발행인 고본화
발 행 반석출판사
2025년 1월 15일 개정 2쇄 인쇄
2025년 1월 20일 개정 2쇄 발행
반석출판사 | www.bansok.co.kr
이메일 | bansok@bansok.co.kr
블로그 | blog.naver.com/bansokbooks

07547 서울시 강서구 양천로 583, B동 1007호
(서울시 강서구 염창동 240-21번지 우림블루나인 비즈니스센터 B동 1007호)
대표전화 02) 2093-3399   팩 스 02) 2093-3393
출 판 부 02) 2093-3395   영업부 02) 2093-3396
등록번호 제315-2008-000033호

Copyright ⓒ FL4U컨텐츠

ISBN 978-89-7172-987-8 (13740)

30일만에 끝내는 토텝

영숙어

900

반석출판사

숙어는 영어의 독특한 맛을 내기도 하지만 학습자에게 무거운 짐을 지게 하기도 한다.

　단어나 문법을 잘 알아도 숙어를 모르면 영어 정복에 한 걸음도 나아갈 수 없다. 왜냐하면 원어민은 쉬운 단어로 이루어진 쉬운 표현인 idiom을 즐겨 사용하기 때문이다.

　그래서 문어체로만 쓰이는 어려운 단어는 Vocabulary 책을 보고 외워 어렵지 않지만, 오히려 쉬운 단어 몇 개로 이루어진 숙어표현은 문맥으로 짐작하려 해도 잘 되지 않는다.

　숙어라는 존재는 단어와 문장의 중간에 위치하고 있다. 영어를 공부하는 데 가장 기본적인 요소는 역시 단어다. 몇 개의 단어가 모여 숙어를 이루고 단어와 숙어가 모여 문장을 이루는 것이다. 숙어는 또 단어의 약점을 보충해 주는 역할을 한다. 수많은 의미 단위를 모두 단어로만 채운다면 영어 학습자에게는 더 힘겨울 것이다. 익숙한 단어 몇 개가 모여 새로운 의미를 형성하는 숙어의 묘미를 알고 나면 영어 정복은 그만큼 가까워진다.

　본 서에는 영어를 읽고 구사하는 데 필요한 900개의 필수 숙어와 2,000개의 각종 시험 대비 기출 숙어가 실려 있다. 필수 숙어는 모두 Q&A의 짧은 대화로 이루어진 상황에 들어 있으므로 학습내용을 기억하기 쉬울 것이다. 그리고 토플, 토익이나 여타 시험에 자주 출제된 문제를 수록하여 새로운 어휘를 확장할 수 있도록 편집했다.

　독자님들이 아무쪼록 본 서를 디딤돌로 삼아 영어에 자신감을 가지게 되시기를 바란다.

FL4U컨텐츠

이 책의 활용법

단어를 외우는 것은 지겨운 일이기도 하지만 단기간에 끝낼 수 없는 영어 실력이라는 건축의 기초 작업을 세우는 일입니다. 요즘은 웹사이트에서 영어사전을 제공하기도 하지만 편리하게 단어 검색을 하면 그만큼 쉽게 단어가 기억의 창고에서 사라지고 맙니다. 단어를 외울 때는 고생을 하며 외워 봅시다.

1 큰 소리로 읽는다.
소리 내어 읽으면 쉽게 외워집니다. 노래를 외울 때처럼 소리 내어 발음하면 쉽게 외워지므로 열 번, 스무 번 정도 읽어 봅시다.

2 사전으로 찾아본다.
단어의 의미를 모를 때 무슨 뜻일까 생각하면서 사전을 뒤져거립니다. 알파벳 순서를 생각하면서 앞으로 넘겼다가 뒤로 넘기는 과정을 통해 외워집니다.

3 mp3로 학습한 부분을 듣는다.
청취력을 겸하여 입체감 있게 학습을 하면 기억에 오래 남아 내 것이 됩니다.

4 해당 단어가 들어 있는 재미있는 문장을 읽는다.
이렇게 하면 기억에 오래 남습니다. 그 문장이 단서로 남아 기억을 도와줍니다. 영화에서 멋진 배우가 그 단어를 발음하는 걸 듣는다면 잊을 수가 없겠지요.

5 손으로 적어 본다.
전통적인 방법이지만 손과 뇌의 기능이 연결되어 있으므로 손의 작업을 통해 머릿속에 쉽게 기억됩니다.

목차

목차

목차

PART 1

30일에 끝내는
Essential Idiom
900

1st Day

001 a piece of cake

:: 식은 죽 먹기

↳ something very easy to do

Q Was the exam difficult?
그 시험 어려웠니?

A No, it was a piece of cake.
아니, 식은 죽 먹기였어.

002 blow a fuse

:: 노발대발하다

↳ get very angry

Q Did your mother get angry when she saw your report card?
네 어머니가 성적표를 보고 화내셨니?

A Yes, she blew a fuse.
그래, 노발대발하셨어.

003 mind one's own business

:: 당신 일에나 신경 쓰시오! 남의 일에 참견 마시오!

↳ don't interfere in one's affairs

Q May I ask what your salary is?
당신 봉급이 얼마인지 물어도 됩니까?

A No! Mind your own business!
안 됩니다! 남의 일에 참견 마세요!

004 not on your life
:: 결코 안 하겠다

↳ never, ever

Q Will you marry me?
나와 결혼하시겠소?

A No, not on your life!
아뇨, 결코 안 하겠어요!

005 pick up the tab
:: 지불하다

↳ pay the bill

Q Are you paying for lunch today?
오늘 점심 값은 네가 낼래?

A No, it's your turn to pick up the tab.
아니, 요금을 내는 것은 네 차례야.

006 peter out
:: 용두사미로 끝나다

↳ end small after a big and impressive beginning

Q Was the anti-smoking campaign a success?
금연운동은 성공했습니까?

A No, it petered out after about three weeks.
아뇨, 3주 후 용두사미로 끝났습니다.

007 look down one's nose at
:: 얕잡아보다

↳ treat with disrespect, despise

Q Does he admire rock 'n' roll musicians?
그는 록 가수를 존경합니까?

A No, he looks down his nose at them.
아뇨, 그는 그들을 깔봐요.

008 in hot water
:: 궁지에 처한

↳ in big trouble

Q Are you in big trouble with your husband again?
네 남편과 또 불화 중이니?

A Yes, I'm in hot water because I got into another traffic accident.
그래, 내가 교통사고를 당해서 몹시 난처한 상태에 빠졌어.

009 get cold feet
:: 용기(배짱)를 잃다

↳ nervous about doing something because of fear of failure

Q Did you find the courage to ask her out for a date?
그녀에게 데이트를 신청할 용기가 생겼니?

A No, I got cold feet right after I picked up the phone to call her.
아니, 수화기를 집어들자 곧 용기를 잃었어.

010 call off
:: 취소하다

↳ stop from happening

Q Was the baseball game cancelled?
야구 경기가 취소됐니?

A Yes, it was called off because of rain.
그래, 비 때문에 취소됐어.

011 out of order
:: 고장난

↳ not working properly

Q Have they fixed the vending machine yet?
그들은 벌써 자판기를 고쳤니?

A No, it's still out of order.
아냐, 아직도 고장 상태야.

012 keep one's shirt on   :: 침착하다

↪ try to be calm and patient

Q Can't you get ready and faster?
좀 더 빨리 준비할 수 없니?

A No, so keep your shirt on!
없어, 그러니 침착하라구!

013 on the house   :: 주인이 공짜로 내는

↪ provided free of charge by the owner

Q You mean we don't have to pay for our cocktails?
우리가 칵테일 값을 낼 필요가 없다는 뜻이니?

A Yes, the bartender said they were on the house.
그래, 주인이 공짜로 내는 것이라고 바텐더가 말했어.

014 from one's point of view   :: ~의 의견으로는

↪ in one's opinion

Q Is she a good teacher?
그녀는 훌륭한 선생님이니?

A No, from my point of view she's terrible.
아니, 내 의견으로는 형편없어.

015 run out of   :: 다 떨어지다

↪ have no more left

Q Do you have any sugar I could borrow?
내가 빌릴 수 있는 설탕 좀 있니?

A No, sorry but I ran out of it this morning.
없어, 미안하지만 오늘 아침에 다 떨어졌어.

016 **for the time being** :: 당분간

↪ for the present

> Q Have you found an apartment yet?
> 벌써 아파트를 찾았니?

> A No, so for the time being I'll have to stay with my aunt.
> 아니, 그래서 당분간 아주머니와 함께 있어야 해.

017 **turn over a new leaf** :: 심기일전하다

↪ stop behaving in a bad way

> Q Have you really stopped smoking and drinking?
> 너 정말로 담배와 술을 끊었니?

> A Yes, I've turned over a new leaf and started to watch my health.
> 그래, 마음을 고쳐먹고 건강을 돌보기 시작했어.

018 **pass on** :: 전달하다

↪ deliver to

> Q Did you give him the report yourself?
> 너 자신이 그 보고서를 그에게 주었니?

> A No, I passed it on to his secretary.
> 아니, 그의 비서에게 전했어.

019 **look after** :: 돌보다

↪ take care of

> Q Are you going to work during summer vacation?
> 여름 휴가 중 일할 거니?

> A Yes, I'm going to look after my neighbor's two children.
> 그래, 이웃집 애들 2명을 돌볼 거야.

020 **in other words** :: 다른 말로 하면, 환언하면

↳ to say it differently

Q Did you say you won't be home for dinner?
너 오늘 저녁 집에서 밥을 못 먹을 거라고 했니?

A Yes. In other words, I have to work late tonight.
그래. 달리 말해서, 밤늦게까지 일해야 돼.

021 **make ends meet** :: 수지를 맞추다, 예산을 맞추다

↳ balance the budget

Q Are you and your wife going to have another child?
너희 부부는 아기를 또 가질 거야?

A No, because we can't even make ends meet with only one child.
아니, 아기 하나만으로도 감당할 수 없는 걸.

022 **catch a cold** :: 감기 걸리다

↳ get sick with a cold

Q Did you get sick over the weekend?
주말에 아팠니?

A Yes, I caught a cold.
그래, 감기 걸렸어.

023 **get in touch with** :: 연락하다

↳ contact

Q Will you write or call me as soon as you arrive in Rome?
로마에 도착하자마자 편지하거나 전화해 줄래?

A Yes, I'll get in touch with you the minute I get off the plane.
그러지. 비행기에서 내리자마자 연락할게.

024 take one's breath away

:: 기막히게(놀라게) 하다

↳ amaze

Q Wasn't that a wonderful rainbow we saw yesterday?
어제 우리가 본 무지개 멋지지 않았니?

A Yes, it really took my breath away.
응, 정말로 기막혔어.

025 tear up

:: 찢다

↳ rip into pieces

Q Are you going to keep all your old love letters?
너 옛날 연애편지 모두 간직할거니?

A No, I'm going to tear them up and then burn them.
아니, 모두 찢어서 태워버릴 거야.

026 on purpose

:: 고의로

↳ intentionally

Q Did you really step on that old lady's foot?
너 정말로 저 연로한 여성의 발을 밟았니?

A Yes, but I didn't do it on purpose.
그래, 하지만 고의로 그런 건 아냐.

027 at any rate

:: 여하튼, 하여간

↳ any how

Q Is the used car you just bought in good condition?
네가 방금 산 중고차는 괜찮니?

A No, but at any rate I didn't have to pay much for it.
아니, 그러나 여하튼 돈을 많이 줄 필요가 없었어.

028 cut back on
:: 줄이다, 감축하다

↪ reduce

Q Will you be able to save enough to buy your own house someday?
언젠가는 네 집을 살 수 있을 만큼 충분히 저축할 수 있니?

A Yes, but only if I cut back on unnecessary expenses.
응, 하지만 불필요한 경비를 줄여야만 하지.

029 tell apart
:: 구분(구별)하다

↪ distinguish

Q Are they twins?
그들은 쌍둥이니?

A Yes, and I can hardly tell them apart.
그래, 그래서 난 거의 구별할 수 없어.

030 run over
:: (차가) 치다

↪ hit (while driving a vehicle)

Q Did you hear that? It sounded like breaking glass.
저 소리 들었니? 유리 깨지는 소리 같았는데.

A Yes, our car just ran over a bottle.
그래, 우리 차가 병을 치고 지나갔어.

영숙어 문제 단번에 공략하기

001. Geysers have often been compared to volcanoes _____ they both emit hot liquids from below the Earth's surface.

(A) due to   (B) because
(C) in spite of   (D) regardless of

> 어휘 **geyser** 간헐천(間歇泉) / **emit** 방출하다, 분출하다 / **due to** ~때문에(because of, owing to) / **in spite of** ~에도 불구하고(despite) / **regardless of** ~에 상관없이
>
> 해석 간헐천은 흔히 화산에 비유되곤 하는데, 둘 다 지표면 아래에서 뜨거운 액체를 분출시키기 때문이다.

---

002. You should try to _____ yourself with the facts before you express an opinion.

(A) familiar   (B) inform
(C) acquaint   (D) apprise

> 어휘 **acquaint oneself with** ~에 대해 잘 알다 / **familiarize oneself with** (= be familiar with) ~에 정통하다, 익숙하다 / **apprise** 통고하다, 알리다
>
> 해석 의견을 표명하기 전에 사실을 잘 알도록 노력해야 한다.

---

003. They had a terrible quarrel, but later <u>became reconciled</u>.

(A) made out   (B) made over
(C) made up   (D) made with

> 어휘 **reconcile** 화해시키다 / **make out** 성취하다, 이해하다 **make over** 양도하다 / **make up** 화해하다 / **make with** ~을 만들어 보이다
>
> 해석 그들은 심하게 다퉜지만, 나중에 화해했다.

004. During nuclear fission, uranium atoms <u>disintegrate</u> into lighter elements.

(A) dry up
(B) speed up
(C) break up
(D) heat up

어휘 **fission** (핵)분열 / **disintegrate** 분해되다, 붕괴되다 / **dry up** 바짝 마르다
speed up 속도를 높이다 / **break up** 분해하다, 해체하다 / **heat up** 가열하다

해석 핵이 분열되는 동안 우라늄 원자들은 더 작은 입자들로 분해된다.

---

005. <u>In the midst of</u> the Civil War, Abraham Lincoln signed a bill for the founding of Yosemite National Park.

(A) Before
(B) At the start of
(C) During
(D) At the end of

어휘 **in the midst of** 한창 ~중에 / **the Civil War** 미국의 남북전쟁 / **bill** 법안

해석 남북전쟁이 한창 진행중일 때, 에이브러햄 링컨은 Yosemite 국립공원을 설립하는 법안에 서명했다.

---

006. Fish oil mainly <u>consists</u> of unsaturated fats which can be margarine.

(A) is in need
(B) is made up
(C) is indicative
(D) is in place

어휘 **fish oil** 어유(魚油) / **unsaturated** 불포화의 / **consist of** ~로 구성되다(be made up of) / **be in need of** ~이 필요하다 / **be indicative of** ~을 나타내다 / **in place of** ~대신에

해석 어유(魚油)는 주로 마가린을 만드는 불포화 지방질로 구성된다.

2nd Day

---

031 **as a rule** :: 대체로, 일반적으로

↳ generally

Q Do you exercise every morning?
너 매일 아침 운동하니?

A Yes, as a rule I jog about 3 miles a day.
그래, 대체로 하루 약 3마일을 조깅해.

---

032 **all thumbs** :: 아주 서툰

↳ unskillful

Q Is your husband good at fixing broken furniture?
네 남편은 부서진 가구를 잘 고치니?

A No, he's all thumbs when it comes to such things.
아니, 그런 일에는 아주 서툴러.

---

033 **run into** :: 우연히 만나다

↳ meet by chance

Q Have you seen him lately?
그를 최근에 보았니?

A Yes, I ran into him downtown yesterday.
그래, 어제 시내에서 우연히 만났어.

034 fall in love with

:: 사랑에 빠지다

↳ start to like romantically

Q Does Joe have a new girlfriend?
Joe에게 새 여자친구가 있니?

A Yes, he's fallen in love with one of the secretaries.
그래, 비서 한 명과 사랑에 빠졌어.

Day

02

035 on the rocks

:: 파산(파멸) 직전인

↳ near collapse

Q Did she hire a divorce lawyer?
그녀가 이혼 변호사를 고용했습니까?

A Yes, so I guess her marriage is now on the rocks.
예, 그녀의 결혼은 거의 파경 상태 같아요.

036 throw up

:: 토하다

↳ vomit

Q Is this the first time you've ever eaten raw octopus?
산낙지를 먹어 보는 것이 처음이니?

A Yes, and I think I'm going to throw up.
그래, 그래서 토할 것 같아.

037 feel like a fish out of water :: 어색하다, 서먹서먹하다

↳ feel uncomfortable and nervous

Q Do you feel uncomfortable in this disco?
이 디스코장이 불편하니?

A Yes, I feel like a fish out of water around all these young people.
응, 젊은이들뿐이니 어색하다구.

038 call it a day

:: 오늘은 그만하다

↳ finish for the day

Q Shall we study one more chapter?
1장 더 공부할까요?

A No, let's call it a day.
아뇨, 오늘은 그만해요.

039 go fifty-fifty

:: 절반으로 (똑같이) 나누다

↳ divide equally

Q Shall we divide the prize money equally?
그 상금을 똑같이 나눌까요?

A Yes, let's go fifty-fifty.
예, 반반으로 해요.

040 make a beeline for

:: 직행하다

↳ go straight toward

Q Did you go somewhere else after the party late last night?
어젯밤 늦게 파티가 끝난 후 다른 곳에 갔니?

A No, I made a beeline for home.
아니, 집으로 직행했어.

041 pull one's leg

:: 놀리다, 농담하다

↳ tease

Q Did I ever tell you that I once won an Olympic gold medal?
내가 올림픽 금메달을 땄다고 말했지?

A No, and I think you're just trying to pull my leg.
아니, 나를 놀리려는 거겠지.

042 hold one's tongue

:: 닥치다, 잠자코 있다

↳ shut up

Q Did you make another stupid mistake?
너 또 미련한 실수를 했구나?

A Yes, but you'd better hold your tongue or I might get angry!
그래, 하지만 너 잠자코 있는 게 좋아. 그렇지 않으면 화낼지도 몰라!

043 little by little

:: 조금씩

↳ gradually

Q Is your English getting better these days?
요즘 네 영어실력은 좋아지니?

A Yes, it's improving little by little.
그럼, 조금씩 향상되고 있어.

044 all day long

:: 하루종일

↳ from morning till night

Q Were you in the library yesterday?
어제 도서관에 갔었니?

A Yes, I was there all day long.
응, 하루종일 거기 있었어.

045 step down

:: 물러나다, 사퇴하다

↳ resign

Q Is he going to resign soon?
그는 곧 사임할 거니?

A Yes, he'll probably step down before August.
그래, 아마 8월 전에 물러날 거야.

046 **get even with** :: 앙갚음하다, 복수하다

↳ take revenge on

Q Is she now treating him the way he used to treat her?
그녀는 지금 그가 그녀에게 하던 대로 그를 대하고 있지?

A Yes, she's finally getting even with him.
그래, 그녀는 마침내 그에게 앙갚음을 하고 있어.

047 **cheer up** :: 격려하다, 위로하다

↳ make happy

Q Is she still in the hospital?
그녀는 아직도 병원에 있니?

A Yes, so let's go there and cheer her up with some flowers.
그래, 그러니까 꽃을 사가지고 병원에 가서 그녀를 위로하자.

048 **take apart** :: 분해하다

↳ disassemble

Q Will it take you a long time to fix my radio?
내 라디오 고치는 데 오래 걸리니?

A Yes, because I'll have to take it all apart and look inside.
그래, 그것을 모두 분해해서 속을 들여다봐야 하니까 말이야.

049 **put on weight** :: 뚱뚱해지다, 살찌다

↳ get fatter

Q Are you going to go on a diet?
너 다이어트 할거니?

A Yes, I've been putting on too much weight these days.
그래, 요즘 너무 뚱뚱해졌어.

050 tear down
:: 헐다, 부수다

↳ demolish

Q Did the city demolish the old apartment building where you used to live?
시에서 네가 살던 아파트를 철거했니?

A Yes, it tore it down a few years ago.
그래, 몇 년 전에 헐었어.

051 as a matter of fact
:: 사실은

↳ actually

Q Did you see their new baby?
너 그들의 새 아기 봤니?

A Yes, as a matter of fact I saw him yesterday.
그래 사실은 어제 그를 봤어.

052 take into account
:: 고려하다

↳ consider

Q Do you think the judge will consider the fact that the thief is only 19?
그 도둑이 겨우 19살이라는 사실을 판사가 고려할 것 같니?

A Yes, I'm sure he'll take that into account when he sentences him.
응, 판사가 선고할 때 그것을 고려할 것이 틀림없어.

053 point out
:: 지적하다

↳ indicate

Q Should I tell him to wear a necktie to his job interview?
면접시험에 넥타이를 매고 가라고 그에게 말할까?

A Yes, and point out that first impressions are very important.
응, 그리고 첫 인상이 매우 중요하다고 지적해 줘.

054 **take turns** :: 교대하다

↳ alternate

Q Do you want to drive the entire distance to Chicago?
시카고까지 혼자 운전하고 싶니?

A No, let's take turns driving every 100 miles.
아니, 100마일마다 교대하자구.

055 **throw the book at** :: 엄벌하다

↳ punish severely

Q Did the judge give him the maximum punishment?
판사가 그에게 중벌을 내렸니?

A Yes, he really threw the book at him — 25 years in prison.
그래, 정말로 엄벌에 처했어. 25년 징역형을 내렸거든.

056 **save one's breath** :: 입을 다물고 있다

↳ do not waste one's time talking about it

Q Do you think he'll help me if I ask him?
그에게 요청하면 그가 나를 도와줄 것 같니?

A No, so save your breath.
아니, 그러니까 입 다물고 있어.

057 **make sure** :: 확실히 하다

↳ be certain

Q Is there anything else you want me to do tonight, Boss?
사장님, 오늘 밤 제가 하기를 바라시는 게 뭐 또 있습니까?

A Yes, make sure all the computers are turned off before you go home.
있지, 퇴근 전 모든 컴퓨터를 껐나 꼭 확인하게.

058 ## in the red   :: 적자인

↳ operating at a loss

Q Did your company do well last year?
네 회사는 지난해 잘 됐니?

A No, we were in the red most of the time.
아니, 거의 일년 내내 적자였어.

059 ## in the black   :: 흑자인

↳ operating at a profit

Q Did your company earn a profit last month?
네 회사는 지난달 이윤을 보았니?

A Yes, we were in the black for the first time this year.
그래, 금년 처음 흑자였어.

060 ## bump into   :: 우연히 만나다

↳ meet by chance

Q Did anything interesting happen to you when you went downtown today?
오늘 시내에 갔을 때 뭐 재미있는 일이 있었니?

A Yes, I bumped into one of my old high school friends.
그럼, 고등학교 친구 한 명을 우연히 만났지.

영숙어 문제 단번에 공략하기

007. Provocation will often cause an animal to attack an object not necessarily <u>associated</u> with the source of irritation.

(A) connected   (B) compared
(C) confronted   (D) confused

어휘 **provocation** 도발, 자극 / **irritation** 초조, 성냄 / **confront** ~에 직면하다 / **confuse** 혼란시키다

해석 동물을 자극하면 때때로 화를 내게 만든 원인과 그다지 관계없는 대상을 공격하도록 만들게 될 것이다.

- -

008. Some doubt has been _____ on the reliability of the witness' statement.

(A) shown   (B) offered
(C) cast   (D) indicated

어휘 **cast[throw] doubt on** ~에 의문을 제기하다 / **reliability** 신뢰도, 확실성

해석 그 증인의 진술에 대한 신빙성에 의문이 제기되어 왔다.

- -

009. Heavy income taxes, which exert a stranglehold on the economy, have _____ sources of new investment capital.

(A) swallowed up   (B) crippled
(C) choked off   (D) tied up

어휘 **exert** (힘을) 쓰다 / **stranglehold** 활동을 저해하는 것 / **swallow up** 들이키다 / **cripple** 절름거리게 하다, 무력하게 하다 / **tie up** 매매할 수 없게 조건을 달다 / **choke off** (계획 등을) 포기하게 하다

해석 과중한 소득세는 경제 활동을 위축시켜 신규 자본 투자의 통로를 막아버렸다.

010. The snake slowly _____ itself around the branch of the tree.

(A) circulated   (B) hinged

(C) focused   (D) coiled

어휘 circulate 빙빙 돌다 / hinge 경첩을 달다 / coil oneself around ~에 똬리를 감다

해석 뱀은 천천히 나뭇가지를 휘감았다.

---

011. Steam _____ to water when it comes into contact with a surface.

(A) reflects   (B) condenses

(C) detects   (D) constitutes

어휘 condense (in)to 응축하여 ~가 되다 / detect 발견하나, 간파하나

해석 수증기는 지표면에 닿으면 물로 응결된다.

---

012. The Athenians charged Socrates with corrupting the youth and he was _____ to death by a jury of five hundred citizens.

(A) faced   (B) blamed

(C) invoked   (D) condemned

어휘 charge A with B A에게 B의 죄를 묻다 / corrupt 타락시키다 / jury 배심, 심사 위원회 / invoke 법령을 발하다 / condemn A to B A에게 B를 선고하다

해석 아테네인들은 소크라테스에게 젊은이들을 타락시킨 죄를 물어서 소크라테스는 500명의 시민들로 구성된 배심원단에게 사형 선고를 받았다

Answers ★ 7.(A) 8.(C) 9.(C) 10.(D) 11.(B) 12.(D)

29

3rd Day

061 **all ears**
:: 열심히 듣는, 몹시 듣고 싶은

↳ listening attentively

Q Do you want to hear some interesting gossip?
재미있는 가십을 듣고 싶니?

A Yes, I'm all ears!
응, 아주 듣고 싶은데

062 **in a nutshell**
:: 요컨대, 한마디로 하면

↳ briefly

Q Could you briefly describe his personality?
간단히 그의 인품을 설명할 수 있니?

A Yes, in a nutshell, he's generous and hardworking.
그러지, 한마디로 그는 관대하고 열심히 일해.

063 **never mind!**
:: 걱정마!

↳ forget it!

Q Did you just say something to me?
너 내게 뭔가 말했지?

A Yes, but never mind, it wasn't important.
그래, 하지만 걱정 마. 중요한 게 아니었으니까.

064 **short of**　　　　　　　　　　　　　　　　　　　　:: 부족한

　↳ lacking

　　Q　Can you lend me $50?
　　　　나한테 50달러 빌려줄 수 있겠니?

　　A　No, because I'm a little short of money this month.
　　　　안돼, 이 달에는 돈이 약간 부족해서 말이야.

065 **sick and tired of**　　　　　　　　　　　　　:: 진저리가 난

　↳ dislike very much

　　Q　Is mother serving leftovers for dinner again tonight?
　　　　엄마가 오늘밤 또 다시 먹다 남은 음식을 주니?

　　A　Yes, and I'm as sick and tired of them as you are.
　　　　그래, 난 너만큼 그 음식엔 진저리가 난다구.

066 **right under one's nose**　　　　　　　　　:: 바로 코밑에

　↳ right in front of one

　　Q　Have you seen my fountain pen?
　　　　내 만년필을 보았니?

　　A　Yes, it's right there under your nose.
　　　　그럼, 바로 네 코밑에 있잖아.

067 **put one's foot down**　　　　　　　　　:: 단호히 반대하다

　↳ refuse strongly

　　Q　Is your father going to let you quit college?
　　　　네 아버지는 네가 대학을 그만두게 하실까?

　　A　No, he put his foot down and insisted that I get my degree.
　　　　아냐, 반대하시면서 내가 학위는 따야 한다고 주장하신 걸.

068 read between the lines   :: 글 속의 숨은 뜻을 파악하다

↳ determine the hidden meaning of

Q Are your country's newspapers censored?
네 나라 신문들은 검열을 받지?

A Yes, so to understand what's going on you have to read between the lines.
그래, 그래서 무슨 일이 있는지 알려면 행간의 뜻을 파악해야 한다구.

069 work one's fingers to the bone   :: 뼈빠지게 일하다

↳ work very hard

Q Have you completed your project yet?
벌써 너의 프로젝트를 끝마쳤니?

A No, but I've been working my fingers to the bone trying to.
아니, 하지만 끝마치려고 뼈빠지게 일하고 있어.

070 take after   :: 닮다

↳ resemble

Q Is she as smart as her father in math?
그녀는 아버지를 닮아서 수학을 잘하지?

A No, but she takes after him in personality.
그렇지 않아, 하지만 인품은 닮았어.

071 drop out of   :: 도중에 그만두다

↳ leave before finishing

Q Is our school's runner still in the marathon?
우리 학교의 선수는 마라톤에서 아직도 뛰고 있니?

A No, he had to drop out of it because of a broken shoelace.
아니, 신발 끈이 풀어져서 도중에 그만두지 않을 수 없었어.

072 **fill in** :: 기입하다

↪ write down on a blank

Q Do I have to write something down for every blank in this form?

이 양식의 공백을 모두 써넣어야 하니?

A No, just fill in your name, address and telephone number.

아냐, 이름, 주소 그리고 전화번호만 기입해.

073 **crocodile tears** :: 거짓 눈물

↪ false sadness

Q Is she just pretending to be sad over her rich husband's death?

그녀는 돈 많은 남편이 죽자 슬퍼하는 척하는 거니?

A Yes, those are just crocodile tears. Inside, she's overjoyed.

그래, 거짓 눈물일 뿐이야. 속으론 좋아한다구.

074 **bring home the bacon** :: 생계를 꾸려 나가다

↪ support one's family

Q Is your father still out of work?

네 아버지 아직도 실직중이시니?

A Yes, so in my family it's my mother who brings home the bacon.

응, 그래서 어머니가 생계를 꾸려 나가셔.

on the tip of one's tongue

:: 입에서 뱅뱅 돌고 안 나오다

↳ I think I know it, it's, ah, it's …

Q Do you know her telephone number?
너 그녀의 전화번호를 아니?

A Yes, wait a minute. It's right on the tip of my tongue.
It's, ah…
응, 잠깐만. 입에서 뱅뱅 돌고 안 나오네.

find out

:: 알아보다

↳ ask about

Q Do you know what's for dinner tonight?
오늘 저녁식사가 뭔지 아니?

A No, so why don't you go into the kitchen and find out?
몰라, 부엌에 가서 알아보렴.

give the cold shoulder

:: 냉대하다

↳ treat coldly

Q Is she ignoring me intentionally?
그녀는 날 고의로 무시하고 있지?

A Yes, she's giving you the cold shoulder because she
doesn't like you.
그래, 너를 좋아하지 않기 때문에 냉대하는 거야.

once in a blue moon

:: 아주 드물게

↳ very rarely

Q Do you ever take your wife out to eat?
너는 부인을 외식시켜주니?

A Yes, but only once in a blue moon.
응, 하지만 아주 드물어.

079 live from hand to mouth :: 하루 벌어 하루 생활을 하다

↳ barely survive

Q Are you getting along okay these days?
요즈음 지내기 괜찮아?

A No, because ever since I lost my job I've been living from hand to mouth.
아냐, 실직한 후 하루 벌어 하루 살아가고 있지 뭐.

080 look up to :: 존경하다

↳ think highly of

Q Do you respect the minister in your church?
너는 너희 교회 목사님을 존경하니?

A Yes, I really look up to him.
응, 난 정말로 그를 존경해.

081 hit the ceiling :: 노발대발하다

↳ get very angry

Q Did your father get angry when you told him you lost your purse again?
네가 지갑을 또 잃어버렸다고 아버지께 말씀드렸을 때 아버지가 화를 내셨니?

A Yes, he hit the ceiling.
응, 노발대발하시더라.

082 turn a deaf ear :: 들은 척도 않다

↳ ignore

Q Did you ask your father if you could borrow the car tonight?
오늘 밤 승용차를 빌릴 수 있는지 네 아버지께 여쭈어봤니?

A Yes, but he just turned a deaf ear.
응, 하지만 들은 척도 안 하시더라.

hand out :: 나누어주다

↳ distribute

Q Do you need some help, professor?
교수님, 도움이 필요하세요?

A Yes, please hand these papers out, one to each student.
그래, 이 시험지들을 나눠줘요. 한 학생에 한 장씩.

sink in :: 이해하다

↳ understand

Q Don't people realize how important my new invention is?
나의 새로운 발명이 얼마나 중요한지 사람들은 이해를 못하지?

A No, and I guess it will take some time for that fact to sink in.
맞아, 그 사실을 이해하려면 시간이 좀 걸리겠지.

talk back :: 말대꾸하다

↳ answer in rude way, especially to a teacher or parent

Q Did you scold Johnny in class this morning?
오늘 아침 수업 중 조니를 꾸짖었니?

A Yes, because he kept talking back to me when I told him to be quiet.
응, 조용히 하라고 하니까 계속 말대꾸를 했기 때문이야.

hit the spot :: 시원하게 하다

↳ satisfy and refresh

Q Would you like some ice tea?
냉차 좀 드릴까요?

A Yes, that would really hit the spot right now.
예, 그거 마시면 참 시원해질 것 같군요.

087 **neck and neck** :: 막상막하

↳ even

Q Does our race car driver still have a big lead?
우리 경주차가 아직도 크게 리드하고 있는 거야?

A No, he's now neck and neck with Car No. 5.
아니, 지금은 5번차와 막상막하야.

088 **cut corners** :: 극도로 절약하다

↳ economize, perhaps excessively

Q Do you think you'll be able to afford sending all your kids to college?
네 아이들을 모두 대학에 보낼 수 있을 것 같니?

A Yes, if we cut corners as much as we can.
그래, 할 수 있는대로 절약한다면.

089 **eat out** :: 외식하다

↳ eat in a restaurant

Q Did your husband take you to a restaurant last night?
네 남편은 어젯밤 너를 음식점으로 데리고 갔니?

A Yes, and that was the first time we had eaten out in three months.
응, 우리가 외식한 것은 3개월만에 처음이었어.

090 **get around to (verb + ~ing)** :: 어떻게든 해보다

↳ finally manage to do

Q Did you wash the windows yet?
벌써 창문을 닦았니?

A No, but I'll get around to doing them right after I take a nap.
아니, 하지만 낮잠을 잔 후 즉시 어떻게든 닦아 볼게.

영숙어 문제 단번에 공략하기

013. Jack won't really mention his problems; he'll only
_____ to them.

(A) whimper (B) allude
(C) molest (D) blur

어휘 whimper 흐느껴 울다 / molest 희롱하다 / blur 흐리게 하다 / allude to
~을 암시하다 cf. mention 직접 언급하다 / them=his problems

해석 잭은 자신의 문제를 실제로 언급하지 않고, 다만 암시하는 선에서 그칠 것이다.

---

014. Because the sale of bonds is a convenient means of
raising capital, corporations often issue bonds <u>as well
as</u> stocks.

(A) as good as (B) as substitutes for
(C) in addition to (D) instead of

어휘 bond 채권, 공채 / issue 발행하다 / as well as ~뿐만 아니라, 아울러
(in addition to, besides) / stock 주식 / as good as ~와 다름없는, 거의 /
substitute 대체(물)

해석 채권 판매는 자본을 증식시키는 편리한 방법이라서 기업들은 종종 주식뿐만
아니라 채권도 발행한다.

---

015. A prominent advocate of woman suffrage, Susan B.
Anthony <u>gave speeches</u> throughout the United States
for the cause of women's rights.

(A) raised money (B) arranged meetings
(C) wrote articles (D) lectured

어휘 advocate 주창자 / suffrage 투표, 참정권, 선거권 / give speech 연설하
다 / cause 주장 / raise money 돈을 모으다 / arrange meeting 회합을
준비하다

해석 저명한 여성 참정권 주창자인 수전 B. 앤서니는 여성의 권리 주장을 위해 미
국 전역에 걸쳐 강연을 했다.

016. The cotton plant produces fluffy pods called bolls, which contain long and short fibers <u>stuck to</u> each seed.

(A) facing toward   (B) attached to
(C) related to   (D) preserved in

어휘 fluffy 솜털의 / pod 꼬투리, 고치 / boll (목화 등의) 둥근 꼬투리 / fiber 섬유질 / stick to 붙어 있다(attach to) / face toward ~쪽으로 향하다 / relate to ~와 관계하다 / preserve in ~에 보존되어 있다

해석 목화나무에는 둥근 꼬투리라고 불리는, 솜털이 있는 봉오리가 생기는데, 이 봉오리는 씨앗에 붙어 있는 길고 짧은 섬유조직을 가지고 있다.

017. The works of poet Denise Levertov are <u>rooted in</u> her experience as a woman of the mid-twentieth century.

(A) based on   (B) upheld by
(C) valued for   (D) contrasted with

어휘 be rooted in ~에서 유래하다 / be based on ~에 근거하다 / uphold 지탱하다 / contrasted with ~와 대조되는

해석 시인 Denise Levertov의 작품들은 20세기 중반을 산 여성으로서의 자신의 경험에 뿌리를 두고 있다.

018. Many Seoulites _____ with their irregular bus services.

(A) find fault   (B) criticize
(C) condemn about   (D) complain

어휘 find fault with 비난하다(criticize) / condemn 힐난하다 / complain of ~을 불평하다

해석 많은 서울 시민들은 불규칙적인 버스 운행을 비난한다.

091   see off
:: 전송하다

↳ say goodbye at the station, airport etc.

Q Are you going to the airport this afternoon?
오늘 오후 공항에 갈거니?

A Yes, I have to see off my cousin who's going back home.
응, 귀국하는 사촌을 전송해야 해.

092   trade in
:: 신제품과 교환하다

↳ exchange the old for the new

Q Did you buy a new car?
새 차 샀어?

A Yes, because the dealer let me trade in my old one.
응, 딜러가 내 헌차와 교환해 주었어.

093   step on it
:: 빨리 가다, 서두르다

↳ hurry up!

Q Do I have to finish this report before Friday?
금요일 전에 이 보고서를 끝내야 하니?

A Yes, so step on it, because it's already Thursday.
그래, 벌써 목요일이니 서둘러.

on pins and needles :: 매우 초조한

↳ very nervous

Q Are you nervous?
너 초조하니?

A Yes, I'm on pins and needles.
응, 몹시 초조해.

taper off :: 차차 끊다

↳ reduce gradually

Q Should I quit smoking completely?
담배를 완전히 끊어야 하니?

A No, I think it would be easier if you just tapered off.
아니, 차차 끊는 것이 쉬울 거야.

Day
04

rain or shine :: 비가 오나 눈이 오나

↳ always

Q Does the city bus stop here once every 30 minutes?
시내 버스는 30분마다 여기에 서니?

A Yes, rain or shine.
그래, 비가 오나 눈이 오나 항상 서.

on the blink :: 고장난

↳ not working properly

Q Is your TV set broken?
네 TV가 고장났니?

A Yes, it's on the blink.
그래 고장이야.

come in handy :: 유용하다

↳ useful

Q Is fluency in French of any value these days?
프랑스어를 잘 하는 것이 요즘 유용할까?

A No, not much, but it could come in handy if you ever become a diplomat.
그렇게 유용하지는 않겠지만, 네가 외교관이 되면 유용할거야.

on the whole :: 대체로

↳ generally

Q Did your son get a good report card this semester?
네 아들은 이번 학기에 좋은 성적을 얻었니?

A Yes, on the whole his grades were excellent.
응, 대체로 점수가 우수했어.

look into :: 조사하다

↳ investigate

Q Do you know why our office has been using so much copy paper this month?
우리 사무실에서 이 달에 복사지를 그렇게 많이 사용한 이유를 아니?

A No, but I'll look into the problem the first thing tomorrow morning.
몰라, 하지만 내일 아침 무엇보다도 먼저 그 문제를 조사할게.

in charge of :: ~을 책임지는, ~을 담당하고 있는

↳ responsible for

Q Do you have many responsibilities in your new job?
너 새 직장에서 책임이 많니?

A Yes, I'm in charge of overall planning.
그래, 총괄계획을 담당하고 있어.

102 not hear of
:: 결코 허락하지 않다

↳ never give permission for

Q Did you give permission to your daughter to go camping with her boyfriend?

자네 딸이 남자친구와 캠핑가는 것을 허락했나?

A No, of course not! I told her I would not hear of such nonsense.

아니, 물론 아니지! 그런 얼토당토않은 이야기는 결코 허락할 수 없다고 말했네.

103 on one's toes
:: 조심하는, 대비하는

↳ alert and ready for action

Q Is he a good baseball shortstop?

그는 훌륭한 유격수지?

A Yes, because he's always on his toes.

그래, 그는 항상 준비하고 있으니까.

104 rock the boat
:: 평지풍파를 일으키다

↳ upset a stable situation

Q Don't you think the time has come to start letting women join our club?

여성을 우리 클럽에 가입시킬 때가 됐다고 생각지 않니?

A No, and stop trying to rock the boat!

아직 안됐어. 평지풍파를 일으키려 하지마!

105 on the point of doing
:: ~할 지경인, ~하기 직전

↳ on the verge of

Q Do you think the economy is in bad shape these days?

요즈음 경기가 나쁘다고 생각하니?

A Yes, it's on the point of collapsing.

그래, 붕괴 직전이야.

106 on the contrary
:: 반대로

↳ the opposite is true

Q It looks like you don't like my new dish very much!
너는 내 새로운 요리를 몹시 싫어하는 것 같구나!

A No, on the contrary, I think it's delicious. But I'm full already.
아냐, 반대로 맛있다고 생각해. 하지만 난 벌써 배불러.

107 on the side
:: 부업으로

↳ in addition to

Q Did you buy another car? I thought you were just a garbage man!
너 또 차 샀니? 난 네가 그저 청소부인 줄 알았는데!

A Yes, I am, but I've got a few other small jobs on the side.
맞아, 하지만 부업으로 조그만 일을 하고 있어.

108 around the corner
:: 임박한

↳ soon to arrive

Q Is it December already?
벌써 12월이니?

A Yes, and Christmas is just around the corner.
그래, 성탄절이 임박했어.

109 act one's age
:: 나이값을 하다

↳ behave like an adult

Q Is Mr. O'brian playing hide-and-seek with our kids again?
O'brian 씨가 우리 애들과 또 숨바꼭질을 하고 있지?

A Yes, and I wish he'd start acting his age.
그래, 나이값을 했으면 좋겠어.

110 a slip of the tongue

:: 실언

↳ an unintentional verbal mistake

Q Hey, did you say you don't like my new hairdo?
이봐, 내 새 머리스타일을 좋아하지 않는다고 말했어?

A No, sorry, it was just a slip of the tongue.
아니, 미안해. 그건 단지 실언이었어.

111 sew up

:: 지배권을 쥐다, 독점하다, 확보하다

↳ certain to be obtained

Q Do you think you'll get the job?
그 직장에 취직될 것 같아?

A Yes, my resume is so good I'm sure I've got the position sewed up.
응, 내 이력이 너무 좋아. 확실히 그 일자리를 얻을 수 있을 거야.

Day

04

112 mess up

:: 망쳐놓다

↳ ruin

Q Is it still raining outside?
아직도 밖에는 비가 오니?

A Yes, so that really messes up our plans for a picnic today.
응, 그래서 오늘 우리 소풍계획은 정말로 엉망이 됐어.

113 feel ill at ease

:: 마음이 편치 않은, 불안한

↳ feel uncomfortable

Q Do you like to dance?
춤추고 싶니?

A No, because I always feel ill at ease in front of a lot of people.
아니, 많은 사람들 앞에선 항상 불안해서.

like water off a duck's back

:: 아무 효과가 없는

↳ have absolutely no effect

Q Did the minister's sermon about the evils of drinking upset you?

음주의 해악에 관한 목사님의 설교에 화가 났니?

A No, it was like water off a duck's back. After church I drank five beers.

아니, 아무 영향 없었어. 예배 후 맥주를 다섯 잔이나 마셨거든.

poles apart

:: 정반대인, 완전히 다른

↳ exactly opposite

Q Have labor and management reached an agreement yet?

노조와 경영자 측은 벌써 합의했니?

A No, both sides are still poles apart.

아니, 양측은 아직도 정반대 입장이야.

scratch the surface

:: 겉만 핥다

↳ just begin to find out about a subject

Q Did you learn a lot about computers last semester?

지난 학기에 컴퓨터에 관해 많이 배웠니?

A No, I barely scratched the surface.

아니, 겨우 겉만 핥았어.

once in a while

:: 가끔

↳ sometimes

Q Do you often eat out?

종종 외식하니?

A No, only once in a while.

아니, 가끔 할 뿐이야.

118 make a mountain out of a molehill

:: 침소봉대하다

↳ exaggerate the importance of

Q Jane wouldn't talk to you for a whole week because you laughed at her hairdo?

제인은 네가 그녀의 머리 모양을 비웃었기 때문에 일주일 동안은 네게 말을 하지 않을 거야, 그렇지?

A Yes, she always makes a mountain out of a molehill.

그래, 그녀는 항상 과장해서 얘기한다구.

119 spill the beans

:: 비밀을 누설하다

↳ reveal a secret

Q Are you planning a surprise party for him?

너는 그를 위해 몰래 파티를 준비해서 그를 놀래줄 계획이니?

A Yes, so be careful not to spill the beans and let him know.

응, 그러니 비밀을 누설해서 그가 사전에 알지 않도록 주의해.

120 tell off

:: 책망하다, 야단치다

↳ scold

Q Did you scold him for using bad language in front of ladies?

너는 그가 숙녀들 앞에서 나쁜 말을 한 것을 책망했니?

A Yes, I really told him off and insisted he apologize.

응, 난 정말로 그를 야단치고 그가 사과하도록 했어.

영숙어 문제 단번에 공략하기

019. It _____ Smith as an only child to support his mothers as his father died.

(A) drew upon   (B) fell upon
(C) insisted upon   (D) pulled on
(E) bound upon

어휘 **draw upon** 요구하다, 서서히 다가오다 / **fall upon** 엄습하다, 해당하다, …의 의무가 있다 / **pull on** 급히 입다

해석 아버지가 돌아가시자 어린 아이인 스미스는 어머니를 부양해야만 했다.

- -

020. He is convinced that reducing air rather than _____ completely is the best solution to the problem.

(A) seeing to it   (B) resigning it
(C) ignoring it   (D) cutting it off
(E) fulfilling it

어휘 **be convinced that**절 ~라고 확신하다 / **see to** 주의하다, 배려하다 / **cut off** 중단하다, 끊다

해석 그는 공기를 완전히 차단시키기보다는 점차 줄여나가는 것이 그 문제에 대한 최선의 해결책이라고 확신한다.

- -

021. The secretary of the interior decides whether a building is worthy of designation as a national historic site.

(A) requires   (B) deserves
(C) suggests   (D) provides

어휘 **be worthy of** ~할 가치가 있다, ~에 족하다 / **designation** 지정, 지명, 명칭 / **the secretary of the interior** 내무성 장관 / **historic site** 사적지(史蹟地)

해석 내무성 장관은 어떤 건물이 국가 유적물로 지정을 받을 가치가 있는지를 결정한다.

022. <u>As a rule</u>, catfish live in freshwater lakes, ponds, or streams.

(A) Surprisingly   (B) Generally

(C) Fortunately   (D) Currently

어휘 **as a rule** 대개, 일반적으로(on the whole) / **catfish** 메기의 일종 / **freshwater** 민물, 담수 / **currently** 현재, 널리

해석 일반적으로 메기는 담수호(淡水湖)나 연못 혹은 개울에 산다.

---

023. The United States Senate <u>carries out</u> much of its work by means of committees.

(A) accomplishes   (B) sorts through

(C) looks at   (D) follows up

어휘 **Senate** 상원 / **carry out** 실행하다, 성취하다(perform, fulfill) / **by means of** ~에 의해 / **sort through** 정리하다, 정돈하다 / **follow up** 끝까지 추적하다

해석 미(美) 상원은 위원회를 통해 많은 일을 수행한다.

---

024. Jimmy is so unreliable you can never <u>count on</u> him.

(A) respect   (B) plan for his participation

(C) expect   (D) be in agreement with

(E) depend upon

어휘 **count on** ~을 의지하다 / **be in agreement with** ~에 동의하다

해석 지미는 정말 못믿을 사람이므로 결코 그를 믿어서는 안 된다.

5th Day

121 under arrest

:: 체포된, 수감된

↳ seized by the police

Q Have the police caught the kidnappers yet?
경찰은 벌써 그 납치범들을 잡았니?

A Yes, and they're now under arrest in the city jail.
응, 그들은 지금 시 교도소에 수감돼 있어.

122 cut short

:: 단축하다

↳ end early before it is finished

Q Did this morning's staff meeting last its usual two hours?
오늘 아침 중역회의도 통상적으로 2시간 동안 계속했니?

A No, the boss cut it short because of a luncheon appointment.
아니, 사장이 오찬 약속 때문에 단축했어.

123 by way of

:: ~경유로

↳ passing through

Q Isn't there a quicker route than this to the airport?
공항으로 가는 길이 이것보다 더 빠른 것이 없니?

A Yes, by way of 7th Street.
있어, 7번가를 경유하는 길이 있어.

124 **at random** :: 되는대로, 아무렇게나

↳ without any particular order

Q Have they picked the lottery winners yet?
벌써 복권 당첨자를 선정했니?

A Yes, they drew their names at random out of a big glass bowl.
응, 큰 유리사발에서 되는대로 끄집어냈어.

125 **promise the moon** :: 불가능한 것, 너무 많은 것을 약속하다

↳ promise too much

Q Do the citizens of your country also distrust politicians?
네 나라 시민 역시 정치인들을 불신하지?

A Yes, because they always promise the moon in order to get elected.
그래, 그들은 당선되기 위해 항상 불가능한 것을 약속하기 때문이야.

126 **same here!** :: 나도 같은 것으로!

↳ me, too!

Q Did he say he wanted a strawberry ice cream cone, too?
그 사람 역시 딸기 아이스크림을 달라고 말했니?

A Yes, he said, "Same here!"
그래, "나도 같은 것으로!"라고 했어.

127 **wide of the mark** :: 엉뚱한

↳ far from what is adequate or expected

Q Did you attend Prof. Smith's special lecture on economics last night?
너는 어젯밤 스미스 교수의 경제학 특강에 참석했니?

A Yes, I did, but I found most of his opinions wide of the mark.
응, 그러나 그의 의견은 대부분 기대와는 동떨어졌어.

128 sooner or later

:: 조만간

↳ eventually

Q Are you ever going to fix the leaky faucet in the bathroom?
욕실의 새는 수도꼭지를 고칠 거지?

A Yes, I'll do it sooner or later, if I ever find the time.
그래, 시간이 나면 조만간 할 거야.

129 take the bull by the horns

:: 위험을 무릅쓰고 용감히 행동하다

↳ meet a challenge directly

Q Are you scheduled to see your boss this morning?
오늘 아침 사장을 만날 예정이니?

A Yes, I've decided to take the bull by the horns and
demand a pay raise.
그래, 용감하게 봉급인상을 요구하기로 했어.

130 make one feel at home

:: 마음을 편하게 해주다

↳ make one feel comfortable

Q Is she a good hostess?
그녀는 좋은 여주인인가요?

A Yes, she always tries to make her guests feel right at home.
예, 그녀는 항상 손님한테 마음을 편하게 해주려고 애쓰지요.

131 follow one's nose

:: 똑바로 나아가다

↳ go straight ahead

Q Excuse me, but is there a rest room in this building?
실례지만 이 건물에 화장실이 있습니까?

A Yes, just follow your nose down this hall and you can't
miss it.
예, 그냥 이 홀을 똑바로 내려가세요. 그러면 찾을 수 있을 거예요.

every time one turns around

:: 매우 자주

↳ constantly

Q Is Mrs. Williams wearing another new dress?
윌리엄스 부인은 다른 새 옷을 입고 있나요?

A Yes, and I think she buys one just about every time she turns around.
예, 그녀는 매우 자주 옷을 사는 것 같아요.

cool as a cucumber

:: 침착한, 냉정한

↳ very calm

Q Is he a good pilot?
그는 뛰어난 조종사인가요?

A Yes, he's cool as a cucumber especially in difficult situations.
예, 그는 특히 위기 상황일 때 침착하지요.

take over

:: 인수하다

↳ assume control of

Q Do you think the company will be sold when the founder finally retires?
창립자가 결국 은퇴할 때 그 회사가 팔릴 거라고 생각하니?

A No, because his oldest son will probably take over the company.
아니, 아마 그의 장남이 그 회사를 인수할 것이니까.

on the level

:: 정직한

↳ honest

Q Do you believe the fortune-teller your wife is seeing is an honest person?
네 아내가 만나는 점쟁이가 정직한 사람이라고 믿니?

A No, of course not! I have never met one who was on the level.
물론 안 믿지! 정직한 점쟁이는 만나본 적이 없어.

136 make friends with   :: ～와 사귀다

↳ establish a friendly relationship with

Q Are you bringing her flowers plus a box of chocolates?
초콜릿 상자에다 꽃을 넣어서 그녀에게 갖다 줄거니?

A Yes, and what's wrong with trying to make friends with people?
응, 사람들과 사귀려는 게 뭐 잘못됐니?

137 get off the ground   :: 출발하다

↳ get started

Q Do you think his plan will succeed?
그의 계획이 성공할까요?

A No, it'll never even get off the ground.
아뇨, 그것은 시작조차도 못할 거에요.

138 make one's hair stand on end
:: 머리칼이 곤두서게 하다

↳ terrify

Q Was the movie frightening?
그 영화 무서웠니?

A Yes, it made my hair stand on end.
응, 내 머리칼을 곤두서게 할 정도였어.

139 not have a fat chance

:: 가능성이 별로 없다

↳ have not much of a chance at all

Q Do you think he'll do well in the next Olympics, too?
그가 다음 올림픽에서도 잘 할까?

A No, he won't have a fat chance of winning a medal because he's getting old.
아니, 그 사람은 늙어가니까 메달 하나도 따기 어려울 걸.

140 lend one a hand

:: 도와주다

↳ help

Q Do you need some help?
좀 도와줄까요?

A Yes, could you lend me a hand and carry some of these packages?
네, 날 도와서 이 짐들을 좀 날라주시겠어요?

Day

05

141 on the other hand

:: 다른 한편

↳ conversely

Q John is a very generous guy with his friends, isn't he?
존은 친구들한테 아주 관대한 녀석이지?

A Yes, but on the other hand, he spends little time with his family.
그래, 하지만 다른 한편으로 자기 가족과는 시간을 보내지 않아.

142 on the button

:: 정확한

↳ exactly right

Q Did he answer the questions correctly?
그는 질문에 정확히 대답했니?

A Yes, all of his answers were right on the button.
응, 그의 대답은 모두 아주 정확했어.

143   get out of hand   :: 수라장이 되다

↳ become chaotic

Q Did you have some trouble at your party last night?
어젯밤 파티에서 말썽이 있었니?

A Yes, it got out of hand when some idiot started a food fight!
응, 어떤 바보 같은 자가 음식 싸움을 시작하자 수라장이 됐지.

144   one of these days   :: 근일중

↳ at some time in the future

Q Haven't you fixed the leaky roof yet?
아직도 새는 지붕을 고치지 않았니?

A No, but don't worry, I'll do it one of these days.
응, 하지만 걱정마. 근일중 수리할게.

145   see to it   :: ~하도록 하다

↳ make sure

Q Is there anything you need me to do for you while you're on vacation?
당신 휴가 동안 내가 해줬으면 하는 일이 있어요?

A Yes, please see to it that all my plants are watered regularly.
예, 규칙적으로 내 화초에 물을 주도록 하세요.

146   give one a ring   :: 전화하다

↳ call one on the telephone

Q Should we call grandma tonight?
할머니께 오늘 밤 전화해야 하나요?

A Yes, let's give her a ring and tell her how much we miss her.
응, 전화해서 우리가 할머니를 얼마나 보고 싶어 하는지 말씀드리자.

as is :: 현재 그대로

↳ in its present condition without any changes

Q If I agree to buy your car, will you repaint it for me first?
내가 네 차를 사겠다면, 먼저 그 차를 다시 칠해줄거니?

A No, you'll have to buy it *as is*.
아니, 넌 차를 현 상태 그대로 사야 해.

---

148 **fly off the handle** :: 몹시 화내다

↳ get angry

Q Does your downstair's neighbor ever get angry about your noisy kids?
아래층 사람이 당신의 소란스러운 애들에 대해 화낸 적이 있나요?

A Yes, in fact just yesterday he *flew off the handle* and shouted at them.
예, 사실 어제 그 사람이 몹시 화내며 애들에게 고함치더군요.

Day
05

---

149 **ring a bell** :: 상기시키다

↳ remind

Q Do you know a certain John Smith?
존 스미스라는 사람 아세요?

A Yes, I think the name does *ring a bell*.
예, 그 이름을 들으니 생각나네요

---

150 **out of one's mind** :: 정신이 나간

↳ crazy

Q Is Sam going to try to swim across the English Channel?
샘이 영국해협을 헤엄쳐서 건너려고 하니?

A Yes, and he must be *out of his mind*.
응, 그 사람 미친 게 분명해.

영숙어 문제 단번에 공략하기

025. Don't <u>rule out</u> the possibility of the plan failing.

(A) worry about   (B) underestimate

(C) forget   (D) dismiss

> **어휘** **rule out** 배제하다(exclude) / **underestimate** 과소평가하다 / **dismiss** 잊어버리다, 없애버리다
>
> **해석** 그 계획이 실패할 수도 있다는 가능성을 배제하지 마라.

---

026. I wish some of those guys would <u>come up with</u> a bright idea.

(A) suggest   (B) realize

(C) overtake   (D) perceive

> **어휘** **come up with** 제안하다 / **overtake** 따라잡다 / **perceive** 인지하다
>
> **해석** 저 녀석들 중 몇 놈이라도 재치 있는 아이디어를 제안한다면 좋겠다.

---

027. Psychologists have done extensive studies of how well patients <u>comply with</u> doctor's orders.

(A) obey   (B) understand

(C) improve with   (D) agree with

> **어휘** **extensive** 광범위한 / **comply with** (요구, 규칙에) 따르다, 순응하다
>
> **해석** 심리학자들은 환자들이 의사의 지시에 얼마나 잘 따르는지에 대한 광범위한 연구를 했다.

028. He was stubbornly persistent; nothing or nobody could
_____ him from his self-appointed mission.

(A) prevent   (B) dissuade
(C) pervade   (D) jeopardize

어휘 **dissuade from** ~하지 못하게 단념시키다 / **self-appointed** 독단적인, 자기가 추천한 / **pervade** 만연하다 / **jeopardize** 위태롭게 하다

해석 그는 아주 고집이 강해서, 어떤 무엇도, 어느 누구도 그 스스로 정한 독단적인 임무를 단념시킬 수가 없었다.

---

029. It was hard for him to realize that because he had
a weaker character than that of Queen Elizabeth
and because, unlike her, he had a large family
and extravagant tastes, he could not hope to hold
Parliament _____ quite as she had done.

Day

05

(A) responsible   (B) in power
(C) up   (D) in cheek

어휘 **character** 성격, 기질 / **extravagant** 사치스런, 엄청난 / **hold ~ in power** 장악하다 / **hold up** 지탱하다

해석 그는 엘리자베스 여왕보다 나약한 기질을 지녔으며, 그녀와 달리 가족이 많은 데다 낭비벽이 심해서 그녀가 했던 만큼 의회를 수중에 넣기가 힘들다는 것을 깨닫지 못했다.

---

030. A skilled carpenter often <u>dispenses with</u> detailed plans.

(A) give away   (B) does without
(C) completes   (D) adapts

어휘 **dispense with** ~없이 해내다 / **give away** 거저주다 / **adapt** 적응시키다
해석 유능한 목수는 때때로 세부 계획서 없이 일을 해낸다.

151 turn down
:: 거절하다

↳ reject or deny

Q Did the publisher agree to publish your manuscript?
출판사가 네 원고를 출판하기로 동의했니?

A No, and this is the third time it's been turned down!
아니, 이번이 세 번째 거절이야.

152 much less
:: 말할 것도 없이

↳ not to mention

Q Do you know much about algebra?
대수에 대해 많이 아니?

A No, I can hardly understand arithmetic much less algebra.
아니, 대수는커녕 산수도 거의 몰라.

153 or so
:: 약 ~이나 그 정도쯤

↳ or a little more

Q Did the doctor say you could leave the hospital soon?
네가 곧 퇴원할 수 있다고 의사께서 말씀하시던?

A Yes, and maybe in a week or so.
응, 아마 1주일 후나 그 정도쯤.

154 **sit on one's hands** :: 아무것도 하지 않다

↳ not give any help

Q Did your rich uncle help you much during your campaign for governor?
당신의 주지사 선거 운동 동안 부유한 당신 아저씨께서 많이 도와 주셨나요?

A No, he just sat on his hands and watched me lose.
아뇨, 그는 아무것도 하지 않고 내가 지는 것을 보기만 했지요.

155 **by all means** :: 어떻게 해서든지, 어서 하세요

↳ please go ahead and do it

Q Can I have another piece of this delicious apple pie?
이 맛있는 사과 파이 한 개 더 먹어도 되나요?

A Yes, by all means.
예, 어서 드세요

156 **break out** :: 발생하다

↳ occur

Q Do you know when the Korean War occurred?
한국전쟁이 언제 발발했는지 아니?

A Yes, it broke out in 1950.
응, 1950년에 일어났지.

157 **at fault** :: 잘못한

↳ to blame

Q Did your wife cause the traffic accident?
당신 부인이 교통 사고를 일으켰나요?

A No, the other driver was at fault.
아뇨, 다른 운전사가 잘못한 겁니다.

158 throw one a curve

:: 속이다

↳ deceive

Q You mean the President's press secretary deliberately deceived you?
대통령의 공보비서가 고의로 당신들을 속였다는 말입니까?

A Yes, he threw the press corps a curve to distract it from the real story.
예, 그는 진실에서 눈을 돌리기 위해 기자단을 속였죠.

159 sign off

:: 방송을 끝내다

↳ stop broadcasting for the day

Q Do you want me to switch to Channel 9?
내가 채널 9번으로 바꾸길 원하니?

A No, don't bother. The station signed off over 30 minutes ago.
아니, 내버려 둬. 30분 전에 방송이 끝났어.

160 hit bottom

:: 최저이다

↳ reach the lowest point

Q Do you think the economy will get any worse?
경제가 더 악화될까?

A No, it can't because it's already hit bottom.
아니, 이미 경제는 최악이야.

161 go up in smoke

:: 헛되이 없어지다, 무산되다

↳ end in vain

Q Did she finally fulfill her dream to go to college?
그녀가 드디어 대학가는 꿈을 이루었니?

A No, it went up in smoke when her boyfriend got her pregnant.
아니, 남자친구가 그녀를 임신시켰을 때 무산되었지.

162 do away with   :: 제거하다

↳ get rid of

Q Do you have any good ideas on how to reduce crime in
   New York City?
   뉴욕의 범죄를 줄일 좋은 생각이 있나요?

A Yes, doing away with all handguns would help a lot.
   예, 모든 권총을 제거하면 꽤 효과가 있을 겁니다.

163 break off   :: 단절하다

↳ sever

Q Does your country have an embassy in Israel?
   당신 나라는 이스라엘에 대사관이 있습니까?

A No, we broke off diplomatic relations with it several
   years ago.
   아뇨, 우린 수년 전에 외교관계를 끊었습니다.

164 at worst   :: 나빠봤자, 최악의 경우에는

↳ in the worst possible case

Q What's going to happen to Ted for cheating on his
   exam?
   Ted가 시험에서 부정행위를 했으니 그에게 무슨 일이 있을까?

A At worst, he could get kicked out at college.
   나빠봤자 퇴학당하겠지.

165 at best   :: 기껏해야

↳ in the best possible case

Q If he gets thrown out, where will he be able to find a
   job?
   그가 쫓겨나면 어디서 일자리를 찾지?

A At best, he'll be able to find work in his uncle's bakery.
   기껏해야, 그는 아저씨네 빵집에서 일할 수 있겠지.

166 go into
:: ~을 화제로 삼다

↳ discuss

Q During dinner tonight shall I tell Daddy I lost my purse again?
오늘밤 식사할 때 아빠한테 또 지갑을 잃어버렸다고 얘기할까?

A No, don't go into any subject that might spoil his appetite.
아니, 아빠 식욕을 잃게 할 만한 얘긴 꺼내지마.

167 in the long run
:: 마침내, 결국

↳ eventually

Q Do I have to memorize all these stupid idioms for the next test?
다음 시험 때문에 이 귀찮은 숙어를 다 외워야 하나요?

A Yes, because in the long run knowing them will be very useful.
그래, 결국에는 그것들을 알아두는 것이 매우 유용할 것이니까.

168 inside out
:: 안쪽이 바깥쪽으로 가 있는

↳ the inside is incorrectly on the outside

Q Are you wearing two different socks?
서로 다른 양말을 신은 거니?

A No, one of them is just turned inside out.
아냐, 하나를 뒤집어 신은 거야.

169 turn thumbs down
:: 거절하다

↳ reject

Q Did your dad approve of your plan to hitchhike across Europe next summer?
내년 여름 유럽으로 무전여행할 계획을 아빠가 허락하셨어?

A No, he turned thumbs down on the idea.
아니, 그 제안을 거부하셨어.

170 go out on a limb

:: 틀릴지 모른다

↳ make a risky prediction

Q Do you think he'll win the election?
그가 선거에서 이길 것 같니?

A Yes, and I'll go out on a limb and predict he'll win by a landslide.
그럼, 내가 틀릴지 모르지만 압도적으로 그가 이길 것이라고 예상해.

171 up a tree

:: 곤란한

↳ in an embarrassing situation

Q Haven't you left for your dental appointment yet?
치과의사와 약속이 있는데 아직도 떠나지 못했니?

A No, and I'm really up a tree because I can't find my car keys.
못 떠났어. 승용차 키가 없어서 난 정말 곤란해.

172 run in the family

:: 유전이다, 혈통을 물려받다

↳ be hereditary

Q Did you know that his three daughters are all concert violinists?
그의 세 딸이 모두 콘서트 바이올리니스트인 것을 알았니?

A Yes, musical talent must run in the family.
그래, 음악적 재능이 그 가문의 유전임에 틀림없어.

173 lose face

:: 체면을 잃다

↳ be humiliated in front of others

Q Did he resign?
그가 사임했니?

A Yes, because he lost face when the boss scolded him in front of everybody.
응, 사장이 모든 사람 앞에서 그를 꾸짖자 체면을 잃었기 때문이지.

174 hit below the belt
:: 규칙위반이다, 비겁한 짓이다

↳ be unfair

Q Did you know that she is gossiping about you behind your back?
그녀가 너 없는 데서 네 험담하는 것을 알았니?

A No, I didn't. Boy, that's really hitting below the belt!
아니, 몰랐어. 야, 그거 참 비겁한 짓인데.

175 in labor
:: 진통중인

↳ starting to give birth to a child

Q Did your wife give birth yet?
부인이 벌써 출산했니?

A No, she's still in labor.
아니, 아직도 진통중이야.

176 cross one's mind
:: 생각이 떠오르다

↳ think about

Q Are you really planning to get a divorce?
너 정말 이혼할 계획이니?

A No, of course not! The thought has never even crossed my mind.
아니, 물론 아니야! 그런 생각은 꿈에도 가져본 적이 없어.

177 in season
:: 한철인, 한창인

↳ available

Q Do you want me to buy you anything at the fruit market?
과일 시장에서 뭔가 내가 사주길 원하니?

A Yes, some peaches. I think they're in season now.
그래, 복숭아 좀. 지금 한창일 것 같은데.

178 out of season
:: 철이 지난

↳ not available

Q Does your grocery store have any tomatoes?
토마토 있어요?

A No, sorry, but they're now out of season.
없어요, 미안하지만 철이 지났어요.

179 in common
:: 공통적인

↳ shared

Q Did you stop dating him?
그와 데이트를 중단했니?

A Yes, after I found out we have almost nothing in common.
응, 우린 공통점이 아무 것도 없는 것을 안 후 그만두었어.

180 in a fog
:: 헤매는, 오리무중인

↳ mentally confused

Q Does your wife have a good sense of direction?
네 부인은 방향 감각이 좋지?

A No, she's always in a fog whenever she drives.
아니, 운전할 때마다 항상 헤맨다구.

Day
06

영숙어 문제 단번에 공략하기

031. The scars of battle were <u>effaced</u> during the incident.

(A) wiped off (B) effective
(C) groped (D) stashed
(E) none of these

어휘 scar 상처, 흉터 / efface 지우다 / incident 사건, 사변 / wipe off 닦아내다, 말소하다 / grope 손으로 더듬다 / stash 감추다
해석 전쟁의 상처들은 그 사변이 일어난 동안 잊혀졌다.

032. He should ideally have a wide range of experience and personal anecdotes to <u>draw upon</u>.

(A) make use of (B) describe
(C) bring out (D) keep in mind

어휘 ideally 이상적으로 말하면 / anecdote 일화 / draw upon 이용하다, 끌어들이다 / make use of 이용하다(utilize) / bring out 발표하다 / keep[bear] in mind 명심하다
해석 그가 이용할 만한 폭넓은 경험과 개인적인 일화들을 가지고 있다면 더할 나위 없을것이다.

033. The planet best known and most studied is, <u>of course</u>, our own.

(A) naturally (B) currently
(C) by and large (D) by the way

어휘 currently 현재, 널리 / by and large 대체로(on the whole, in general) / by the way 도중에, 그런데
해석 제일 유명하고 또 가장 많이 연구된 행성은 당연히 우리 자신의 행성이다.

034. The government should <u>do away with</u> the regulations restricting working hours.

(A) keep   (B) uphold

(C) abandon   (D) perform

(E) abolish

어휘 **do away with** 폐지하다(abolish) / **uphold** 지지하다

해석 정부는 노동 시간을 제한하고 있는 법규들을 철폐해야 한다.

---

035. The student <u>broke in on</u> the conversation without waiting for speaker to stop talking.

(A) withdrew from   (B) heard

(C) regarded   (D) interrupted

어휘 **break in on** ~을 방해하다, 중단시키다(interrupt) / **withdraw from** 물러나다

해석 그 학생은 상대방의 말이 끝나기를 기다리지도 않고 불쑥 대화에 끼어들었다.

---

036. This should make quite a comfortable and attractive house if it's <u>done up</u> a bit.

(A) swept   (B) cleared

(C) repaired   (D) produced

어휘 **do up** 수리하다, 손질하다 / **sweep** 청소하다

해석 약간 수리를 하면 이 집은 아주 편안하고 매력적인 집이 될 것이다.

7th Day

181 that is to say
:: 바꿔 말하면, 즉

↳ in other words

Q Does he go to church every Sunday?
그는 매주 일요일 교회에 가니?

A No, he's an atheist, that is to say, he doesn't believe in god.
아니, 그는 무신론자야. 바꿔 말하면 신을 믿지 않아.

182 stab one in the back
:: 배반하다, 중상 모략하다

↳ betray

Q Are you and Bill still not speaking?
너는 아직도 Bill과 말을 하지 않니?

A Yes, he stabbed me in the back by telling my teacher I copied my homework.
그래, 그는 날 배신해서 내가 숙제를 베꼈다고 선생님에게 말했지 뭐야.

183 right off the bat
:: 즉시, 즉각

↳ right away

Q Did you meet your old boyfriend at your high school class reunion?
고등학교 동창회 모임에서 옛날 남자친구를 만났니?

A Yes, this afternoon, and right off the bat my heart started beating wildly.
응, 오늘 오후에 만났는데 즉시 내 가슴이 크게 뛰기 시작했어.

184 over the hill
:: 한물 간

↳ gotten old and weak

Q You don't jog anymore in the mornings?
너 아침에 더이상 조깅 안 하니?

A No, I just don't seem to have the energy. Maybe I'm now over the hill.
안 해. 힘이 없는 것 같아. 아마 이젠 한물 갔나 봐.

185 lose one's shirt
:: 알거지가 되다

↳ lose everything

Q Did you win a lot of money in Las Vegas last weekend?
지난 주 라스베가스에서 돈을 많이 땄니?

A No, I almost lost my shirt.
아니, 거의 알거지가 됐어.

186 made to order
:: 안성맞춤인

↳ perfect

Q Did you fly your kite yesterday?
어제 연을 날렸니?

A Yes, and the weather was made to order : clear and windy.
응, 날씨가 안성맞춤이었지. 맑고 바람이 있어서.

Day
07

187 lose one's head
:: 이성을 잃다

↳ act irrationally

Q Aren't you ashamed to be dating a girl who has such a bad reputation?
이렇게 평판이 나쁜 여자와 데이트를 하다니 부끄럽지도 않니?

A Yes, but because she's so beautiful I guess I just lost my head.
그래, 하지만 그녀가 너무 아름다워서 내가 정신을 잃었나봐.

188 in the line of duty
:: 근무중

↳ while on the job

Q Was the young policeman killed while on patrol last night?
그 젊은 경찰이 어젯밤 순찰중 살해됐니?

A Yes, he lost his life in the line of duty trying to stop a bank robbery.
응, 은행강도를 제지하려다 근무중 생명을 잃었어.

189 give someone a piece of one's mind
:: 책망하다

↳ scold

Q Is that man over there staring at us?
저기 저 사람이 우리를 노려보고 있니?

A Yes, and I should go and give him a piece of my mind for such rudeness.
응, 내가 가서 그런 무례함을 야단쳐야겠어.

190 give away
:: 거저 주다

↳ give as a present

Q Have you sold all the kittens yet?
벌써 새끼 고양이를 모두 팔았니?

A No, unfortunately I can't even give them away.
아니, 공교롭게도 거저 줄 수 없어서.

191 bail out
:: 구해주다

↳ save

Q Did his company go bankrupt?
그의 회사는 파산했니?

A No, his rich uncle bailed him out with a low-interest loan.
아니, 그의 돈 많은 아저씨가 저리융자로 구해주셨어.

192 give off

:: 풍기다, 발산하다

↳ emit

Q Do you like roses?
장미꽃을 좋아하니?

A Yes, they give off such a pleasant smell.
그럼, 그것들은 기분 좋은 냄새를 풍기거든.

193 in the saddle

:: 집권중인

↳ in power

Q You didn't vote for the Republican presidential candidate?
공화당 대통령 후보에 투표하지 않았지?

A Yes, because I'd rather have a Democrat in the saddle.
그래, 난 민주당이 집권하는 게 좋으니까.

194 make it snappy

:: 서두르다

↳ hurry up

Q Do we have much time before the plane's departure?
비행기가 떠나기 전 시간이 많지?

A No, so make it snappy and get all the suitcases packed.
아니, 그러니 서둘러서 모든 짐을 꾸리라구.

Day

07

195 pin one down

:: 꼼짝 못하게 하다

↳ force one to explain

Q Did he finally admit to the police that he accepted a bribe?
그는 마침내 뇌물을 받았다고 경찰에 인정했니?

A No, they haven't been able to pin him down and get a confession.
아니, 경찰은 그를 꼼짝 못하게 하여 자백을 받아낼 수 없었어.

73

196 in the wind

↳ rumored

Q Did the President's cabinet reshuffle surprise you?
대통령의 개각에 놀랐니?

A No, it was in the wind around Seoul for weeks.
아니, 서울에선 수주 전부터 그런 소문이 있었어.

197 stir up

:: 선동하다

↳ agitate

Q Is he a member of a radical political group?
그는 급진 정치단체의 일원인가?

A Yes, one that always seems to be trying to stir up trouble.
응, 항상 말썽을 선동하려는 듯 보이는 사람이라구.

198 walk on air

:: 하늘을 날 듯이 기쁘다

↳ feel very happy

Q Were you surprised that your daughter won the Miss Universe contest?
자네 딸이 미스 유니버스 대회에서 우승하여 놀랐나?

A Yes, and I'm so happy I feel like I'm walking on air.
그래, 너무 기뻐서 하늘을 날 것 같은 기분이야.

199 boil down to

:: 요약해서 말하다

↳ briefly mean

Q Can you summarize his economic predictions in just a few words?
몇 마디로 그의 경제 예측을 요약할 수 있겠니?

A Yes. They all boil down to this : the economy will soon collapse.
응, 이렇게 요약할 수 있어. 경제는 곧 붕괴할 거라고.

200 put one's finger on

:: 꼭 집어 말하다

↳ determine exactly

Q Isn't he acting a little strange these days?
그는 요즈음 좀 이상하게 행동하지 않니?

A Yes, but I can't put my finger on the exact reason.
그래, 하지만 정확한 이유를 꼭 집어 말할 수 없어.

201 wear out one's welcome

:: 반가운 손님이라도 오래 있으면 싫어지다

↳ stay too long

Q Have your relatives been staying with you now for over a week?
네 친척들은 일주일 이상이나 네 집에 있는 거니?

A Yes, and they're beginning to wear out their welcome.
그래, 그래서 그들이 싫어지기 시작했어.

202 give the green light

:: 청신호를 보내다

↳ allow

Q Did the boss like your plan?
사장이 당신 계획을 좋아하시던가요?

A Yes, and he gave us the green light to put it into operation.
그래, 그래서 실행하도록 허락하셨어.

203 keep one's chin up

:: 용기를 잃지 않다

↳ be brave

Q Did I tell you that my wife has gone and left me?
아내가 날 버리고 떠나갔다고 내가 말했지?

A Yes, but just keep your chin up because I'm sure she'll come back soon.
그래, 하지만 곧 돌아올 것이 확실하니까 용기를 잃지마.

204 roll out the red carpet

:: 정중히 환영하다

↳ welcome warmly

Q Did the returning astronauts receive a warm welcome?
그 귀환하는 우주비행사들은 따뜻한 환영을 받았니?

A Yes, the city really rolled out the red carpet for them.
그래, 도시가 정말로 그들을 따뜻하게 환영했어.

205 in good hands

:: 도움을 잘 받는

↳ under good care

Q Is Dr. Smith a competent physician?
스미스 박사는 유능한 의사니?

A Yes, you'll be in good hands if you visit him.
그래, 그를 방문하면 너는 도움을 잘 받을 거야.

206 frown upon

:: 눈살을 찌푸리다

↳ disapprove

Q Do you mind if I smoke?
담배 피워도 될까?

A No, I don't, but my wife frowns upon people who smoke in her house.
음, 난 괜찮지만 아내가 집에서 담배 피우는 사람을 싫어해.

207 going on

:: 거의

↳ nearing

Q Is your sister older than you?
네 누이가 너보다 나이가 많니?

A Yes, she's 13 going on 14.
응, 14살이 다 된 13살이야.

a run for one's money

:: 상대가 이기기 힘들도록 잘 싸움, 선전

↪ a good fight

Q You lost the game, didn't you?
너는 그 경기에서 졌지?

A Yes, but at least we gave our opponents a run for their money.
응, 하지만 최소한 우린 상대가 힘들도록 잘 싸웠어.

nail down

:: 결말나다

↪ conclude

Q Has an agreement been reached yet?
벌써 합의에 도달했니?

A No, but we expect to have one nailed down by next week.
아니, 하지만 우리는 다음 주면 해결을 볼 것 같아.

tune in

:: 다이얼(채널)을 맞추다

Day
07

↪ set your radio/TV dial to a particular station/channel

Q Let's watch Channel 5 tonight, okay?
오늘밤은 5번 채널을 시청하자, 괜찮지?

A No, I'd rather tune in to Channel 13— it's got a better late movie.
싫어, 난 13번으로 맞추고 싶어, 거기에 더 좋은 심야영화가 있어.

영숙어 문제 단번에 공략하기

---

037. To avoid him you <u>dodge into</u> the nearest cafe.

(A) enter slowly   (B) enter quickly

(C) enter bravely   (D) leave slowly

(E) leave quickly

어휘 **dodge into** 재빨리 몸을 피하다

해석 그를 피하려면 가장 가까이에 있는 카페로 재빨리 몸을 숨기는 게 좋아.

---

038. In order to reach some agreement they need to _____ their differences.

(A) trade   (B) negotiate

(C) liberate   (D) consent

(E) hammer out

어휘 **hammer out** 문제를 해결하다 / **liberate** 해방하다(set free) / **consent** 동의하다

해석 어떤 합의점에 도달하려면 그들은 서로의 차이점을 해결해야 한다.

---

039. Try to remain capable of <u>entering into</u> other people's states of mind.

(A) demonstrating   (B) beginning

(C) releasing   (D) developing

(E) sympathizing

어휘 **capable of** ~할 능력이 있는 / **demonstrate** 보여주다 / **enter into** 공감하다

해석 다른 사람들의 마음 상태에 공감할 수 있도록 애써라.

040. I certainly got something <u>analogous to</u> religious satisfaction out of it.

(A) different from　　　　(B) similar to
(C) suggestive of　　　　(D) contrary to

어휘 **analogous to** ~와 유사한 / **suggestive of** ~을 암시하는 / **contrary to** ~에 반대인

해석 나는 그것에서 분명히 종교적인 만족감과 유사한 뭔가를 얻었다.

---

041. Chlorophyll cannot be produced unless the plant is <u>exposed to</u> light.

(A) protected against　　　(B) developed with
(C) subjected to　　　　　(D) kept from
(E) raise with

어휘 **chlorophyll** 엽록소 / **subject to** ~을 받다, ~을 쬐다

해석 엽록소는 빛에 노출되어 있지 않으면 생성될 수 없다.

---

042. The novelist can only <u>fall back on</u> that—on his recognition that man's constant demand for what he has to offer is simply man's general appetite for a picture.

(A) turn to for help　　　(B) meet by chance
(C) admit　　　　　　　(D) keep up with

어휘 **fall back on** ~에 의존하다 / **recognition** 인식 / **appetite for** ~에 대한 욕구, 흥미 / **turn to for** ~에 의지하다 / **meet by chance** 우연히 만나다 / **keep up with** 뒤지지 않다

해석 소설가는 소설가가 제공해야 되는 것을 인간이 끊임없이 요구하는 것은 단순히 심미적인 묘사에 대한 인간의 일반적인 욕구라는 인식에만 단지 의존할 수 있다.

Answers ★ 37.(B) 38.(E) 39.(E) 40.(B) 41.(C) 42.(A)

211 wink at
:: 눈감아 주다

↳ overlook

Q Did the traffic cop give you a ticket for over parking?
교통순경이 시간을 넘겨 주차했다고 딱지를 뗐니?

A No, he winked at it because it's the Christmas holidays.
아니, 크리스마스 휴가이기 때문에 눈감아 주었어.

212 put a stop to
:: 중지시키다

↳ halt

Q Don't you think the drug problem in this city is getting worse and worse?
이 도시의 마약문제가 점점 악화된다고 생각지 않니?

A Yes, but the mayor doesn't seem to be doing much to put a stop to it.
응, 하지만 시장은 이를 중지시키려고 큰 노력을 하는 것 같지 않아.

213 on the spur of the moment
:: 순간적으로

↳ without careful consideration

Q Did she give it a lot of thought before she decided to change jobs?
그녀는 전직을 결정하기 전에 생각을 많이 했니?

A No, I think her decision was made on the spur of the moment.
아니, 순간적으로 결정한 것 같아.

lay eyes on :: 보다

↳ look at

Q Our new art teacher is a little strange, isn't he?
새로 오신 미술 선생님이 좀 이상해 보이지 않아?

A Yes, from the minute I laid eyes on him I knew he was not normal.
그래, 그를 본 순간부터 정상이 아닌 것을 알았어.

keep a stiff upper lip :: 이를 악물고 견디다, 용감하다

↳ be brave

Q Do you admire the British people?
너는 영국사람을 존경하니?

A Yes, because even when things are bad they try to keep a stiff upper lip.
응, 그들은 어려운 때라도 이를 악물고 견디려 하기 때문이지.

in public :: 공개적으로

↳ not privately

Q Did she refuse Mr. Lopez's request for a date?
그녀는 Lopez 씨의 데이트 요청을 거절했니?

A Yes, because she was ashamed to be seen in public with a foreigner.
그래, 공개적으로 외국인과 함께 있는 게 눈에 띄는 것이 창피했기 때문이야.

Day
08

in private :: 사적으로

↳ not publicly

Q He's a very entertaining TV personality, isn't he?
그는 매우 재미있는 TV 배우지 않니?

A Yes, but in private he's gloomy and humorless.
그래, 하지만 개인적으로는 우울하고 유머가 없어.

one's heart goes out to
:: 동정이 가다

↳ feel sorry for

Q Did you see the TV documentary last night about the boat people?
어젯밤 보트 피플(선박 피난민)에 관한 TV 기록물을 보았니?

A Yes, and my heart really went out to them.
그래, 정말로 그들에게 동정이 갔어.

have a way with
:: 잘 다루다

↳ know how to handle

Q Is he an excellent veterinarian?
그는 우수한 수의사니?

A Yes, he really has a way with animals, especially dogs.
그래, 그는 정말 동물들을 잘 다뤄. 특히 개를 말이야.

a man of one's word
:: 약속을 잘 지키는 사람

↳ the man who keeps his promises

Q Are you sure he'll keep his promise?
그가 약속을 지킬 것이라고 확신하니?

A Yes, and don't worry. He's a man of his word.
그래, 염려 마. 그는 약속을 잘 지키는 사람이야.

hold over
:: 연장하다

↳ make stay for a longer period

Q Is " Terminator II" still playing at the Myungbo Theater?
"터미네이터 II"가 아직도 명보극장에서 상영중이니?

A Yes, it's so popular it's being held over for more weeks.
응, 너무 인기가 좋아서 몇 주 동안 더 연장되고 있어

222 crop up

:: 뜻밖에 발생하다

↳ happen unexpectedly

Q Will you be home for dinner tonight on time?
오늘 저녁은 제때에 식사하기 위해 귀가할 건가?

A No, something has cropped up at the office so I'll be a few hours late.
아니, 사무실에 무슨 일이 갑자기 생겨서 몇 시간 늦을 거야.

223 play cat and mouse with

:: 괴롭히다, 놀리다

↳ make miserable and frustrated

Q Did the State Department reject your visa application again?
국무성이 또 네 비자 신청을 거절했니?

A Yes, for the third time! I think they're playing cat and mouse with me.
그래, 세 번째야. 날 골탕먹이고 있나봐.

224 screw up

:: 엉망으로 만들다

↳ make a big mess of

Q Are you going to vote Republican again in the next election?
다음 선거에서 또 공화당에 투표할거니?

A Yes, unless the party screws up the economy before then.
응, 그 이전에 경제를 크게 망치지 않는 한.

Day
08

225 come out of nowhere

:: 뜻밖에 갑자기 나타나다

↳ appear suddenly and unexpectedly

Q Do you know which car was responsible for the accident?
어느 차가 그 사고에 책임이 있는지 아니?

A Yes, the blue one. It came out of nowhere and crashed into the white one.
응, 파란 차야. 그게 갑자기 나타나서 흰 차를 들이받았어.

look up :: 찾아보다

↳ search for

Q Do you know how to spell "truly"?
"truly"를 어떻게 쓰는지 아니?

A No, I'm not sure. Why don't you look it up in my dictionary?
확실히 몰라. 내 사전을 찾아보지 그래?

screen out :: 심사하다, 걸러내다

↳ remove what is not wanted

Q Are many people applying for jobs these days?
취직하려는 사람들이 많이 있니?

A Yes, so we have to screen them out through personality and IQ tests.
응, 그래서 인성검사와 지능검사로 걸러내야 해.

get together :: 모이다, 만나다

↳ meet

Q Shall we eat out sometime soon?
우리 조만간 외식할까?

A Yes, let's get together next Saturday night.
그러지, 다음 토요일 밤에 만나자.

in any event :: 어떠한 경우에도, 좌우간

↳ anyway

Q Will you be able to tutor my son next semester, too?
다음 학기에도 내 아들의 가정교사가 될 수 있겠습니까?

A No, but in any event I'll try to help you find someone else.
아뇨, 좌우간 다른 사람을 찾는 일을 도와드리죠.

230 hush up

:: 쉬쉬하다, 은폐하다

↳ keep secret

Q Is the Secretary of Defense going to resign soon?
국방장관이 곧 사임할거니?

A Yes, he's been accused of trying to hush up the Department of Defense scandal.
그래, 국방부 추문을 은폐하려 했다는 혐의를 받았어.

231 at a loss

:: 당황한

↳ confused about what one should do

Q Does he have any secret to his success as a salesman?
그가 판매원으로 성공한 무슨 비결이 있니?

A Yes, he's never at a loss for persuasive words in front of his customers.
응, 그는 고객 앞에서 결코 설득할 말을 몰라서 쩔쩔매지 않아.

232 never say die

:: 결코 포기하지 않다, 실망하지 않다

↳ never surrender or lose hope

Q I'm going bald and I'm still single. I'll never find a girl to marry me!
머리는 벗겨지고 있는데 난 아직도 총각이야. 하지만 나와 결혼할 여자는 절대 찾지 못할 거야.

A Yes, you will, so don't worry. Never say die, okay!
아니, 찾을 수 있을 거야. 그러니 걱정하지마. 결코 실망하지 말라구, 알았지!

Day

08

233 bring down the house

:: 집이 떠나갈 정도로 갈채를 받다

↳ get an ovation

Q Did the audience like his concert?
청중이 그의 연주회를 좋아했나요?

A Yes, and the last song he played brought down the house.
예, 끝으로 연주한 곡은 대단한 갈채를 받았죠.

fire off
:: 빨리 보내다

↳ send right away

Q Did you read this morning's editorial page?
오늘 아침의 사설면을 읽었니?

A Yes, and I'm so mad I'm going to fire off a letter to the editor right now!
응, 그런데 너무 성나서 지금 바로 편집자에게 편지를 부칠거야.

---

out of the question
:: 불가능한, 고려할 가치가 없는

↳ not worth considering

Q Can't you postpone my dental appointment until after summer vacation, Mom?
엄마, 내 치아 치료 약속을 여름 방학 후로 연기시킬 수 있어요?

A No, it's out of the question. You've got to have that rotten tooth pulled.
아니, 그건 불가능해. 넌 충치를 뽑아내야 해.

---

plan on
:: 기대하다

↳ expect

Q Does it take months for a package to get from here to Chicago?
소포를 여기서 시카고까지 보내는데 여러 달 걸릴까요?

A No, but you'd better plan on 2 to 3 weeks.
아뇨, 2, 3주 정도라고 생각하는 게 좋아요.

---

see about
:: 알아보다

↳ inquire into

Q Do you need some help finding out how the new tax law will affect you?
신 세법이 당신께 어떤 영향을 줄지 알아보는데 도와줄까요?

A Yes, could you see about it for me? I'm a little busy these days.

예, 저를 위해 알아봐 주겠어요? 저는 요즘 좀 바빠서요.

238 round off

:: 개략하다

↳ raise to the nearest whole number

Q Do you know how much we still have in our checking account?

우리 당좌구좌에 얼마 있는지 아니?

A Yes, we have $40, if we round off the sum to the nearest dollar.

응, 달러로 개략하면 40달러 갖고 있지.

239 no matter what

:: 무엇이라 해도

↳ regardless of what

Q Do you believe he's telling us the whole truth?

그가 우리에게 모든 진실을 얘기하고 있다고 믿니?

A No, because no matter what comes from his mouth I'm sure it's a lie.

아니, 그가 뭐라고 하든 난 거짓이라고 확신해.

240 put off

:: 연기하다

↳ postpone

Q Are Sally and Sam getting married next Sunday as planned?

Sally와 Sam이 예정대로 다음 일요일에 결혼하니?

A No, they decided to put off the wedding until he finds a job.

아니, Sam이 직장을 구할 때까지 연기됐어.

Day

08

영숙어 문제 단번에 공략하기

043. The clerk knew that if he embezzled the funds the company would <u>find him out</u>.

(A) detect his identity
(B) discover that he stole money
(C) learn about his motive
(D) know where he did the money
(E) locate his residence

어휘 **embezzle** 횡령하다 / **find out** 범인을 찾아내다, 간파하다 / **residence** 거주
해석 그 점원은 자신이 자금을 횡령한다면 회사가 그의 소행임을 밝혀낼 거라는 걸 알았다.

---

044. When he bowed his head, the other members <u>followed suit</u>.

(A) did the same   (B) went forward
(C) retorted   (D) disobeyed
(E) picked up the same cards

어휘 **follow suit** 선례를 따르다 / **retort** 반박하다 / **go forward** 진행되다 / **disobey** ~에 따르지 않다
해석 그가 머리를 숙여 인사를 하자 다른 회원들도 그대로 따라했다.

---

045. I _____ myself in work so as to stop thinking about the problem.

(A) intercepted   (B) imputed
(C) inspired   (D) immersed

어휘 **immerse oneself in** ~에 열중하다 / **intercept** 가로막다 / **impute** 전가하다 / **inspire** 고무하다
해석 나는 그 문제에 대한 생각을 그만두려고 일에 열중했다.

046. He was wrong. I knew that. He looked shocked. He <u>stuck to his gun</u>.

(A) He was ready to fight   (B) He remained firmly
(C) He pulled his gun out   (D) He lost his courage
(E) He was about to shoot

어휘 **stick to one's gun** 입장을 고수하다 / **be about to** 막 ~하려고 하다
해석 그가 틀렸다. 난 그걸 알고 있었다. 그는 충격을 받은 듯 보였다. 그는 자기 입장을 완강히 고수했다.

---

047. Mrs. Thatcher could not <u>hold back</u> the tides of the world history.

(A) control   (B) support
(C) delay   (D) follow
(E) go against

어휘 **hold back** 늦추다, 주저하다 / **go against** 반대하다, 거스르다
해석 대처 여사는 세계 역사의 조류를 저지할 수 없었다.

---

048. It was difficult to <u>pin down</u> what it was that made him seem different from others.

Day
08

(A) conceive   (B) define exactly
(C) make known   (D) estimate
(E) discern

어휘 **pin down** 꼭 집어내서 말하다 / **make known** 공표하다, 알리다 /
estimate 평가하다 / **discern** 분별하다
해석 무엇이 그를 다른 사람들과 달라 보이게 하는지 꼭 집어서 말하기는 어려웠다.

241 snap out of

:: 벗어나다, 꿈깨다

↳ come back to reality

Q Is he still taking singing lessons?
그 사람 여전히 노래 강습 받니?

A Yes, and I wish he'd snap out of it and realize he has no future in music.
응, 그 사람 그걸 관두고 노래에 장래성이 없다는 걸 깨달으면 좋겠는데.

242 polish off

:: 끝마치다

↳ finish

Q Aren't you going to bed soon?
곧 잠자지 않을 거니?

A No, I have to polish off history term paper first.
안 자, 역사과목 학기말 논문을 먼저 끝내야 돼.

243 eke out a living

:: 간신히 생계를 이어가다

↳ manage to keep from starving

Q Is your friend Bill getting along okay these days?
네 친구 Bill은 요즘 잘 지내니?

A No, he's barely eking out a living selling cookbooks door-to-door.
아니, 집집마다 요리책을 팔러 다니며 근근이 살고 있어.

244 in view of

:: ~을 고려하여, ~에 비추어

↳ considering

Q He's been with this company 20 years! Do you have to
fire him?

그 분은 이 회사에서 20년이나 근무했어요. 그 분을 해고해야만 해요?

A Yes, in view of the rising costs of labor these days a
robot is much cheaper.

예, 요즘 인건비가 오르기 때문에 로봇이 훨씬 싸게 먹힙니다.

245 egg on

:: 선동하다

↳ stir up

Q Did the strike turn violent?

파업이 난폭해졌니?

A Yes, the strikers were egged on by some of the more
radical union members.

응, 파업자들이 더 과격한 노조원들에게 선동되었지.

246 spruce up

:: 정돈하다, 깨끗이 하다

↳ straighten up so it looks neater

Q Are guests coming over for dinner tonight, Mom?

엄마, 손님들이 오늘밤 식사하러 오세요?

A Yes, so help me spruce up the living room a little before
they arrive.

그래, 그러니 그분들이 오기 전에 거실 청소하는 걸 도와다오.

Day
09

247 check in

:: 숙박 수속하다

↳ register at a hotel

Q Shall we go to the beach first?

우리 먼저 해변에 갈까요?

A No, let's check in a hotel, get unpacked and then go
swimming.

아뇨, 호텔에 투숙하고, 여장을 풀고, 수영하러 갑시다.

248 go with
:: 같이 지내다, 사귀다

↳ date

Q Is she still dating your brother?
그녀는 여전히 네 동생과 사귀니?

A No, she's now going with someone else.
아니, 지금은 다른 사람과 사귀어.

249 bow and scrape
:: 굽실거리다

↳ act like a slave

Q Do you like your new boss?
새 사장님을 좋아하니?

A No, because he likes us to bow and scrape before him all the time.
아니, 그는 우리가 자기 앞에서 언제나 굽실거리길 바라거든.

250 stack the cards against
:: 불공정하게 하다

↳ arrange in an unfair way

Q Will your company be able to compete successfully on the world market?
당신 회사가 세계 시장에서 성공적으로 경쟁할 수 있을까요?

A No, because the Japanese have stacked all the cards against us.
아뇨, 왜냐하면 일본인들이 우리에게 불리한 수단을 쓰기 때문이죠.

251 dawn on
:: ～에게 (생각이) 분명해지다

↳ occur to

Q Did you forget that yesterday was your wife's birthday?
어제가 자네 부인 생일인 거 잊고 있었나?

A Yes, until it finally dawned on me why she wasn't speaking to me.
응, 왜 그녀가 내게 말을 걸지 않았는지 깨닫고서야 생각났지.

out of kilter   :: 똑바르지 않은, 정상이 아닌

↳ not straight

Q Is the picture straight now?
그림이 똑바릅니까?

A No, move it left a little. It's still out of kilter.
아뇨, 왼쪽으로 조금 옮기세요. 아직 불완전합니다.

make fun of   :: 놀리다

↳ ridicule

Q Did you scold Billy this morning?
오늘 아침 Billy를 야단쳤소?

A Yes, because he was making fun of my son who's a little overweight.
예, 그 애가 좀 비만인 우리 아들을 놀려서요.

put a damper on   :: 기를 꺾다

↳ suppress

Q Do you like our new chairman?
우리 새 회장님이 좋니?

A No, because all he seems to do is put a damper on every suggestion I make.
아니, 왜냐하면 그가 하는일이라곤 내가 하는 제안마다 트집잡는게 다야.

Day
09

make eyes at   :: 추파를 던지다

↳ look at with lust

Q Is something bothering you?
뭐 귀찮게 하는 거라도 있니?

A Yes, I think that old man over there is trying to make eyes at me.
응, 저 노인이 내게 추파를 던지고 있는 것 같애.

256 all the same

:: 그래도

↳ in any case

Q Do you think your mother will mind if I sleep over at your house tonight?
내가 네 집에서 오늘 밤 잔다면 네 어머니께서 싫어하실까?

A No, but all the same let me ask her first.
아니, 하지만 그래도 먼저 내가 어머니께 부탁할게.

257 lose one's way

:: 길을 잃다

↳ get lost

Q Do you know exactly where we are now?
우리가 지금 어디에 있는 건지 정확히 알고 있니?

A No, I'm afraid I've lost my way.
아니, 아무래도 우리가 길을 잃었나봐.

258 over again

:: 반복해서

↳ repeat

Q Is this the correct answer, Professor?
교수님, 이것이 정답입니까?

A No, so do the equation over again and this time get it right!
아냐, 그러니 그 방정식을 다시 풀어보게. 그리고 이번엔 옳게 해봐.

259 out-and-out

:: 철저한(나쁜 의미)

↳ thorough

Q Is he dishonest?
그는 정직하지 않니?

A Yes, he's an out-and-out liar.
응, 철저한 거짓말쟁이야.

through thick and thin :: 만난(萬難)을 무릅쓰고

↳ in good times and in bad times

Q Will you always be my friend?
당신, 언제나 제 친구가 되어 주실래요?

A Yes, through thick and thin I'll stay by your side.
예, 물불을 가리지 않고 당신을 곁에서 돕겠습니다.

in no time flat :: 곧

↳ very soon

Q Will the report be finished soon?
보고서가 곧 완성됩니까?

A Yes, it'll be ready in no time flat.
예, 곧 준비됩니다.

pass off as :: ~로 통하다, ~인 체하다

↳ be regarded as

Q Is she an American?
그녀는 미국인이니?

A No, but her English is so good she could easily be
passed off as one.
아니, 그러나 영어를 아주 잘해서 쉽게 미국인 행세를 할 수 있지.

Day
09

something else again :: 별개의 것

↳ another matter

Q Can I borrow $50, Dad?
아빠, 50달러 빌려 주실래요?

A Yes, for books. But if it's for beers, well that's something
else again.
책 살 거라면 좋다. 하지만 술 마신다면 문제가 다르지.

264 shut off

:: 잠그다

↳ turn off

Q Why's there no water? Is there something wrong with this faucet?
왜 물이 안 나와? 이 수도꼭지가 잘못 됐나?

A Yes, I shut off the valve to fix the leak.
응, 새는 곳을 고치려고 내가 밸브를 잠갔지.

265 take the reins

:: 권력을 잡다

↳ take power

Q Do you think he's qualified to be president?
그가 회장이 될만하다고 생각해?

A No, he's still too young to take the reins of such a big company.
아니, 그는 그렇게 큰 회사를 장악하기엔 아직 너무 어려.

266 simmer down

:: 진정하다

↳ calm down

Q We're going to be late! Isn't that stupid brother of yours here yet?
우리 지각하겠어! 그 멍청한 네 동생은 아직 안 온 거야?

A No, so just simmer down and don't get excited!
응, 그러니 진정하고 흥분하지 마!

267 in luck

:: 운이 좋은

↳ fortunate

Q Do you have any aspirin tablets in your purse?
핸드백에 아스피린 좀 있나?

A Yes, you're in luck. I've got a whole bottle of them.
예, 당신 운이 좋아요. 한 병 가득 있어요.

268 put up with

:: 참다

↳ endure

Q Did you hear what the Mayor proposed yesterday?
시장님이 어제 무엇을 제안했는지 들었니?

A Yes, and I'm getting tired of putting up with his shallow ideas.
응, 그리고 그의 피상적인 얘기를 참느라 피곤해졌어.

269 every now and then

:: 자주

↳ sometimes

Q Do you still go bowling since you got married?
너 결혼하고서도 볼링 치러 다니니?

A Yes, my wife lets me go every now and then.
응, 아내가 자주 가게 해.

270 make off with

:: ~을 가지고 달아나다

↳ take away

Q Did the robber steal anything from your garage?
강도가 당신 차고에서 뭔가 훔쳤나요?

A Yes, he made off with my son's motorcycle.
예, 아들의 오토바이를 갖고 가버렸죠.

Day

09

영숙어 문제 단번에 공략하기

049. Long journey <u>took it out of me</u>.

(A) made me happy   (B) took away my desire
(C) made me tired   (D) taught me a lot of things
(E) troubled me

> 어휘 **take it out of** 피곤하게 하다 / **take away** 가져가다, 덜다
> 해석 오랜 여행은 나를 지치게 했다.

---

050. Nobody wants to go out for dinner with Sam, because he doesn't enjoy eating, nor does he <u>pick up the tab</u>.

(A) serve   (B) ask for
(C) drink   (D) order
(E) pay for

> 어휘 **pick up (the tab)** 계산을 치르다 / **(pay for) tab** 계산서, 꼬리표
> 해석 아무도 샘과 함께 저녁 식사하러 나가기를 원치 않는다. 그는 먹는 것을 즐기지도 않을뿐더러 계산도 하 지 않기 때문이다.

---

051. Harry was a capable lawyer, but it was difficult for him to _____ to the reputation established by his more brilliant father.

(A) live up   (B) compete
(C) live on   (D) compel
(E) submit

> 어휘 **live up to** ~에 따라 생활하다 / **brilliant** 찬란한, 훌륭한 / **live on** ~을 먹고 살다 / **compel** 억지로 시키다 / **submit to** ~에 복종시키다
> 해석 해리는 유능한 변호사였지만, 그보다 더 훌륭했던 아버지가 이룩한 명성을 따라잡기는 힘들었다.

052. Frequent mistakings _____ against your promotion.

(A) mitigate   (B) militate
(C) deploy   (D) darken
(E) take

어휘 mitigate 완화시키다 / militate against ~을 방해하다 / deploy 전개·배
치하다 / take against 반항하다, 반감을 갖다
해석 잦은 실수들은 당신의 승진을 방해한다.

---

053. He _____ a longstanding grievance against theoretical antirealism and the academic glorification of the modernist aesthetics.

(A) knelled   (B) freckled
(C) scraped   (D) nursed

어휘 longstanding 오래 계속되는 / nurse + 불만 + against ~에게 불만을 품
다 / glorification 찬미, 축연, 미화 / aesthetics 미학 / knell 종을 울려
알리다 / freckle 주근깨가 생기다 / scrape 문지르다
해석 그는 이론적인 반리얼리즘과 모더니스트 미학의 아카데믹한 미화(美化)에 오
랜 반감을 품고 있었다.

---

054. Charles was not sure which profession to enter, but finally _____ for the law.

(A) chose   (B) opted
(C) preferred   (D) selected

Day
09

어휘 be sure ~을 확신하다 / opt for ~을 선택하다(choose)
해석 찰스는 어떤 직장에 들어가야 할지 확신할 수 없었으나, 마침내 법조계를 선택
했다.

10th Day

271 every inch
:: 완전히, 빈틈없이

↳ completely from head to foot

Q Mr. Smith is a kind and wonderful man, isn't he?
Smith 씨는 친절하고 훌륭한 분이야, 그렇지?

A Yes, he's every inch a gentleman.
응, 완벽한 신사이지.

272 hit upon
:: 우연히 찾다

↳ come up with

Q Isn't this an ingenious tool?
이거 독창적인 기구 아냐?

A Yes, and the inventor hit upon the idea while he was taking a bath!
그래, 발명가가 목욕하다 떠오른 착상이래.

273 take the rap for
:: 벌받다

↳ be punished for

Q Did aunt Blanda accuse you of breaking her expensive vase?
Blanda 아줌마가 비싼 꽃병을 깼다고 너를 나무랐니?

A Yes, but I'm not going to take the rap for it. I wasn't even in her house.
응, 하지만 그것 때문에 벌받지는 않을 거야. 나는 아줌마 집에 있지도 않았으니까.

274 squeak through

:: 간신히 성공하다

↳ pass but with difficulty

Q Did you have an easy time passing your driver's license test?
운전 면허 시험에 합격하기 쉬웠니?

A No, I barely squeaked through.
아니, 겨우 합격했어.

275 shake off

:: 제거하다

↳ get rid of

Q Are you still taking cough medicine?
아직도 기침약 먹니?

A Yes, because I'm having trouble shaking off my cold.
응, 감기를 떼버리기 어려워서.

276 pull for

:: 후원하다, 응원하다

↳ support

Q Will you be supporting the Dallas Cowboys next Sunday?
다음 일요일 Dallas Cowboys를 응원할거니?

A No, I'll be pulling for the Chicago Bears.
아니, Chicago Bears를 응원할 거야.

277 spell out

:: 상세히 설명하다

↳ explain in detail

Q Did he finally understand what you were trying to explain to him?
네가 설명하려는 걸 그가 결국 이해했을까?

A Yes, but he's so dumb I had to almost spell it out for him.
응, 하지만 그가 너무 둔해서 일일이 얘기해야만 했지.

Day

10

278 hold down

:: 유지하다

↳ maintain

Q Don't you resent always being bypassed for a promotion?

승진에서 빠진 걸 늘 원망하고 있지 않니?

A No, because I'm having a hard time just holding down my present position.

아냐, 왜냐하면 그저 지금 자리를 지키는데도 고생하고 있거든.

279 all but

:: 거의

↳ almost

Q Was she shocked to hear that her cousin was involved in a traffic accident?

조카가 교통사고에 관계되었다는 얘기를 듣고 그녀가 충격 받았니?

A Yes, she all but fainted when she heard the news.

응, 그 소식을 듣고 거의 기절했어.

280 end up

:: ~로 끝나다

↳ finish as

Q Are you worried because your daughter still hasn't gotten married?

따님이 아직 결혼하지 않아서 걱정이세요?

A Yes, of course! I don't want her to end up an old maid.

예, 정말! 난 그 애가 노처녀로 끝나는 것을 원치 않습니다.

281 put something over

:: 속이다

↳ trick

Q Sir, do you mind if I examine the contents of your wallet?

선생님, 제가 선생님의 지갑품목을 조사해도 괜찮을까요?

A Yes, of course! Are you trying to put something over on me?
아니요! 당신 나를 속이려는 거요?

drag on and on

:: 질질 끌다

↳ seem to last forever

Q Are we having another staff meeting tomorrow morning?
우리 내일 아침에 또 참모회의를 하니?

A Yes, and don't you just hate the way they always seem to drag on and on?
응, 그 사람들 늘 질질 끄는 것 같은 게 짜증나지 않니?

hear from

:: 소식을 듣다

↳ receive news from

Q Has she written you recently?
그녀가 최근에 편지를 했나요?

A No, in fact I haven't heard from her in over 6 months.
아뇨, 사실 6개월 이상 소식을 듣지 못했어요.

pull rank on

:: 계급(지위)으로 누르다

↳ use one's higher position to gain an unfair advantage

Q Did you get to sit at the head table during the Boss's birthday party?
사장님의 생일잔치 때 연설자 테이블 옆에 앉았었나?

A No, the section chief pulled rank on me and sat there instead.
아뇨, 과장님이 나를 지위로 누르고 대신 거기 앉았죠.

Day

10

285   luck out

:: 뜻밖에 운이 좋다

↳ be lucky

Q Did your father get to the airport late yesterday?
네 아버지께서 어제 공항에 늦게 도착하셨니?

A Yes, but he really lucked out—his plane was delayed one hour.
응, 하지만 정말 운이 좋아서 그 비행기가 한 시간 지체되었지.

286   show off

:: 과시하다

↳ try to attract attention

Q Did he break his leg riding his bicycle?
그 사람 자전거 타다가 다리가 부러졌나?

A Yes, he crashed into a tree when he was showing off in front of a girl.
응, 여자 앞에서 과시해 보이다 나무에 부딪혔지.

287   it's about time

:: ~할 때가 됐다

↳ it's long overdue

Q Am I late for dinner?
저녁 식사에 제가 늦었나요?

A Yes, and it's about time you came! I'm going to have to reheat the food!
그래, 벌써 왔어야 했다구! 다시 음식을 데워야 하잖아!

288   tide one over

:: 극복하다, 어려운 때를 넘기다

↳ help get through a difficult period

Q Will you need more money next semester, Son?
다음 학기에 돈이 더 필요하니, 얘야?

A Yes, but only about $100 more will be enough to tide me over.
예, 하지만 그저 백불 이상 정도면 충분히 지낼 거예요.

289 keep in touch

:: 연락하다

↳ contact regularly

Q Do you think we'll ever see each other again?
우리가 다시 보게 될까?

A Yes, of course! Let's keep in touch by writing frequently.
그럼, 물론이지! 자주 편지로 연락하자구.

290 put in a good word for

:: 말을 잘해주다

↳ speak on someone's behalf

Q Has your son found a job yet?
댁의 아들이 벌써 취직했나요?

A No, so would you be kind enough to put in a good word for him?
아뇨, 그러니 그를 위해 말씀 좀 잘 해주시겠어요?

291 under fire

:: 공격을 받고 있는

↳ criticized

Q Did the mayor resign this morning?
시장이 오늘 아침 사직했나요?

A Yes, and I would too if I were under fire all the time like he was.
예, 그분처럼 비난당한다면 저라도 그랬을 겁니다.

292 mean well

:: (잘못됐지만) 선의로 하다

↳ have good intentions

Q He was only trying to help you. Did you have to yell at him?
그는 그저 널 도우려는 거야. 그에게 고함쳐야만 했니?

A No, but even though he meant well he made the work twice as difficult!
아니예요, 비록 선의라 해도 그 일을 두 배나 어렵게 만들었다구요!

Day
10

105

293 scrape through

↳ succeed but with difficulty

Q Is your checking account empty already?
네 구좌가 벌써 비었니?

A Yes, but I'm not worried. I'll scrape through somehow.
응, 하지만 걱정 안해. 어떻게든 해 나갈 수 있어.

294 let one's hair down

:: 자연스럽게 행동하다, 경계를 풀고 얘기하다

↳ speak frankly and informally

Q Do you like her personality?
그 여자 성격을 좋아하니?

A Yes, because she always lets her hair down when we talk
together.
응, 그녀는 함께 얘기할 때 늘 스스럼 없어서.

295 touch upon (or on)

:: 언급하다

↳ mention or write briefly about

Q Did you study Reaganomics in your economics class?
경제학 수업 때 레이건의 경제정책을 공부했니?

A Yes, but because it was for only one semester we could
only touch upon it.
응, 하지만 한 학기동안 뿐이었기 때문에 살짝 맛보는 정도야.

296 dead as a doornail

:: 아주 죽은

↳ dead beyond any doubt

Q Is Israel's tourism industry doing well these days?
이스라엘 관광산업은 요즘 잘 됩니까?

A No, it's dead as a doornail because of all the terrorism
recently.
아뇨, 빈발하는 테러 때문에 아주 죽었어요.

297 buy up

:: 매점하다

↳ buy everything available

Q Is your uncle one of the wealthiest men in town?
네 삼촌이 마을에서 가장 부자니?

A Yes, and he got rich buying up all the real estate he could find.
그래, 그는 눈에 띄는 부동산은 전부 매점하는 부자라구.

298 out of character

:: 걸맞지 않은, 이례적인

↳ unlike one's usual behavior

Q Are you sure he really donated $10,000 to an orphanage?
그가 고아원에 1만 달러를 기증한 것이 확실하니?

A Yes, and it was completely out of character for him—he's worse than Scrooge.
그래, 완전히 그 사람답지 않았어. 스크루지보다 지독한 구두쇠인데.

299 beat around the bush

:: 변죽만 울리다

↳ talk indirectly, thereby tiring the listeners

Q Do you really want to hear all the bad things he said about you?
그가 너에 대해 나쁘게 말한 것 모두를 정말 듣고 싶니?

A Yes, and don't beat around the bush. Tell me everything.
그래, 변죽만 울리지 말구 모든 걸 말해 봐.

300 butt in

:: 간섭하다

Day

10

↳ interfere

Q Don't you think you're spending too much time away from your family?
넌 가족과 너무 많은 시간을 떨어져서 보낸다고 생각하지 않니?

A No, and will you stop butting in other people's problems!
아니, 남의 일에 간섭하지 말아줄래?

영숙어 문제 단번에 공략하기

055. Someone has <u>made off</u> with my umbrella.

(A) departed suddenly   (B) made a mistake
(C) attacked a person   (D) got rid of a thing
(E) appeared

> 어휘 **make off with** ~을 가지고 급히 달아나다 / **make a mistake** 실수하다 /
> **get rid of** ~을 없애다
>
> 해석 누군가 내 우산을 갖고 달아나 버렸다.

---

056. It will be necessary to monitor the mills constantly to make sure they are <u>complying with</u> the government standard.

(A) voting for   (B) defying
(C) conforming to   (D) appealing to
(E) compromising with

> 어휘 **mill** 공장 / **make sure** 확인하다 / **comply with** 순응하다 / **vote for** 찬
> 성 투표하다 / **defy** 얕보다, 도전하다 / **conform to** ~에 따르다 / **appeal
> to** ~에 호소하다 / **compromise with** 타협하다
>
> 해석 공장들이 정부 기준을 잘 따르고 있는지 확인하기 위해서는 항상 공장들을 감
> 시해야 할 것이다.

---

057. That was a form of amusement that was never <u>gone in for</u> by the working class.

(A) taken part in   (B) come up with
(C) put up with   (D) looked forward to
(E) run around with

어휘 **go in for** 참석하다, 좋아하다, 열중하다 / **take part in** ~에 참석하다 / **come up with** ~를 따라 잡다 / **put up with** 참다(endure) / **look forward to** 기대하다 / **run around with** 불륜을 저지르다

해석 그것은 노동자 계층에서는 결코 즐기지 않던 오락 양식이었다.

---

058. He is the kind of person who always <u>calls a spade a spade</u>.

(A) has no common sense
(B) speaks plainly
(C) talks about small things
(D) gossips about others
(E) knows everything

어휘 **call a spade a spade** 사실대로 말하다(speak frankly) / **have no common sense** 상식이 없다 / **plainly** 명백히, 솔직히

해석 그는 늘 사실은 사실대로 말하는 그런 사람이다.

---

059. John <u>lost his temper</u> and kicked the vending machine.

(A) was late   (B) lost his time
(C) became angry   (D) misplaced his wallet

어휘 **lose one's temper** 화를 내다 / **vending machine** 자동판매기 / **misplace** 잘못 두다 / **wallet** 지갑

해석 존은 화가 나서 자동판매기를 발로 찼다.

---

060. In his curricula vitae, he <u>put down</u> simply 'businessman' for profession.

Day

10

(A) wrote   (B) reduced
(C) considered   (D) attributed

어휘 **curricula vitae** 이력서 / **put down** 적다(write)

해석 이력서 직업란에다 그는 단순히 '사업가'라고만 적었다.

Answers ★ 55.(A) 56.(C) 57.(A) 58.(B) 59.(C) 60.(A)

301 **beyond question** :: 의심할 여지가 없는

↳ without any doubt

Q Are you sure he's the criminal?
그가 범인인 것이 확실하니?

A Yes, it's beyond question—the lab tests prove him to be the guilty one.
그래, 의심의 여지가 없어. 실험 결과 그가 유죄임이 입증됐어.

302 **beside the point (or question)** :: 핵심을 벗어난

↳ of no importance

Q You mean I still haven't persuaded you?
내가 아직도 너를 설득시키지 못했다는 뜻이니?

A No, because most of what you said is beside the point.
그래, 네가 말한 것은 대부분 핵심을 벗어난 거야.

303 **put the screws on** :: 압박하다

↳ force to do against one's will

Q Don't you feel guilty not giving more money to the church?
교회에 더 많은 돈을 내지 않는 게 죄스럽지 않니?

A No, and stop trying to put the screws on me like this, okay?
아니, 그러니 이렇게 나를 압박하려고 하지마, 알겠니?

304 one at a time
:: 따로 따로, 한번에 하나씩

↳ one by one

Q Are you going to interview all three applicants at the same time?
동시에 세 명의 응시자들을 모두 면접할 거니?

A No, this time I want to meet them one at a time.
아니, 이번엔 한 명씩 만나고 싶어.

305 hear one out
:: 끝까지 듣다

↳ listen to a person or their words until they finished

Q Did mom accept your excuse for coming home very late last night?
어젯밤 늦게 귀가한 변명을 엄마가 들어줬니?

A No, she was so angry she wouldn't even hear me out.
아니, 몹시 화가 나서 끝까지 들으려고도 하지 않으셨어.

306 at stake
:: 위태로운, 내기에 걸려 있는

↳ to be won or lost

Q Are you going to sue him for libel?
그를 중상모략으로 고소할 거니?

A Yes, because my reputation as a public official is at stake.
그래, 공무원으로서 내 명예가 걸려 있기 때문이야.

307 skin-deep
:: 피상적인

↳ shallow

Q Is Joe such a kind person to everyone?
Joe는 누구에게나 몹시 친절하지?

A No, his kindness is just skin-deep. At home he's cold and irritable.
아니, 그의 친절은 아주 얄팍해. 집에선 냉혹하고 화를 잘 내.

111

308 **do one a favor**

:: 부탁을 들어주다

↳ help one

Q Did you have something to ask me?
내게 요청할 게 뭐 있니?

A Yes, could you do me a favor? Could you open this jar for me?
그래, 부탁 하나 들어줄 수 있니? 이 병을 열어줄래?

309 **rub elbows with**

:: ~와 어울리다

↳ meet and mix with

Q Do you like attending movie premieres?
영화 시사회에 참석하기를 좋아하십니까?

A Yes, because I get to rub elbows with some famous film people.
예, 유명한 영화인들과 어울리고 싶거든요.

310 **up one's alley**

:: 취미에 맞는

↳ what I really like doing

Q Do you like golf?
골프를 좋아하니?

A Yes, it's a sport that's right up my alley.
응, 그건 내 취미에 꼭 맞는 운동이야.

311 **not in the least**

:: 전혀 ~않다

↳ not at all

Q Are you too tired to help me do the dishes tonight?
너무 피곤해서 접시 닦는 것을 도와줄 수 없니?

A No, not in the least. I'll be glad to help.
아니, 전혀 안 그래. 기꺼이 도와줄게.

312 **not make any difference with** :: 상관이 없다

↳ not matter with or care about

Q Do you mind if we study in the library tonight instead of at my house?

오늘밤 집 대신 도서관에서 공부해도 괜찮아요?

A No, it doesn't make any difference with me.

괜찮아. 나에겐 전혀 상관이 없어.

313 **get behind in** :: (일이) 밀려 있다

↳ go more slowly than others, letting them move ahead

Q Shall we go to a movie tonight?

우리 오늘밤 영화관에 갈까?

A No, I have to stay home. I've gotten too far behind in my studies.

안 가, 난 집에 있어야 돼. 공부가 너무 많이 밀려 있어.

314 **hold good** :: 유효하다, 지속하다

↳ continue to be true or valid

Q Do you think the cease-fire will last much longer?

휴전이 더 오래 계속될 것 같니?

A No, it will hold good less than three more weeks.

아니, 3주 이상도 지속될 수 없어.

315 **shut down** :: 문닫다, 휴업하다

↳ closed

Q You don't have to go to work again today?

너 오늘 또 일을 나갈 필요가 없니?

A Yes, my factory was shut down temporarily for repairs.

그래, 공장이 수리 때문에 잠시 문 닫았어.

113

316 pull through

:: 회복하다

↳ regain health

Q Does he have any chance of surviving the accident, Doctor?
선생님, 그가 그 사고에서 살아날 가능성이 있습니까?

A Yes, if he pulls through his operation tomorrow.
예, 내일 수술에서 회복한다면요.

317 it goes without saying

:: 말할 것도 없다

↳ it is so obvious that it need not even be said

Q Do you mind if I visit you tonight?
오늘밤 너를 방문해도 괜찮니?

A No, and it goes without saying you're always welcome in my home.
괜찮아. 말할 것도 없이 넌 항상 우리 집에서 환영이야.

318 on the lookout for

:: 찾고 있는

↳ watching closely for

Q Did an FBI agent visit your police station this morning?
FBI요원이 오늘 아침에 경찰서를 방문했니?

A Yes, and he told us to be on the lookout for a bearded man in a gray suit.
그래, 회색 정장에 수염기른 자를 찾고 있다고 말했어.

319 get to the point

:: 요점을 말하다

↳ talk about the most important part

Q Did you learn much from Prof. Smith's lecture on women's rights last night?
어젯밤 여성의 권리에 대한 Smith 교수 강의에서 많은 것을 배웠니?

A No, because he didn't seem to ever get to the point.
아니, 그는 항상 요점을 말할 줄 모르는 것 같아서.

320 bear in mind
:: 기억하다, 명심하다

↳ remember

Q Did Mr. Smith forget to return our lawn mower he borrowed last week?
스미스 씨는 지난 주 빌린 잔디깎기를 되돌려 주는 것을 잊었소?

A Yes, but please bear in mind that he's now almost 90 years old.
그래요, 하지만 그가 지금 아흔 살이라는 것을 기억하세요.

321 run out
:: (시간 등이) 끝나다

↳ come to an end

Q Did your hockey team do well in the tournament?
네 하키팀은 경기에서 잘했니?

A No, time ran out before we could score even one goal.
아니, 한 골도 넣지 못하고 경기가 끝났어.

322 in part
:: 일부는

↳ to some degree

Q Did he hit the car in front of him?
그가 그의 앞차를 받았니?

A Yes, but it was also to blame in part. The tail lights weren't working.
그래, 하지만 그 차도 일부는 책임이 있어. 후미등이 고장나 있었거든.

323 out to
:: ~하려고 애쓰는

↳ trying to

Q Do you now consider him an enemy?
넌 그를 지금 적으로 여기니?

A Yes, I think for the past few months he's been out to do me great harm.
그래, 지난 몇 개월 동안 나를 해치려고 했다고 생각해.

pass judgment on   :: 판단하다

↳ judge

Q Do you think he was the one who committed the
murder?
넌 그가 살인자라고 생각하니?

A No, it's still too early to pass judgment on him before
the trial.
아니, 재판 전에 그를 판단하는 것은 너무 일러.

take something lying down   :: (모욕을) 감수하다

↳ accept without making any protest

Q Did your political opponent call you an incompetent
fool in his TV ads?
정적(政敵)이 TV 광고에서 당신을 무능한 바보라고 불렀습니까?

A Yes, but I'm not going to take it lying down. I'm going
to sue him for libel.
그래요, 하지만 난 그 모욕을 감수하지 않을 겁니다. 명예 훼손죄로 고소하
겠습니다.

get out of line   :: 순종치 않다

↳ not act according to orders

Q Did you kick 10 students out of your class on the first
day?
첫날 너희 반에서 학생 10명을 쫓아냈니?

A Yes, because they were starting to get out of line.
그래, 말을 듣지 않아서.

stick something out   :: 끝까지 참다

↳ endure to the end

Q Do you like your new job?
새 일이 좋니?

A No, I hate it, but I'll stick it out until I can find a better one.

아니, 싫어. 하지만 더 좋은 일을 찾을 때까지 꾹 참을 거야.

328 so far, so good   :: 지금까지는 좋아

↳ until now things have gone pretty well

Q Is your English conversation class going well these days?

요즘 영어회화 수업은 잘 되니?

A Yes, so far, so good.

그래, 지금까지는 좋아.

329 good-for-nothing   :: 쓸모 없는

↳ worthless

Q Does Mary have a night job along with her regular one?

Mary는 본업에다 야간 일도 하니?

A Yes, because her good-for-nothing husband wastes all their money gambling.

그래, 그녀의 쓸모 없는 남편이 도박에 돈을 모두 낭비하기 때문이지.

330 hand down to   :: 물려주다

↳ give as an inheritance

Q Did you buy that lovely vase in a department store?

저 예쁜 꽃병을 백화점에서 샀니?

A No, it was actually handed down to me by my greatgrandfather.

아니, 증조부 때부터 나에게 물려 내려온 거야.

영숙어 문제 단번에 공략하기

061. The matter can't be <u>put off</u>.

(A) hesitated   (B) extended

(C) cancelled   (D) postponed

(E) enlarged

어휘 **put off** 연기하다(postpone) / **extend** 연장하다 / **cancel** 취소하다(call off) / **enlarge** 확대하다

해석 그 사안은 연기될 수 없다.

---

062. How do you <u>account for</u> that phenomenon?

(A) allow for   (B) find

(C) explain   (D) consider

어휘 **account for** 설명하다(explain) / **phenomenon** 현상 **phenomena** (pl.) / **allow for** ~을 참작하여 공제해 주다

해석 어떻게 그 현상을 설명하겠어요?

---

063. The contract <u>holds good</u> for five years.

(A) is drawn up   (B) is well kept

(C) is remembered well   (D) remains effective

어휘 **contract** 계약 / **hold good** 유효하다 / **draw up** (문서를) 작성하다 / **effective** 유효한, 효과적인

해석 그 계약은 5년간 유효하다.

064. Who can <u>shed light on</u> the reasons?

(A) turn on   (B) explain
(C) dissipate   (D) appall

어휘 **shed light on** 명백히 밝히다 / **turn on** 켜다 / **dissipate** 흩뜨리다, 낭비
하다 / **appall** 오싹하게 하다

해석 누가 그 이유들을 명확히 밝혀낼 수 있을까?

065. The president and his wife <u>showed up</u> at the party last
night.

(A) showed off   (B) appeared
(C) brought something   (D) showed themselves

어휘 **show up** (모임 등에) 나타나다 / **show off** 자랑하다(brag about, boast of)
/ **show oneself** 참석하다, 모습을 보이다

해석 사장과 그의 부인이 지난 밤 파티에 나타났다.

066. The protesters <u>handed out</u> leaflets describing their
grievances.

(A) distributed   (B) proved
(C) exchanged   (D) deleted

어휘 **hand out** 나눠주다 / **leaflet** 광고 전단, 인쇄물 / **grievance** 불평 /
distribute 분배하다, 배포하다 / **delete** 삭제하다

해석 시위자들은 자신들의 불만사항을 적은 전단을 나눠주었다.

---

331 **call for**

:: 전화로 깨우다

↳ telephone to wake up in the morning

Q Do you want the desk clerk to wake you up early tomorrow, sir?
접수직원이 내일 일찍 깨워드리기를 원하십니까?

A Yes, please have him call for me at 6:00 a.m.
6시에 전화로 깨우도록 해 주세요.

---

332 **ahead of**

:: 미리, 시간 전에

↳ sooner than it starts

Q Are you leaving for the concert already?
벌써 음악회에 가니?

A Yes, I want to get there a little ahead of time and get a good seat.
그래, 약간 미리 가서 좋은 좌석을 차지하고 싶어.

---

333 **grow on**

:: 점점 더 ~마음에 들다

↳ become more accepted or even liked

Q Do you hate modern art as much as I do?
너도 나만큼 현대 예술을 싫어하니?

A No, it's starting to grow on me.
아니, 점점 마음에 들기 시작했어.

334 a matter of course

:: 당연한 일

↳ not unusual but actually quite normal

Q Do Korean students resent having to study English so hard?
한국 학생들은 열심히 영어 공부하는 것을 싫어합니까?

A No, they take it as a matter of course.
아뇨, 당연한 일로 생각해요.

335 a white lie

:: 악의 없는 거짓말

↳ a harmless lie

Q Did you say to Mary you thought her new outfit was lovely?
Mary의 새옷이 예쁘다고 그녀에게 말했니?

A Yes, but sometimes telling a white lie is necessary.
악의 없는 거짓말은 때때로 필요해.

336 a tempest in a teapot

:: 사소한 소동

↳ great excitement or confusion about almost nothing

Q Are the two countries still arguing over trade issues?
양국이 아직도 무역 문제로 논쟁하고 있습니까?

A Yes, but this time it's just a tempest in a teapot.
예, 그러나 이번에는 사소한 분쟁입니다.

337 not have anything to do with

:: 아무 관계가 없다

↳ not have any relationship with

Q Are you going to let your daughter date him?
네 딸이 그와 데이트하게 내버려둘 거니?

A No, because I don't want her to have anything to do with divorced men.
아니, 난 그 애가 이혼한 남자와 관계하는 것을 원치 않아.

338 louse up

:: 망치다

↳ spoil

Q Are you eagerly expecting our annual picnic next
weekend?
다음 주말 연례 소풍을 크게 기대하고 있니?

A Yes, and I just hope the weather won't louse up the
occasion like last year.
그래, 그런데 날씨가 지난 해처럼 이 행사를 망치지 않았으면 좋겠어.

339 from now on

:: 지금부터

↳ from this moment

Q Did you do well on the last biology test?
지난 생물 시험을 잘 봤니?

A No, but from now on I'm going to study as hard as I can.
아니, 하지만 지금부터 할 수 있는대로 열심히 공부할거야.

340 red tape

:: 형식주의, 비능률

↳ irritating bureaucratic regulations

Q Do you dislike bureaucrats?
관료들을 싫어합니까?

A Yes, because all they know how to do is create more and
more red tape.
예, 그들이 할 줄 아는 것이라곤 비능률을 더 많이 만드는 것 뿐이기 때문이죠.

341 pull oneself together

:: 기운 차리다

↳ become emotionally stable again

Q Is Mary now seeing a psychiatrist?
Mary는 지금 정신과 의사를 만나고 있니?

A Yes, but I wish she would try to pull herself together first.
그래, 하지만 그녀가 먼저 기운을 차리려 노력했으면 좋겠어.

342 **turn off**   :: 싫게 하다

↳ disgust

Q Did he make a good first impression?
그의 첫인상이 좋았니?

A No, because his chain-smoking really turned me off.
아니, 그가 줄담배 피우는 게 정말 싫었기 때문이야.

343 **butterflies in one's stomach**
:: 가슴이 조마조마한, 떨리는

↳ very nervous

Q Do you get nervous when you have to speak in front of a large audience?
대중 앞에서 말할 때 떨리니?

A Yes, I always get butterflies in my stomach when I have to do that.
그래, 그럴 때면 항상 가슴이 조마조마해.

344 **wine and dine**   :: 융숭하게 대접하다

↳ entertain expensively

Q Did his company sign a contract with yours?
그의 회사가 너의 회사와 계약했니?

A No, because I think they want to be wined and dined a little first.
아니, 그들은 먼저 융숭하게 대접받고 싶어하는 것 같아.

345 **on the take**   :: 뇌물을 받는

↳ accepting bribes

Q Are most policemen in this town honest?
이 마을의 경찰 대부분은 정직하니?

A Yes, but unfortunately there are a few on the take.
그래, 하지만 불행하게도 뇌물을 받는 사람이 다소 있어.

346 **word for word** :: 한 자 한 자 정확히

↳ in exactly the same words

Q Did you memorize the poem?
그 시를 기억하니?

A Yes, word for word.
그래, 한 자 틀리지 않고 정확히.

347 **win by a whisker** :: 간신히 이기다, 간발의 차로 이기다

↳ barely win

Q Did your horse barely win the race?
네 말이 경주에서 간신히 이겼니?

A Yes, he won by just a whisker.
그래, 간신히 이겼어.

348 **for real** :: 신중한, 진실된

↳ serious and not joking

Q Did your teacher give you a 100-page homework assignment?
선생님이 100페이지의 숙제를 주셨니?

A Yes, and for the third time this semester! Is he for real?
그래, 이번 학기에 세 번째야! 선생님이 제정신일까?

349 **in a rut** :: 판에 박혀 재미없는

↳ in a boring routine

Q Are you going to quit your job, go back to college and finish your degree?
사직하고 대학으로 돌아가 학위를 끝낼 거니?

A Yes, I've been in such a rut I've decided to start a new career.
그래, 판에 박힌 일에 몹시 싫증이 나서 새 일을 하기로 했어.

350 as easy as pie
:: 대단히 쉬운

↳ very easy

Q Is learning how to speak English difficult?
영어로 말하기가 어렵니?

A No, if you practice and practice it's as easy as pie.
아니, 연습하고 연습하면 아주 쉬워.

351 can't rule something out
:: 배제할 수 없다

↳ can't exclude something

Q Do you think it will rain this afternoon?
오후에 비올 것 같니?

A Well, I can't rule it out because it's starting to get cloudy.
글쎄, 구름이 끼기 시작하니까 그럴 수도 있지.

352 brag about
:: 자랑하다

↳ be proud of, boast something

Q Did I tell you that I drank 8 bottles of beer last night?
내가 어젯밤 맥주 8병을 마셨다고 말했니?

A No, but I don't think that's anything to brag about.
아니, 하지만 그것은 자랑할 것이 못된다고 생각해.

353 out of stock
:: 재고가 없는

↳ no longer any in supply

Q Do you have any more shoes in that style?
그 모양의 구두가 더 있습니까?

A No, sorry ma'am, but I'm afraid they're out of stock right now.
없어요, 미안합니다만, 지금 재고가 떨어졌어요.

stick up for

:: 변호하다

↪ support and defend

Q He did a very stupid thing last night and you're not
going to criticize him?
그는 어제 어리석은 짓을 했는데 넌 그를 비판하지 않을 거니?

A No, because I've got to stick up for him. He's my best
friend.
아니, 난 그를 변호해야 해. 가장 좋은 친구야.

more often than not

:: 절반 이상은, 비교적 자주

↪ more than half of the time

Q Does he ever forget to return the books you lent him?
그는 네가 빌려 준 책을 잊고 되돌려주지 않지?

A Yes, more often than not.
그래, 비교적 자주 그래.

blow over

:: 잊혀지다, 잠잠해지다

↪ go away without causing harm

Q Are your parents still upset over last semester's report
card?
부모님이 아직도 지난 학기 성적표 때문에 화내고 계시니?

A Yes, but I'm sure everything will blow over in a couple
of weeks.
그래, 하지만 몇 주일만 있으면 모든 것이 잊혀질 거라고 생각해.

on-again, off-again

:: 불확실한

↪ uncertain and unpredictable

Q Are you going to the outdoor rock concert this Friday
night?
이번 금요일 밤 야외 음악회에 갈거니?

A No, because of the on-again, off-again rainy weather
we've been having.
아니, 비가 오락가락해서 안 가.

358 give a rundown   :: 개요를 말하다

↳ inform or summarize

Q Anything interesting in this morning's newspaper?
오늘 아침 신문에 재미있는 거 있니?

A Yes, a lot. Want me to give you a rundown?
그래, 많아. 개요를 말해줄까?

359 take a dim view of   :: 의심하다

↳ doubt or dislike

Q Do you want to come with us on a weekend trip to the
mountains?
너 우리와 함께 주말 여행으로 산에 가고 싶지?

A No, my parents take a dim view of me going anywhere
without them.
아니, 부모님은 내가 부모님과 따로 가는 것을 의심해.

360 be crawling with   :: ~으로 가득 차다, 우글거리다

↳ be full of

Q Are there many KGB agents in New York?
뉴욕에 KGB 요원들이 많니?

A Yes, of course! The place is crawling with them.
물론이지. 뉴욕은 그들로 우글거려.

067. As Japan's elderly <u>whittle away at</u> their nest eggs, the nation's lofty 14 percent savings rate could plummet.

(A) increase the amount of (B) take away by degrees
(C) reserve for emergencies
(D) stay away from

어휘 elderly 중년 / whittle away at 덜다 / nest egg 밑천, 본전 / lofty 우뚝 솟은 / plummet 폭락 하다, 떨어지다 / take away 감하다, 없애다 / by degree 차차 / reserve 비축하다, 예약하다 / stay away from 불참하다

해석 일본의 중년층이 그들의 자산을 줄이면 14%라는 그 나라의 높은 저축률이 떨어질수도 있다.

- -

068. John never arrives at the office on time. I'd like to know how he manages to <u>get away with</u> it.

(A) answer for   (B) make up for
(C) making nothing of   (D) go unpunished for

어휘 on time 정각에(punctually) / get away with 처벌을 면하다 / answer for 책임지다 / make nothing of 예사로 여기다

해석 존은 정시에 출근하는 법이 없다. 그가 어떻게 혼나지 않고 넘어가는지 알고 싶다.

- -

069. The Red River gains its name from the color of the soil it <u>picks up</u> as it flows through rich prairie land.

(A) nourishes   (B) gathers
(C) produces   (D) reaps

어휘 pick up 모으다 / prairie 대초원 / nourish 자양분을 주다 / reap 거두다

해석 레드 강은 비옥한 대평원을 지나가면서 끌어모은 토양의 색깔에서 그 이름이 유래한다.

070. He easily <u>got the better of</u> her in that argument.

   (A) controlled   (B) made the best of

   (C) satisfied   (D) won over

> 어휘 **get the better of** ~을 이기다 / **make the best of** ~을 최대한 이용하다
> 해석 그는 그 논쟁에서 그녀를 쉽게 이겼다.

Day

12

071. I'll <u>get even with</u> James for cheating me.

   (A) ignore   (B) repay

   (C) forgive   (D) criticize

> 어휘 **get even with** 복수하다 / **cheat** 속이다
> 해석 나를 속인 대가로 제임스에게 복수하겠다.

072. A : He's sure he can become a millionaire by buying 100 lottery tickets.

     B : Never mind. He is just <u>talking through his hat</u>.

   (A) invaluable   (B) speaking out

   (C) speaking impolitely   (D) exaggerating

> 어휘 **be sure that**절 ~을 확신하다 / **millionaire** 백만장자 / **lottery ticket** 복권 / **talk through one's hat** 큰소리치다 / **exaggerate** 과장하다
> 해석 A : 그는 자기가 100장의 복권을 사면 백만장자가 될 거라고 확신하더군.
> B : 신경쓰지마. 단지 허풍을 떠는 것뿐이라구.

Answers ★ 67.(B) 68.(D) 69.(B) 70.(D) 71.(B) 72.(D)

361 in vain
:: 헛된, 소용없는

↳ without success

Q Did he take your advice and quit smoking?
그가 너의 충고를 듣고 금연했니?

A No, I'm afraid all my effort to persuade him to stop was in vain.
아니, 안됐지만 그를 설득시키려는 모든 노력이 헛되었어.

362 it stands to reason that
:: 사리에 맞다, 거의 확실하다

↳ it is logical to assume that

Q Do you think I'll get accepted to Yale?
넌 내가 예일대학에 입학될 것이라고 생각하니?

A Yes, since your grades are very good, it stands to reason that you will.
그래, 넌 점수가 좋으니까 네가 입학될 것은 거의 확실해.

363 run one ragged
:: 피곤하게 하다

↳ tire one out

Q Are your kids giving you a hard time these days?
요즈음 아이들 때문에 고생하지?

A Yes, they're running me ragged. I can hardly wait for summer vacation to end.
그래, 애들이 나를 피곤하게 해. 여름방학이 빨리 끝났으면 좋겠어.

364 get the lead out

:: 빨리빨리 하다

↳ hurry, move fast

Q Do you want me to cut the grass in the backyard, too, dad?
아빠, 내가 뒤뜰의 풀을 잘랐으면 좋겠어요?

A Yes, so get the lead out and start cutting!
그래, 서둘러서 자르기 시작해라!

365 cross swords

:: 싸우다, 다투다

↳ argue or fight with

Q Don't you and Bill agree on anything?
Bill과 너는 무슨 일이든지 의견이 다르지?

A No, and one of these days we're going to have to cross swords.
달라, 근일 중 우리는 싸워야 할 것 같아.

366 rant and rave about

:: 야단법석이다

↳ yell or shout about

Q Do you like our new English teacher?
우리 새 영어 선생님을 좋아하니?

A No, because she's always ranting and raving about neat penmanship.
아니, 항상 글씨를 깨끗하게 쓰라고 야단법석이니까.

367 read one loud and clear

:: 똑똑히 알다

↳ understand one completely

Q I want that damn report on my desk by 3 o'clock, understand?
그 보고서를 3시까지 내 책상에 갖다 놓기를 바라오. 알겠소?

A Yes, sir. I read you loud and clear.
예, 사장님, 잘 알겠습니다.

368 set one straight

:: 바로잡다, 바르게 지도하다

↳ correct one regarding one's bad behavior

Q Did he get drunk again last night?
그는 어제밤 또 술에 취했지?

A Yes, and it's time for one of us to set him straight and get him to stop.
그래, 이제는 우리 중 누군가 그를 바로 지도해서 금주하도록 할 때라구.

369 give in

:: 항복하다

↳ surrender

Q Is your son still begging you to buy him a motorcycle?
자네 아들이 아직도 오토바이를 사달라고 조르나?

A Yes, but I'm not going to give in. It's too dangerous for an 18-year-old.
그래, 그러나 난 지지 않을 거야. 18살 먹은 애에겐 너무 위험하거든.

370 in the cards

:: 전망이 밝은

↳ in the future, be expected (or on the cards)

Q Are you going to have to sell your company?
자네 회사를 팔아야 할 것 같은가?

A Yes, because any improvement in the toy export business is not in the cards.
그래, 장난감 수출업 전망이 밝지 않기 때문이야.

371 make the best of

:: 최대한 잘 이용하다, 더 나빠지지 않도록 최대한 애쓰다

↳ try to make a bad situation less bad

Q Did you finally stop feeling bad over losing your job?
실직한 데 대해 기분 나쁘지 않게 되셨습니까?

A No, but I'm trying very hard to make the best of a terrible situation.
아뇨, 하지만 좋지 않은 상황을 덜 나쁘게 하도록 몹시 노력중입니다.

372 draw a blank
∷ 생각이 떠오르지 않다

↳ fail to remember

Q Can't you remember where you left your car keys?
승용차 키를 어디에 두었는지 기억나지 않니?

A No, I keep drawing a blank.
모르겠어요. 영 생각나지 않아요.

373 up for grabs
∷ 먼저 온 사람이 얻을 수 있는

↳ available

Q Has anyone bought your old car?
누가 네 중고차를 샀니?

A No, it's still up for grabs.
아니, 아직 누구든지 먼저 온 사람이 살 수 있어.

374 take a stab at
∷ 시도하다, 해보다

↳ try

Q Do you know how to play this video game?
이 비디오게임을 어떻게 하는지 아니?

A No, I don't, but let me take a stab at it.
아니, 몰라. 하지만 한번 해 볼게.

375 break one's heart
:: 마음을 아프게 하다

↳ cause one's great emotional pain

Q Was your puppy run over by a car?
자네 강아지가 차에 치었지?

A Yes, and it broke my little daughter's heart.
그래, 그것이 내 딸의 마음을 아프게 했어.

376 speak of the devil
:: 호랑이도 제말하면 온다

↳ the person appears just when you're talking about him

Q Where's Bill when we really need him?
Bill이 어디 있지? 그가 정말 필요한데.

A Speak of the devil. He's coming this way now.
호랑이도 제말하면 온다더니 지금 이 쪽으로 오네.

377 stick to one's guns
:: (주장을) 고집하다

↳ remain firm in one's beliefs and values

Q Do you admire the new mayor?
새 시장을 존경하니?

A Yes, because he sticks to his guns and doesn't worry about public opinion.
그래, 그는 자기 주장을 고집하고 여론은 걱정도 안해.

378 split the difference
:: 타협하다, 서로 양보하다

↳ divide the difference with someone else

Q Are you paying for lunch today?
오늘 점심 값은 네가 지불할거니?

A No, I'll pay half and you and Sam split the difference.
아니, 난 반만 낼게. 너와 Sam이 나머지를 부담해.

379 rack up

:: 모으다

↳ gain or gather

Q Did the Republican presidential candidate do well in the South?
공화당 대통령 후보가 남부에서 선전했습니까?

A Yes, especially because he racked up big gains in urban areas.
예, 특별히 도시지역에서 큰 지지를 얻었기 때문이죠.

380 steer clear of

:: 접촉을 피하다, 멀리하다

↳ avoid contact with

Q Should I go onto date with him?
그와 데이트할까?

A No, steer clear of guys like him.
아니, 그런 녀석들은 멀리해.

381 zero in on

:: 주의를 집중하다

↳ aim at or focus on

Q Did the President's speech focus mostly on Latin America?
대통령은 주로 라틴아메리카에 초점을 두고 연설했니?

A Yes, and it zeroed in on Columbia and the drug problem.
응, 콜럼비아와 마약문제에 집중했어.

382 sore over

:: 화난, ~때문에 기분이 상한

↳ angry and upset about

Q Is Jim upset about something?
Jim은 뭔가에 화가 났니?

A Yes, he's sore over the fact that someone scratched the paint on his new car.
그래, 그의 새 차를 누군가 긁은 데 화가 났어.

383 hold on

↳ wait (on the telephone)

Q Bill, this is Sam. Do you know Sally's telephone number?
Bill, 나 Sam인데, Sally의 전화번호 아니?

A Yes, I wrote it somewhere in my notebook. Hold on a
second, okay?
그래, 내 공책 어딘가에 적어놨어. 잠깐 기다려, 알았지?

384 get ahead
:: 성공하다

↳ succeed

Q Do you know the secret to being successful in the
business world?
사업계에서 성공하는 비결을 아니?

A Yes, to get ahead in life you've got to enjoy what you're
doing.
응, 인생에 성공하려면 무엇보다도 먼저 네가 하는 일에 만족해야 해.

385 take the edge off
:: 기세를 꺾다, 무디게 하다

↳ lessen the strength of

Q Would you like a piece of chocolate candy?
초콜릿 과자 한 조각 드시겠어요?

A No, thanks, that would take the edge off my appetite for
dinner.
아뇨, 그것을 먹으면 저녁 식욕이 감소될 거예요.

386 take a load off one's feet
:: 편히 앉다

↳ sit down please

Q Can I sit down here?
여기 앉아도 됩니까?

A Yes, of course. Take a load off your feet.
예, 물론이죠. 편히 앉으세요.

387 wear off

:: 점차 약해지다, 없어지다

↳ become weaker gradually

Q Will the effects of this medicine last long?
이 약효가 오래 지속될까요?

A No, they'll wear off within an hour or so.
아뇨, 한 시간 정도면 점차 사라질 거예요.

388 put on airs

:: 뽐내다, 젠체하다

Day

13

↳ act too proudly

Q Did you hear that Mary got a job at IBM?
Mary가 IBM에 취직했다는 것 들었니?

A Yes, and ever since she started working there she's been putting on airs.
그래, 거기서 일하기 시작하면서부터 그녀는 잘난 척 한다구.

389 lose heart

:: 실망하다, 낙담하다

↳ become discouraged

Q Have they found your lost kitten yet?
그들이 너의 잃어버린 새끼고양이를 벌써 찾았니?

A No, but I'm not going to lose heart and give up hope.
아니, 하지만 난 실망하지 않고 희망을 포기하지 않을 거야.

390 by far

:: 훨씬, 단연

↳ without any doubt

Q Do you think Italy will win the World Cup?
이탈리아가 월드컵에서 우승할 것 같니?

A Yes, because they have the best team by far.
그래, 단연 가장 훌륭한 팀을 가지고 있으니까.

073. A : How are you doing with your new project?
B : We decided to <u>put it on ice</u> till the end of this year.

(A) cancel (B) freeze
(C) reserve (D) skate

어휘 **put it on ice** 보류하다 / **freeze** 동결하다 / **reserve** 연기하다(postpone)
해석 A : 당신들의 새 프로젝트를 어떻게 하실건가요?
　　 B : 올해 말까지 보류하기로 결정을 보았습니다.

---

074. You must <u>look over</u> the contract before you sign it.

(A) glance at (B) cancel
(C) neglect (D) examine
(E) pass over

어휘 **look over** 훑어보다, 조사하다 / **contract** 계약 / **pass over** 넘겨주다
해석 계약서에 서명을 하기 전에 조사해 봐야 한다.

---

075. Susan Jackson <u>made a scene</u> with her husband the other day.

(A) went to the movies (B) wrote a drama
(C) made love (D) became a good wife
(E) had a violent argument

어휘 **make a scene** 울고불고 난리를 피우다 / **the other day** 일전에 (약 일주
일 정도)
해석 수잔 잭슨은 일전에 자기 남편과 한바탕 난리를 피웠다.

076. To <u>look quickly through</u> a book is an important study skill.

(A) skim   (B) outline

(C) summarize   (D) paraphrase

어휘 **look through** 조사하다, 간파하다 / **skim** 스쳐가다, 대충 훑다 / **outline** 개요를 말하다, 약술하다 / **summarize** 요약하다 / **paraphrase** 알기 쉽게 바꾸어 말하다, 부연(敷衍)하다

해석 책을 대충 훑어보고 재빨리 간파해 내는 것은 학습활동에 있어서 중요한 기술 이다.

Day

13

077. Unfortunately he died after ten years of struggle against a disease. He is _____ by his wife and two sons.

(A) succeeded   (B) remained

(C) deceased   (D) survived

(E) followed

어휘 **be survived by** ~보다 먼저 죽다

해석 그는 불행히도 10년간 투병생활을 하다가 죽었다. 그는 아내와 두 아들을 남 겼다.

078. In the book he <u>lays bare</u> his social relationship.

(A) exposes   (B) deals with

(C) emphasizes   (D) discusses

어휘 **lay bare** 드러내다, 폭로하다(expose) / **deal with** ~을 다루다 / **emphasize** 강조하다

해석 그 책에서 그는 자신의 인간 관계를 적나라하게 드러내고 있다.

14th Day

391 well put   :: 잘 표현한

↳ well expressed in words

Q I think he's lazy and incompetent, don't you?
그는 게으르고 무능하지 않니?

A Yes, I think your description of him was very well put.
그래, 네 표현이 아주 적절한 것 같아.

392 lay off   :: 날 좀 내버려둬! 귀찮게 굴지마!

↳ leave me alone!

Q Why don't you cut off that ugly beard?
그 흉한 수염 좀 깎지 그래?

A No, I don't want to! Now lay off okay!
아니, 깎고 싶지 않아. 날 좀 내버려둬!

393 give and take   :: 주고받다, 서로 양보하다

↳ listen to other's opinions and compromise when necessary

Q Have you really been married for over 30 years?
정말 결혼한지 30년 이상이나 됐습니까?

A Yes, and our secret is that we both know how to give and take.
예, 우리의 비결은 서로 양보할 줄 알고 있다는 것입니다.

get away from :: ~을 벗어나 휴가 가다

↳ go on a vacation trip

Q Are you going to New York again this year on your summer vacation?
금년 여름방학에 또 뉴욕에 갈 거니?

A No, this time we're going to Maine to get away from all the pollution.
아니, 이번에는 공해에서 벗어나기 위해 Maine으로 갈 거야.

395 **set in one's ways** :: 습관이 굳어진

↳ one's habits are fixed and unchangeable

Q Do you think Ralph will ever get married?
Ralph가 결혼할 것이라고 생각하니?

A No, I'm afraid he's too set in his ways to ever raise a family.
아니, 가족을 부양하기엔 그의 습관이 너무 굳어진 것 같아.

Day
14

396 **look back on** :: 회고하다

↳ remember

Q We had a pretty good time in high school, didn't we?
우리 고교시절에 아주 재미있었지?

A Yes, I look back on those days as some of the happiest of my life.
그래, 당시를 돌아보면 내 생애에서 가장 행복했던 때였어.

397 **bundle up** :: 옷을 따뜻하게 입다

↳ dress warmly

Q Grandma, can I go outside and build a snowman?
할머니, 밖에 나가 눈사람을 만들어도 돼요?

A Yes, of course, dear. But be sure to bundle up nice and warm.
그래, 물론이지. 하지만 옷을 따뜻하게 입도록 해라.

398 by word of mouth
:: 구두로, 말로

↳ informed by speaking rather than by writing

Q The food is really great in this restaurant. Do you eat here often?

이 레스토랑의 음식은 정말 좋아, 여기서 가끔 먹니?

A Yes, and I learned about this place by word of mouth.

응, 이 음식점에 관해서 말로 들었어.

399 take one's time
:: 천천히 하다

↳ there's no big hurry, so go slowly

Q Are you in a big hurry, Sally?

몹시 급하니, 샐리야?

A No, so just take your time putting on your makeup.

아니, 그러니까 화장을 천천히 해.

400 see the light
:: 사태를 파악하다

↳ realize the true situation

Q Does the Congress still oppose sending military aid to the rebels?

의회가 아직도 반군에 대한 원조를 반대하고 있니?

A No, because the President finally persuaded them to see the light.

아니, 대통령이 마침내 사태를 파악하도록 설득했기 때문이야.

401 for all I know
:: 내가 알기로는

↳ as far as I know

Q It's time for breakfast. Is Billy still upstairs?

아침 밥 먹을 시간이다. 빌리가 아직도 이층에 있니?

A Yes, and for all I know he's probably still sleeping.

그래, 내가 알기로는 그는 아직도 자고 있어.

take a chance
:: 위험을 무릅쓰고 해보다

↳ risk danger

Q Have you ever eaten raw octopus?
너 낙지를 날것으로 먹어본 적 있니?

A No, because I don't want to take a chance and get a
stomachache.
아니, 위험을 무릅쓰고 먹어 배탈나고 싶지 않아.

pure and simple
:: 오직 ~뿐, 순전히

↳ nothing more, nothing less

Q Is Sam having a date with his next-door neighbor's girl?
샘은 그의 이웃집 소녀와 데이트를 했니?

A Yes, and he's a Don Juan, pure and simple.
응, 그는 순전히 바람둥이라구.

stand one up
:: 바람맞히다

↳ do not show up to take one on the date he promised

Q Did your date go well last night?
어젯밤 데이트는 잘 됐니?

A No, the guy stood me up!
아니, 그 남자가 날 바람맞혔어.

take advantage of
:: 이용하다

↳ exploit

Q Could you ask Uncle Bill to loan me $1,000? I need the
money.
빌 아저씨에게 1,000달러를 내게 융자해 달라고 요청할 수 있니?

A No, I can't! And stop taking advantage of our rich
relatives, okay?
아니, 할 수 없어. 그리고 돈 많은 우리 친척을 그만 이용해, 알겠니?

psyched up :: 만반의 준비를 갖춘

↳ mentally prepared to win

Q Is he an outstanding football coach?
그는 뛰어난 축구 코치니?

A Yes, and he's especially good at getting his teams
psyched up for their games.
그래, 특히 그의 팀이 경기에 대비한 준비를 갖추게 하는데 유능해.

throw away :: 저버리다

↳ waste fail to take advantage of

Q Do you think I made a big mistake by dropping out of
Yale?
내가 예일대학을 중퇴한 것이 큰 실수였다고 생각하니?

A Yes, I think you threw away an opportunity you'll never
get again.
그래, 네가 또다시 얻을 수 없는 기회를 저버렸다고 생각해.

had better :: ~하는 편이 좋다

↳ should

Q Should I forget about entering tomorrow's speech
contest?
내일 웅변대회에 참석하지 말아야 하니?

A Yes, you had better because you still haven't gotten over
your cold.
그래, 그러는 게 좋아. 아직도 네 감기가 낫지 않았으니까.

psych out :: 심리적으로 겁먹게 하다

↳ defeat or weaken psychologically

Q Do you think Ali was the greatest heavyweight in boxing
history?
Ali가 권투사에서 가장 위대한 선수였다고 생각하니?

A Yes, because he was an expert at psyching out his opponents.
그래, 그는 상대를 겁먹게 하는데 전문가니까.

410 have half a mind to
:: 할까말까 생각하고 있다

↳ have almost decided to do, unpleasant though it may be

Q Is it true that Jim is secretly dating another girl?
Jim이 다른 여자와 몰래 데이트하는 것이 사실이니?

A Yes, and I have half a mind to tell his fiance.
그래, 그래서 그의 약혼자에게 말해줄까말까 생각하고 있어.

Day

14

411 next to
:: 거의

↳ almost

Q Do you think we will be able to reach Boston by 3:00 this afternoon?
우리가 오늘 오후 3시까지 보스턴에 도착할 수 있을 거라고 생각하니?

A No, that's next to impossible. We still have over 300miles to drive.
아니, 그건 거의 불가능해. 아직도 300마일이나 달려야 해.

412 take the lead
:: 리드하다, 선두를 달리다

↳ go into first place

Q Is Car No.3 still in first place?
3번 경주차가 아직도 1등이니?

A No, I think Car No.8 has taken the lead.
아니, 8번 차가 앞선 것 같아.

413 pride oneself on

:: 자랑하다

↳ is very proud about

Q Alice is a nice dresser, isn't she?
앨리스는 옷을 잘 입지?

A Yes, she prides herself on her fine taste in clothes.
그래, 옷에 대한 멋진 취향을 자랑해.

414 pull one's own weight

:: 자기 역할을 다하다

↳ do the work he's expected or assigned to do

Q Do you still think he's not ready for a promotion?
그는 아직도 승진할 준비가 되어 있지 않다고 생각하니?

A Yes, because he's not pulling his own weight around the office yet.
그래, 그가 여전히 사무실에서 자기 역할을 다하지 못하기 때문이야.

415 put one in one's place

:: 분수를 지키게 하다

↳ embarrass by criticizing one for his foolish pride

Q Sam thinks his girlfriend is the most beautiful on campus, doesn't he?
Sam은 그의 여자친구가 학교에서 가장 예쁘다고 생각하니?

A Yes, and I think it's time for us to put him in his place.
그래, 그래서 우리가 그로 하여금 분수를 지키도록 할 때라고 생각해.

416 have one's fortune told

:: 점치다

↳ have one's future predicted

Q Are you going to an astrologer again?
또 점쟁이에게 가니?

A Yes, this time I want to have my daughter's fortune told.
그래, 이번엔 딸의 점을 보고 싶어.

sleep off

:: 푹 자다

↳ sleep until the effects of a drug or alcohol go away

Q Hasn't Joe come in for work yet?
Joe가 아직도 출근 안 했니?

A No, and maybe he's still home sleeping off last night's drunken party.
안 했어. 어젯밤 과음을 해서 아직도 집에서 자고 있나봐.

keep a straight face

:: 엄숙한 표정을 짓다

↳ keep from laughing

Q Did you compliment Mary on that ugly dress of hers?
그렇게 누추한 옷을 입은 Mary를 칭찬했니?

A Yes, and I could barely keep a straight face when I said it looks nice.
그래, 그리고 멋지게 보인다고 말하면서 엄숙한 표정을 지을 수 없었어.

stamp out

:: 발본색원하다

↳ get rid of

Q Are you going to run for Sheriff, Sam?
Sam, 보안관에 출마할 거니?

A Yes, because I want to stamp out all the drug dealing in our town.
그래, 우리 마을의 마약 거래를 발본색원하고 싶어서.

spring a leak

:: 새기 시작하다

↳ develop a hole so that the liquid escapes

Q Do you need a screwdriver?
드라이버가 필요하니?

A No, get me a wrench right away! My sink has just sprung a leak.
아니, 어서 렌치를 줘! 싱크가 방금 새기 시작했어.

영숙어 문제 단번에 공략하기

079. You <u>hit the nail on your head</u>.

(A) become very strict   (B) always work hard

(C) make someone look bad

(D) arrive at the correct answer

(E) make trouble for someone

어휘 **hit the nail on one's head** 정곡을 찌르다 / **strict** 엄한, 정밀한, 완전한 / **make trouble for** ~에게 폐를 끼치다

해석 당신이 정곡을 찔렀습니다.

- -

080. We haven't got meat, so we'll have to <u>make do with</u> bread.

(A) do without   (B) replace

(C) manage with   (D) purchase

어휘 **make do with** 대용품으로 때우다, 변통하다 cf. **make do without** ~없이 지내다 / **manage with** ~로 그럭저럭 때우다 cf. **manage without** ~없이 그럭저럭 살다 / **purchase** 사다, 구입하다

해석 고기가 없어서 우리는 빵으로 때워야 할거야.

- -

081. Although he is recognized as one of the most brilliant scientists in his field, Professor White cannot seem to <u>make his ideas understood</u> in class.

(A) get his ideas with   (B) recall his ideas

(C) summarize his ideas   (D) get his ideas across

어휘 **make one's ideas understood** ~의 생각을 남에게 이해시키다 / **get one's ideas with** ~의 생각을 이해하다 / **recall** 생각해내다 / **get one's ideas across** ~의 생각을 이해시키다

해석 화이트 교수는 자기 분야에서 가장 훌륭한 과학자로 인식되고 있지만, 수업중에는 자신의 논지를 이해시키지 못하는 것 같다.

082. Try to forget your desire to be a popular musician, <u>let alone</u> your wish to become a recording star.

(A) to do justice to   (B) notwithstanding
(C) not to mention   (D) regarding

어휘 **let alone** ~은 말할 것도 없이 / **do justice to** ~을 정당하게 평가하다 / **notwithstanding** ~에도 불구하고(nevertheless) / **regarding** ~에 관하여

해석 음반계의 스타가 되겠다는 바람은 말할 것도 없고, 유명한 음악가가 되겠다는 희망은 접어버리도록 해라.

---

083. Mr. Barpal said that he once saved a deal by <u>boning up on Japanese</u> when a licensing arrangement was in jeopardy.

Day

14

(A) contacting Japanese   (B) studying Japanese hard
(C) picking on Japanese   (D) employing Japanese
(E) using Japanese

어휘 **bone up on** 열심히 공부하다 / **be in jeopardy** 위험에 처해 있다

해석 Barpal씨가 말하길 전에 면허증 취득이 어려웠을 때 그는 일본어를 열심히 공부해서 많은 돈을 모았다고 한다.

---

084. The heart-lung machine rids the blood of carbon dioxide and replenishes it _____ oxygen.

(A) with   (B) within
(C) for   (D) by

어휘 **heart-lung machine** 인공 심폐기 / **rid A of B** A에게서 B를 제거하다 / **carbon dioxide** 이산화탄소 / **replenish A with B** A에게 B를 채워넣다

해석 심폐기는 혈액에서 이산화탄소를 제거하고 산소를 공급한다.

Answers ★ 79.(D) 80.(C) 81.(D) 82.(C) 83.(B) 84.(A)

149

15th Day

421 hold still
:: 가만히 있다

↳ don't move around

Q Can't you cut my hair a little faster, mom?
엄마, 더 빨리 내 머리를 깎을 수 없어요?

A No, so just hold still and keep your mouth shut, okay?
안돼, 가만히 있어. 입 다물고, 알았지?

422 pick on
:: 괴롭히다

↳ bother or make miserable

Q Haven't you finished doing all your chores around the house yet?
아직 집안의 잡일을 마치지 않았니?

A No, and will you stop picking on me! I only have two hands!
그래, 그러니 날 좀 그만 괴롭혀!

423 lose sight of
:: 잊다

↳ forget the significance of

Q Is Sen. Smith popular among the underprivileged because he also was born poor?
Smith 상원의원은 가난하게 태어났기 때문에 소외계층에게 인기가 있지?

A Yes, and he's never lost sight of that fact.
그래, 그는 그 사실을 결코 잊지 않는다구.

slow down :: 천천히 가다

↳ reduce the speed

Q Can't you walk any faster? We'll be late for the concert.
좀 더 빨리 걸을 수 없니? 음악회에 늦겠다.

A No, I can't, so why don't you just slow down and stop worrying?
그럴 수 없어, 걱정 말고 천천히 가는 게 어때?

---

425 **high-handed** :: 고압적인, 거만한

↳ too proud

Q Why do you think the President was defeated for reelection?
대통령이 재선에 실패한 이유가 뭐니?

A Because of his high-handed methods in dealing with the Congress.
의회를 다루는데 그 방법이 너무 거만했어.

Day

15

---

426 **fix up with** :: 데이트 시켜주다, 만나게 주선해주다

↳ arrange a date for one

Q Do you want me to arrange for you a date with Mary?
Mary와 데이트하게 내가 주선해주길 원하니?

A No, fix me up with a cheerleader instead.
아니, 대신 응원단장과 만나게 해 줘.

---

427 **drop a line** :: 몇 줄 써 보내다, 편지하다

↳ write a letter

Q Are you being transferred to a branch in another city?
다른 도시의 지점으로 전근될 거니?

A Yes, so please drop me a line now and then, okay?
그래, 종종 나에게 편지해 줘, 알겠니?

428 **day in and day out** :: 날이면 날마다

↳ constantly

Q Does your wife ever ask you to help her with the housework?
네 부인은 집안일을 도와달라고 요구하니?

A Yes, she nags me about it day in and day out!
날이면 날마다 바가지를 긁어.

429 **take something off one's hands** :: 떠맡다, 인수하다

↳ help you get rid of your burden

Q Do you want a free kitten?
고양이를 공짜로 원하니?

A Yes, I'll be glad to take it off your hands.
그래, 너에게서 받으면 좋겠어.

430 **call a spade a spade** :: 정직하게 말하다

↳ speak frankly and openly

Q Is she a frank person?
그녀는 솔직한 사람이니?

A Yes, she never hesitates to call a spade a spade.
그래, 결코 정직하게 말하는데 주저하지 않아.

431 **off and on** :: 가끔씩

↳ not regularly

Q Have you and your friend been writing to each other for a long time?
너는 네 친구와 오랫동안 서로 편지했지?

A Yes, we've been corresponding off and on now for over six years.
그래, 우린 지금껏 6년간 가끔씩 편지하고 있어.

432 catch one off balance

:: 허를 찌르다

↳ catch one unprepared

Q Do you have a good game plan against your next opponents, Coach?

코치님, 다음 상대와 싸울 좋은 계획을 가지고 있습니까?

A Yes, we'll catch them off balance by full-court pressing them the whole game.

그래, 경기 내내 풀코트 프레싱전법으로 상대의 허를 찌를 거야.

433 call one names

:: 욕하다

↳ say bad things about one

Q Didn't you do your homework yet, you lazy bum?

아직도 숙제 안 했지, 이 게으름뱅이야?

A Yes, of course I did. And please stop calling me names, okay?

아니, 했어. 그러니 제발 날 욕하지 마, 알겠지?

Day
15

434 cancel out

:: 상쇄하다

↳ balance or remove the effects of

Q Did you really get a C in math?

정말 수학 점수로 C를 받았니?

A Yes, but the A I received in History cancels it out.

그래, 하지만 역사에서 A를 받아 상쇄됐어.

435 die out

:: 소멸하다

↳ disappear forever

Q Are there many blue whales in this part of the ocean?

이 지역 해양에는 푸른 고래가 많니?

A No, they've pretty much died out because of the Japanese.

아니, 일본인 때문에 많이 소멸됐어.

436 dispose of
:: 없애버리다

↳ get rid of

Q Do you want me to keep any of this morning's junk mail?
오늘 아침에 온 이 시시한 우편물을 간수할까요?

A No, just dispose of it in that wastebasket over there.
아니, 저기 쓰레기통에 모두 없애버려요.

437 call to order
:: 개회하다

↳ start a meeting

Q Has the meeting started yet?
회의를 벌써 시작했니?

A No, but I think the chairperson is just about to call it to order.
아니, 하지만 의장이 곧 개최할 것 같아.

438 on duty
:: 당번인, 근무중인

↳ working

Q Do you have time now to have a cup of coffee with me?
나와 커피 한 잔 할 시간 있니?

A No, but maybe a little later. I'm still on duty.
없어, 아직 근무중이니까 잠시 후에는 할 수 있어.

439 off duty
:: 비번인

↳ not working

Q Do you have to work Saturday?
토요일에 일하니?

A No, I'm off duty on weekends.
아니, 주말엔 비번이야.

440 can't help oneself   :: 어쩔 수 없다

↳ can't control oneself

Q Don't you think you're eating too many sweets these days, Sally?
요즘 단 것을 너무 많이 먹는다고 생각지 않니, Sally?

A Yes, but I can't help myself. I love desserts.
그래, 하지만 어쩔 수 없어. 난 디저트를 너무 좋아해.

441 real quick   :: 지금 당장

↳ right now

Q Do you want something to drink, Joe?
뭐 좀 마시고 싶니, Joe?

A Yes, get me an ice-cold beer real quick! I'm dying of thirst.
그래, 지금 당장 찬 맥주 좀 줘. 갈증나 죽겠어.

442 out of necessity   :: 부득이해서, 어쩔 수 없이

↳ because one has to

Q Do you like your new side job?
새 부업이 마음에 드니?

A No, I work there out of necessity. I've got 3 college age kids to support.
아니, 어쩔 수 없이 거기서 일해. 돌봐야 할 대학생 또래의 자식이 3명이나 돼.

443 the upper crust   :: 상류층

↳ the upper class

Q Is the tuition expensive in this school?
이 학교의 수업료가 비싸지?

A Yes, it costs so much only the upper crust can send their kids there.
그래, 너무 비싸서 상류층만이 자녀들을 그곳에 보낼 수 있어.

444 off the top of one's head

↳ if one remember correctly

Q Can you remember the name of the first woman astronaut?
최초의 여자 우주 비행사 이름을 기억할 수 있니?

A Yes, off the top of my head I think her name was Rider.
그래, 언뜻 생각하건대 Rider인 것 같아.

445 under the thumb of

:: ~가 시키는 대로

↳ completely controlled by

Q Is Peter a hen-pecked husband?
Peter는 공처가니?

A Yes, he constantly seems to be under the thumb of his nagging wife.
그래, 그는 항상 바가지 긁는 마누라가 시키는 대로 하는 것 같아.

446 up in the air

:: 미정인

↳ undecided

Q Are you leaving for the Bahamas next Monday?
다음 월요일 바하마로 떠나니?

A No, our winter vacation plans are still up in the air.
아니, 우리 겨울 방학 계획이 아직 미정이야.

447 can't help but do

:: ~하지 않을 수 없다

↳ have no other choice but do

Q Why are you staring at me? Don't you know that's rude?
왜 날 빤히 쳐다보지? 그게 무례하다는 것을 모르니?

A Yes, I know, but I couldn't help but notice that your zipper's down.
알아, 하지만 네 지퍼가 내려가 있으니 보지 않을 수 없었다구.

156

abide by   :: (약속 등을) 지키다

↳ keep

Q Did the umpire kick both managers out of the game?
심판이 양측 감독을 모두 경기에서 추방했지?

A Yes, because he thought they weren't abiding by the rules of baseball.
그래, 그들이 야구 규칙을 지키지 않는다고 생각해서야

safe and sound   :: 무사히

↳ unharmed

Q Are the Johnsons still on their vacation in Europe?
Johnson네 가족이 아직도 유럽에서 휴가중인가?

A No, they arrived back home late last night safe and sound.
아니, 어젯밤 늦게 무사히 집에 돌아왔어.

Day
15

back down   :: 후퇴하다, 물러서다

↳ retreat

Q Did Bill carry out his threat to fight it out with Joe?
Bill은 Joe와 끝까지 싸우겠다는 위협을 실행했나?

A No, he backed down when he found out that Joe has a black belt in Taekwondo.
아니, Joe가 태권도 검은 띠를 매고 있는 것을 알고는 물러섰어.

15th Day

영숙어 문제 단번에 공략하기

085. The country <u>makes up</u> one-twelfth of the continental mass of Asia.

(A) governs
(B) generates
(C) possesses
(D) decorated
(E) constitutes

어휘 make up 구성하다 / generate 발생시키다
해석 그 나라는 아시아 대륙 전체의 1/12을 차지한다.

086. He <u>moved heaven and earth</u> to please her, but she just did not want to stay there with him.

(A) showed evidence of action
(B) changed his clothes everyday
(C) moved actively
(D) did everything possible
(E) took advantage of almost every chances

어휘 move heaven and earth 죽을 힘을 다하다 / take advantage of ~을 이용하다
해석 그는 그녀를 달래느라 사력을 다했지만, 그녀는 그와 함께 거기에 머물기를 원치 않았다.

087. Their old life-styles were <u>passing out of existence</u>.

(A) increasing
(B) developing
(C) disappearing
(D) changing

어휘 pass[go] out of existence 절멸하다, 없어지다
해석 그들의 오랜 생활양식이 점점 없어지고 있었다.

158

088. Paul seems to me to have <u>perjured himself</u>.

(A) been spoiled　　　　　(B) borne false witness

(C) victimized himself　　(D) overexerted himself

어휘 **perjure oneself** 위증하다 / **bear ~ witness** 증언하다 / **victimize** 희생
시키다 / **overexert oneself** 무리하다

해석 폴이 위증을 한 것 같군요.

---

089. The ice in a glacier is <u>packed with</u> soil, trees, rocks, and boulders that have been picked up along the glacier's path.

(A) emptied of　　　　(B) scratched by

(C) blocked with　　　(D) filled with

Day

15

어휘 **be packed with** ~로 채워져 있다 / **glacier** 빙하 / **boulder** 둥근 돌 /
pick up 줍다, 도중에 태우다, 만나다, 저절로 익히다 / **empty A of B** A에
서 B를 비우다 / **scratch** 할퀴다, 휘갈겨 쓰다 / **block A with B** B로 A를
막다, 차단하다

해석 빙하 속 얼음은 빙하가 흘러가면서 주워모은 흙, 나무, 바위 그리고 둥근 돌들
로 채워져 있다.

---

090. Meanwhile, in the drawing room Edith had, <u>of her own accord</u>, told her cousin Sally that she was sorry.

(A) agreeably　　　　　(B) unhesitatingly

(C) voluntarily　　　　(D) enthusiastically

(E) intentionally

어휘 **drawing room** 거실 / **of one's own accord** 자발적으로 / **agreeably** 기
꺼이

해석 한편, 거실에서 Edith는 스스로 사촌 Sally에게 자기가 미안하다고 말했었다.

16th Day

451 **above all**   :: 무엇보다도

↳ most importantly

Q Is patience a very important ingredient in a successful marriage?
인내가 성공적 결혼에서 매우 중요한 요소니?

A Yes, but above all the couple should have a lot of things in common.
그래, 그러나 무엇보다도 부부는 공통점이 많아야 해.

452 **back out**   :: 취소하다

↳ withdraw, failing to keep a promise

Q Is Holmes still going to box Ali?
홈즈가 여전히 알리와 권투 시합할 거니?

A No, he decided to back out of the fight a few minutes ago.
아니, 몇 분전에 시합 취소를 결정했어.

453 **back up**   :: 후원하다

↳ support

Q Are you going to sing without any musical accompaniment?
악기 반주 없이 노래할 거니?

A No, I've asked a pianist friend of mine to help back me up.
아니, 내 친구인 피아니스트에게 반주해 달라고 요청했어.

454 scale down

:: 줄이다

↳ reduce

Q Are you going to make many changes in your company next year?
내년에 회사에 많은 변화가 있겠지?

A Yes, we're planning to scale down production about 30 percent.
그래, 생산을 약 30% 줄일 계획이야.

455 aboveboard

:: 공명정대하게

↳ in an honest way

Q Does this firm have a good reputation?
이 회사는 평판이 좋습니까?

A Yes, because they always try to do business aboveboard.
예, 그들은 항상 사업을 공명정대하게 하려고 하기 때문이지요.

Day

16

456 according to

:: ~에 따르면

↳ as said or indicated by

Q Is the government going to lower interest rates?
정부가 금리를 낮추게 되니?

A Yes, according to what the Treasury Secretary said this morning.
그래, 오늘 아침 재무부 발표에 따르면.

457 the acid test

:: (진짜 가치를 알아보는) 결정적 시험

↳ the true test

Q Is loyalty an important ingredient in a good friendship?
충성은 값진 우정의 중요 요소지?

A Yes, but the acid test of a true friend is to borrow money from him.
그래, 하지만 진정한 친구를 알아보는 결정적 시험은 그에게서 돈을 빌려보는 거야.

settle for second best

:: 차선을 택하다

↪ accept what is less than the best

Q Is Yale such a bad college?
예일대학이 몹시 나쁘니?

A No, but why settle for second best when you can apply
for Harvard?
아니, 하지만 하버드에 응시할 수 있는데도 왜 차선의 대학을 택하니?

on second thought

:: 다시 생각해 보니

↪ after further consideration

Q Would you like to go see a baseball game with me next
Saturday?
다음 토요일 나와 함께 야구 경기를 보러 갈래?

A Yes, I'd love to. Oh, on second thought, I'd better stay
home and study.
그래, 좋지. 아, 다시 생각해 보니 집에서 공부하는 것이 좋겠어.

of one's own accord

:: 자발적으로

↪ by himself

Q Was Bill forced to resign?
Bill이 사임을 강요당했니?

A No, surprisingly he did it of his own accord.
아니, 놀랍게도 그는 자진 사퇴했어.

call on

:: 방문하다

↪ visit

Q Shall we visit our grandparents tonight?
우리 오늘밤 조부모님을 방문할까?

A No, let's call on uncle Bill instead.
아니, 대신 Bill 아저씨를 방문하자.

462 bank on
:: 기대하다, 의지하다

↳ depend on

Q Were you disappointed to hear that the New York Times endorsed your opponent?
뉴욕 타임즈가 반대파를 지지한다는 소식을 듣고 실망했니?

A Yes, because I was banking on their support.
그래, 난 그들의 지지를 기대하고 있었거든.

463 act up
:: 재발하다, 도지다

↳ behave badly

Q Can't you walk any faster, Mr. Jones?
좀 더 빨리 걸을 수 없나요, 존스 씨?

A No, because my sore leg is starting to act up again.
안돼요, 아픈 다리가 다시 도지기 시작했어요.

464 get one's second wind
:: 원기를 회복하다, 기운을 차리다

↳ renewal of regular breathing or energy

Q Do you want to stop jogging?
조깅을 중단하고 싶니?

A No, I'm just starting to get my second wind.
아니, 이제 막 기운이 나기 시작했어.

465 see into
:: 간파하다, 알아차리다

↳ understand

Q Do you know why the Japanese economy is booming?
왜 일본 경제가 활기찬지 아니?

A No, because it's so difficult to see into a culture so different from ours.
몰라, 우리가 다른 문화를 알아보는 것이 너무 어렵기 때문이야.

466 add up

:: 납득이 가다, 앞뒤가 맞다

↳ make any sense

Q Did Sally give you any excuse for coming home late last night?
Sally가 어젯밤 늦게 귀가한데 대해 무슨 변명이라도 했니?

A Yes, but her story just doesn't add up. I think she's hiding something.
그래, 하지만 그녀의 말은 앞뒤가 맞지 않아. 뭔가 숨기는 것 같아.

467 after all

:: 결국

↳ in spite of what had been decided

Q Isn't Bill going to the movies with us tonight?
Bill 이 오늘밤 우리와 함께 영화보러 가지 않을까요?

A No, he called me this afternoon to say he couldn't come after all.
아뇨, 그는 오늘 오후 나한테 전화를 걸어 결국 갈 수 없다고 했어요.

468 to the tune of

:: 무려 ~에 이르는, 총계 ~의

↳ amounting to

Q Did you pay your traffic fine yet?
교통 위반 벌금을 벌써 냈니?

A Yes, to the tune of $50.
그래, 무려 50달러나 냈어.

469 after while

:: 잠시 후에

↳ later

Q Would you like your dessert now, sir?
지금 디저트를 드시겠습니까?

A No, waiter, I'll have some after while.
아뇨, 잠시 후에 먹겠소.

470 **bear up** :: 견디다

↳ endure and keep strong in a difficult situation

Q Is Mary getting along okay since her husband died?
Mary는 남편이 죽은 후 잘 지내고 있니?

A Yes, she's bearing up remarkably well.
그래, 아주 잘 견디고 있어.

471 **not agree with** :: (기후, 음식 등이) 맞지 않다

↳ make ill, especially the stomach

Q Do you like Italian food?
이탈리아 음식이 좋니?

A No, because garlic doesn't usually agree with me.
아니, 나한테 마늘이 맞지 않아서.

472 **say one's piece** :: 소신을 말하다

↳ express openly and frankly what one's thinking

Q You wrote a letter to the editor expressing your feelings about flag-burning?
깃발 소각에 대한 감정을 표시하는 글을 편집자에게 보냈니?

A Yes, I said my piece so now I feel much better.
그래, 난 내 소신을 밝혀서 지금은 기분이 좋아졌어.

473 **bawl one out** :: 크게 꾸짖다

↳ scold severely

Q Did mother just scold you for not cleaning your room?
어머니는 네가 방을 깨끗이 하지 않았다고 꾸짖었니?

A No, she bawled me out for not doing my homework.
아니, 어머니는 내가 숙제를 하지 않았다고 크게 꾸짖으셨어.

474 all eyes

:: 눈을 크게 뜬

↳ wide-eyed with interest or curiosity

Q Did your kids enjoy their trip to the zoo?
네 아이들은 동물원 구경을 즐거워했니?

A Yes, and they were all eyes especially during the dolphin show.
그래, 특히 돌고래 쇼 때 눈이 휘둥그래졌어.

475 see one through

:: 지내다

↳ help one survive through a time of difficulty

Q Will $250 be enough spending money for next semester, son?
애야, 다음 학기 지내는데 250달러면 충분하니?

A No, Dad. I'll need at least $500 to see me through.
아뇨, 아버지. 최소한 500달러는 필요해요.

476 raise a stink about

:: 물의를 일으키다, 한바탕 소동을 벌이다

↳ make a noisy commotion about

Q Did you complain to the manager about the way one of his clerks treated you?
지배인에게, 그의 직원이 당신을 대한 태도에 대해서 항의하셨나요?

A Yes, I raised a big stink about it but I doubt if it did any good.
예, 그 일로 한바탕 소동을 벌였지만 별로 소용이 없을 것 같아요.

477 so to speak

:: 이를테면, 말하자면, 즉

↳ as it were

Q How would you rank Bill among his co-worker in this company?
이 회사에서 동료 가운데 Bill의 지위가 어떠하죠?

A He is, so to speak, the lowest man on the ladder.
말하자면, 그는 최하 말단입니다.

cook up :: 날조하다

↳ make up

Q Do you believe his excuse for coming late?
그 사람이 늦게 온 변명을 믿는가?

A No, I think he just cooked it up to protect his reputation.
아니, 자기 평판을 지키려고 그런 핑계를 지어낸 것 같아.

---

479 **go to pieces** :: 감정이 엉망이 되다, 자제심을 잃다

↳ fall apart emotionally

Q Did June get upset when she heard she failed the entrance exam?
입학시험에 합격하지 못했다는 말을 들었을 때 June은 당황했지?

A Yes, she went to pieces.
그래, 자제심을 잃었어.

Day

16

480 **make a monkey out of** :: 사람을 놀리다, 웃음거리로 삼다

↳ humiliate or try to make look foolish

Q Did you have to swear at him?
너는 그 사람에게 꼭 욕설을 퍼부어야 했니?

A Yes, because he was trying to make a monkey out of me in front of my friends.
예, 내 친구들 앞에서 나를 놀리려고 했거든요.

영숙어 문제 단번에 공략하기

091. In order to understand the concept of infinity, we must think in much <u>accustomed to</u>.

(A) used to   (B) able to
(C) confronted with   (D) aware of

어휘 **accustomed to** 익숙한(used to) / **infinity** 무한대 / **confronted with** ~에 직면한 / **aware of** ~을 알고 있는

해석 무한대의 개념을 이해하기 위해서는 우리가 익숙해져 있는 것보다 훨씬 더 넓은 관점에서 생각해야 한다.

---

092. The song "Yankee Doodle" was originally sung by British troops to <u>make fun of</u> the American colonists.

(A) give inspiration to   (B) ridicule
(C) entertain   (D) discourage

어휘 **doodle** 바보 / **make fun of** 조롱하다(ridicule, deride) / **inspiration** 영감 / **entertain** 대접 하다, 즐겁게 하다, 마음에 품다

해석 "Yankee Doodle" 이라는 노래는 본래 영국 군대가 미국 식민지인들을 비웃기 위해 불렀다.

---

093. He <u>lost his heart</u> when he had failed to win the game.

(A) was surprised   (B) went mad
(C) was discouraged   (D) were sad

어휘 **lose one's heart** 낙담하다 / **fail to** ~하지 못하다
해석 그는 경기에 지자 낙담했다.

094. After Elizabeth Blackwell's medical degree was
<u>bestowed</u> on her in 1849, she spent many years
promoting professional opportunities for women in
medicine.

(A) granted to   (B) contracted to
(C) rejected by   (D) requested by

어휘 degree 학위 / bestow A on B B에게 A를 주다 / contracted to ~와 약
혼한

해석 엘리자베스 블랙웰은 1849년에 의학 박사 학위를 수여받은 후, 여성들이 의학
분야에 진출할 수 있도록 기회를 증진시키는 데 많은 세월을 보냈다.

095. I was able to <u>get a head start</u> on my reading during the
holidays.

(A) start with no experience   (B) get by
(C) start earlier   (D) get around
(E) get started

어휘 get a head start 먼저 시작하다 / get by 그럭저럭 모면하다 / get
around 돌아다니다

해석 나는 휴일 동안 일찌감치 독서를 시작할 수 있었다.

Day

16

096. He <u>came upon</u> the telescope principle when he was
looking over some spectacles.

(A) wrote down   (B) depended upon
(C) found unexpectedly   (D) invented
(E) bought

어휘 come [hit] upon 우연히 발견하다 / telescope 망원경 / look over 조사
하다 / spectacles 안경

해석 그는 우연히 몇몇 안경을 조사하던 중 망원경의 원리를 발견했다.

Answers ★ 91.(A) 92.(B) 93.(C) 94.(A) 95.(C) 96.(C)

481 the low-down
:: 상세한 것, 명세

↳ the details

> Q Did you hear the new gossip about Sally's boyfriend?
> 너 Sally의 남자친구에 관한 새로운 소문 들었어?

> A No, so hurry up and give me all the low-down.
> 아니, 그러니까 빨리 자세한 얘기 좀 해 봐.

482 bottoms up!
:: 잔을 비우자! 쭉 들이키자! 건배!

↳ let's drink!

> Q Well, shall we drink to someone?
> 자아, 누군가를 위해서 건배할까?

> A Yes, to our professors. Bottoms up!
> 그래, 우리 교수님을 위해서, 건배!

483 watch one's language
:: 말조심하다

↳ don't use four-letter words

> Q Damn, mom, can't I borrow the car just one Friday night?
> 제기랄, 엄마, 금요일 하룻밤만 차 좀 쓸 수 없어요?

> A No, and you'd better watch your language, young man!
> 안돼, 그리고 말조심하는 게 좋을 거야, 얘야!

all in all   :: 전체적으로 보아, 대체로

↳ in summary, considering everything that happened

Q Did you enjoy your summer vacation in Canada?
캐나다에서의 여름 휴가는 즐거웠니?

A Yes, all in all my family and I had a wonderful time.
그래, 대체로 내 가족과 함께 멋진 시간을 보냈어.

---

ifs ands of buts   :: 군소리

↳ complaints or exceptions

Q Mom, do I have to go to bed already?
엄마, 벌써 자야 해?

A Yes, and I don't want to hear any ifs ands of buts about it!
그래, 엄마는 다시는 군소리를 듣고 싶지 않아!

---

come on strong
:: 자기 주장이 강하다(특히 애정 문제에서), 너무 뻔뻔스럽다

↳ aggressive, especially romantically

Day

17

Q She's pretty dynamic woman, isn't she?
그녀는 꽤 활력 있는 여자야, 안 그래?

A Yes, but she comes on a little too strong, especially around men.
그래, 하지만 때로는 너무 뻔뻔스러워, 특히 남자들 주변에선 말이야.

---

pin one's ears back   :: 벌주다

↳ punish

Q Are you going to prevent him from dating your daughter?
자넨 그가 자네 딸과 데이트하는 걸 막을 셈인가?

A Yes, of course, and if he ever tries to, I'll pin his ears back.
그럼, 물론이지, 하기만 하면 그를 벌 줄 거야.

have a weakness for
:: 사족을 못 쓰다

↳ like very much or be unable to resist

Q Do you like ice cream as much as I do?
너 나 만큼 아이스크림 좋아하니?

A No, but I have a real weakness for chocolate fudge.
아니, 난 초콜릿 퍼지라면 사족을 못 써.

weasel out of
:: (의무를) 회피하다

↳ escape doing in a cowardly or sneaky way

Q Did you forget you told the kids you'd take them to Disneyland next Saturday?
다음 토요일에 아이들을 디즈니랜드에 데려가겠다고 한 말 잊었어요?

A No, and don't worry, I won't try to weasel out of my promise.
아니, 염려마, 약속을 회피하려고 하진 않을 테니까.

hold one's breath
:: (감동, 놀라움으로) 숨을 죽이다

↳ stop breathing because it will never happen

Q Aren't you ever going to start exercising to lose some weight?
살빼러 운동을 시작하지 않을 거예요?

A No, so don't hold your breath.
아뇨, 그렇다고 놀랄 거 없어요.

listen up
:: 경청하다

↳ listen very carefully

Q Am I doing a good job so far parking the car, dad?
제가 주차를 아주 잘했지요, 아빠?

A No, you're doing it all wrong! Listen up and I'll tell you how it's done.
아니, 아주 잘 못했구나! 잘 듣도록 해, 어떻게 하는 건지 말해줄테니.

take back   :: 취소하다

↳ withdraw or cancel what one has said

Q Are you and Jane ever going to go back to being friends again?
너하고 제인은 다시 친구가 되기로 했니?

A No, not before she takes back all the bad things she said about me.
아니, 그녀가 나에 대해 나쁘게 말한 걸 다 취소하기 전에는 아냐.

own up to   :: 완전히 자백하다

↳ confess fully

Q Did Joey finally confess he was the one who stole your pen?
Joey가 네 펜을 훔친 사람이라고 마침내 자백했니?

A Yes, he owned up to the deed after I threatened to tell his father.
응, 자기 아버지한테 이르겠다고 위협한 후에야 그 짓을 다 말했어.

cash in on   :: 편승하다, 이용하다

Day

17

↳ take advantage of

Q Did you read that he's now the most popular actor in Hollywood?
그가 현재 할리우드에서 제일 인기 있는 배우라는 기사 읽었니?

A Yes, and Madison Avenue is already trying to cash in on his popularity.
응, Madison Avenue는 벌써 그의 인기를 이용하고 있어.

keep pace with :: (떨어)지지 않고 따라가다

↳ keep up with

Q Is your boy doing well in school?
아드님이 학교에서 잘 해나가나요?

A No, he's been having a little trouble keeping pace with the other classmates.
아니오, 다른 급우들을 따라가는 데 약간의 어려운 점이 있어요.

take a calculated risk :: 심사숙고해서 시도하다

↳ attempt to do after careful consideration

Q Is there any secret to winning a lot of money playing poker?
포커놀이에 돈을 많이 따는 비법이라도 있니?

A Yes, it's all a matter of knowing when to take a calculated risk.
있지, 심사숙고해서 시도할 때를 잘 아는 게 요령이야.

lighten up :: 누그러뜨리다, 편안하게 하다

↳ relax and take it easy

Q Can't you work a little faster?
좀 더 빨리 일할 수 없어?

A No, and lighten up a little, okay? We've got plenty of time to do the job.
없어요, 좀 쉬엄쉬엄해요, 네? 그 일을 할 시간이 많이 있잖아요.

barge in on :: 난입하다

↳ enter without an invitation

Q Are you finished taking your shower?
너 샤워 다 끝났니?

A No, and did you have to barge in on me like this without knocking?
아니, 너 노크도 없이 이렇게 나한테 쳐들어 와야 해?

stick one's nose into
:: 간섭하다

↳ interfere in

Q Did Mary ask you another personal question?
그 여자가 사적인 질문을 또 했니?

A Yes, and I wish she'd stop sticking her nose into other people's affairs.
응, 그녀는 다른 사람 일에 간섭 좀 말았으면 좋겠어.

as to
:: ~에 관한, 관하여는

↳ regarding

Q Is Mary a good pianist?
메리는 피아노 잘 치니?

A Well, as to technique, she's one of the best in the school.
테크닉 면에서는 학교에서 최고에 속해.

take something on the chin
:: 어려운 상황을 겪다

↳ experience a direct blow or difficult situation

Day

17

Q Did the IRS decide to audit your company?
국세청이 당신 회사를 감사하기로 했습니까?

A Yes, we're really taking it on the chin this year: exports are down, too.
네, 올해는 정말 어려운 상황에 처해 있어요. 수출도 저조하구요.

get suckered into
:: 속아서 ~를 하다

↳ get cheated into

Q Is your car in the repair shop again?
네 차는 또 정비소에 갔니?

A Yes, I got suckered into buying a pile of junk.
그래, 난 속아서 쓰레기더미를 샀지 뭐야.

503 face the music

:: 벌을 받을 만하다

↳ receive a deserved punishment

Q Do you think he deserved getting such a long prison sentence?
그가 그렇게 장기 복역 선고를 받을 만하다고 생각하니?

A Yes, because when you do something bad like that you have to face the music.
그럼, 그런 나쁜 짓을 하면 벌을 받아야 하기 때문이지.

504 raise one's voice

:: 연장자 앞에서 언성을 높이다

↳ speak loudly in the presence of an elder

Q Did you have to spank your son like that?
자넨 그렇게 아들을 철썩 때려야 했나?

A Yes, because no child should be permitted to raise his voice to his father.
그럼, 아이는 제 애비 면전에서 언성을 높여선 안되기 때문이지.

505 rake in

:: 돈을 긁어들이다

↳ obtain in large amounts

Q This winter is really freezing, isn't it?
올 겨울은 정말 얼어붙는 것 같지 않아?

A Yes, and I'm sure the oil companies are raking in lots of money, too.
그래, 정유회사가 돈을 많이 벌어들일 게 분명해.

506 nose around

:: 낌새를 알아채려 하다

↳ investigate closely and sometimes secretly

Q Did you invite all these reporters into your office?
당신이 이 기자들을 다 당신 사무실로 불렀습니까?

A Yes, I thought if I gave them an interview they'd stop nosing around.
예, 내가 그들과 인터뷰를 하면 뭔가 낌새를 알아내려는 걸 그만 두겠죠.

507 rattle off
:: 줄줄 외다

↳ recite quickly and accurately

Q Do you know the names of the presidents from
Washington to Bush?
자넨 워싱턴에서 부시까지 대통령 이름들을 아나?

A No, but my son can rattle them off without any trouble.
아니, 하지만 우리 아들은 별 어려움 없이 줄줄 욀 수 있지.

508 bear down on
:: 내리 누르다

↳ put pressure on

Q Is there any way to get our factory workers to produce
more?
우리 공장 근로자로 하여금 더 생산케 하는 묘책이 있나?

A Yes, it's easy just bear down on them to work harder.
그럼, 쉽지. 일을 더 열심히 하도록 압력을 주기만 하면 돼.

509 of no great account
:: 유익하지 않은, 중요하지 않은

↳ of no real importance

Q Do you like President's antidrug program?
자넨 대통령의 마약 방지 프로그램을 좋아하나?

A No, I think in the end it will prove to be of no great account.
아니, 그 계획이 소용없다는 게 결국은 판명될 걸.

510 there's no two ways about it
:: 선택의 여지가 없다

↳ there's no alternative

Q Did you threaten to fire him?
자넨 그를 해고하겠다고 위협했나?

A Yes, and there's no two ways about it : either he tries
harder or he's out!
그럼, 그 점에 대해선 선택의 여지가 없네. 일을 더 열심히 하든지 나가든지
말야!

097. Jim spent the whole evening asking me questions about his physics exam. However, he <u>made up for</u> it by washing my car for me.

(A) applauded (B) compensated
(C) complemented (D) conciliated
(E) appreciated

어휘 make up for 보상하다(compensate) / applaud 박수 갈채를 보내다 / complement 보충(하다) / conciliate 달래다

해석 짐은 저녁 내내 나한테 물리학 시험에 대한 질문을 퍼부었다. 그런데 그 보상으로 그는 내 차를 세차해 주었다.

098. Please <u>refrain from</u> doing that.

(A) continue (B) be proud of
(C) stop (D) forget

어휘 refrain from ~ing ~을 삼가다 / be proud of ~를 자랑스럽게 여기다

해석 제발 그런 짓은 삼가 주세요.

099. Do you think he will <u>give up</u> his seat in the Senate?

(A) relinquish (B) stand for
(C) run for (D) hold on
(E) pass through

어휘 relinquish 양도하다, 포기하다 / stand for 대표하다 / run for 입후보하다 / hold on 지속하다 / pass through 수료하다, 경험하다

해석 그가 상원의원 자리를 내놓을까요?

100. The hoodlums were all-<u>rounded up</u>.

(A) given refuge   (B) arrested
(C) put to exercise   (D) put on a list

어휘 **hoodlum** 폭력배 / **round up** (범인을) 검거하다 / **give refuge to** ~를 비
호하다

해석 그 폭력배들이 모조리 검거됐다.

---

101. They had <u>rounded up</u> people at gunpoint.

(A) dispersed   (B) threatened
(C) assembled   (D) dismissed

어휘 **round up** 끌어모으다, 검거하다 / **disperse** 흩어지게 하다 / **assemble**
소집하다 / **dismiss** 해고하다, 처리해버리다

해석 그들은 사람들을 총으로 위협하여 끌어모았다.

---

102. I don't know what he <u>is up to</u>.

(A) is getting up for   (B) is planning
(C) is complaining of   (D) is upstairs doing
something

어휘 **be up to** ~을 꾀하다 / **complain of** ~을 불평하다

해석 나는 그가 무슨 일을 꾀하고 있는지 모른다.

Day

17

18th Day

511 no wonder
:: 당연하다

↳ it is not surprising

Q Do your grandchildren like animals?
자네 손자들은 동물들을 좋아하나?

A Yes, and no wonder — they were all raised on a farm in Iowa.
그래, 그게 당연해. 그 애들은 다 아이오와 주에 있는 농장에서 자랐으니까.

512 nose out
:: 근소한 차이로 이기다

↳ defeat but by a small margin

Q Did your horse win the race without much trouble?
자네 말이 큰 어려움 없이 그 경주에서 이겼나?

A No, he barely nosed out the horse that came in second place.
아니. 2등으로 들어온 말과 근소한 차이로 가까스로 이겼네.

513 balled up
:: 뒤죽박죽이다

↳ in a confused and disorganized state

Q Did you have trouble finding our house?
우리 집 찾느라고 애썼니?

A Yes, the directions you gave me were all balled up.
응, 너가 나한테 준 약도는 모두 뒤죽박죽이었어.

take exception to
:: 동의하지 않다, 이의가 있다

↳ disagree with

Q Do you agree with most of Prof. Smith's new theory?
넌 Smith 교수의 새 이론에 대체로 동의하니?

A Yes, though I guess I'll have to take exception to a few minor details.
응, 몇 개의 세부사항은 동의하지 않겠지만.

answer for
:: 책임을 지다, 벌을 받다

↳ take the punishment for

Q Why should I tell you the truth?
내가 왜 당신한테 사실을 말해야 합니까?

A Well, if you don't, you may have to answer for it before a judge.
그렇지 않으면 당신은 판사 앞에서 벌을 받아야 할지도 몰라요.

at will
:: 마음대로, 뜻대로

↳ when one wishes

Q Why do you think there's been so many bank robberies this year?
자넨 금년에 왜 그렇게 은행 강도가 많았다고 생각하나?

A Criminals are now able to rob at will because of the easy availability of weapons.
요즘은 무기를 쉽게 얻을 수 있어서 은행강도들이 마음대로 약탈할 수 있거든.

Day

18

every other
:: 하나 걸러, 격일로

↳ every second one

Q How often do you have to work the night shift?
넌 얼마 간격으로 야간 작업을 해야 하는 거니?

A Every other day.
격일이야.

518   on the ball

:: 빈틈없이, 기민한

↪ alert and ready for action

Q Is there any secret to your magazine's popularity?
당신네 잡지의 인기에는 무슨 비법이라도 있습니까?

A Yes, we've got a staff or writers who are always on the ball.
예, 우린 언제나 기민하게 움직이는 집필진이 있지요.

519   fall behind

:: 뒤지다

↪ move more slowly than others

Q Do you think our country will ever regain its lead in technology?
우리 나라가 기술면에서 선두를 회복할 것 같습니까?

A No, because it's already fallen too far behind Japan and Germany.
아니오, 이미 일본과 독일에 너무 많이 뒤져 있어요.

520   under way

:: 진행중에

↪ started or operating

Q Has the blood drive started?
헌혈 운동이 시작됐니?

A Yes, it's already under way. Have you donated yet?
응, 벌써 진행중이야. 넌 헌혈했니?

521   get a raise

:: 봉급인상을 받다

↪ receive a higher paycheck

Q Did you finally convince the boss to give you the transfer you want?
결국 자네가 원하는 이동을 해주도록 사장을 납득시켰나?

A No, but at least I got a raise out of him this time.
아니야, 하지만 최소한 이번 기회에 그에게서 봉급인상은 받아냈지.

522 **out for blood** :: 복수할 기회를 노리는, 해치울 작정인

↳ seeking revenge

Q Did your basketball team lose to UCLA both times this season?
너희 농구팀이 이번 시즌에서 UCLA에게 두 번 다 졌니?

A Yes, but next year you can be sure we'll be out for blood!
그래, 하지만 내년에는 우리가 꼭 복수할걸.

523 **face-to-face** :: 직접 얼굴을 대하는

↳ directly and in person

Q Have you ever seen the Queen of England?
너 영국 여왕을 직접 본 적 있니?

A Yes, in fact I once met her face-to-face.
응, 실제로 한 번 만난 적이 있어.

524 **rise through the ranks** :: 자수성가하다

↳ advance from lower positions to higher positions

Q Did he inherit his company from his father?
그는 자기 아버지에게서 그 회사를 물려받았습니까?

A No, he became president in an unusual way : he rise through the ranks.
아니오, 특이한 방법으로 사장이 됐어요. 자수성가를 한 거죠.

Day

18

525 **have an ax to grind** :: 원한을 품다, 감정이 있다

↳ have an interested or selfish motive

Q Why did Joe tell the professor that Bill cheated on his final exam?
Joe가 왜 교수한테 Bill이 기말시험에서 부정을 저질렀다고 일러바쳤니?

A He has an ax to grind. Bill went on a date with Joe's girlfriend last week.
악감정이 있어서 그래. 지난주 Bill이 Joe의 여자친구와 데이트했거든.

183

526 all of a sudden
:: 갑자기, 뜻밖에, 돌연

↳ suddenly

Q Why do you look so upset, Jane?
Jane, 안색이 왜 그래요?

A Last night at dinner my husband all of a sudden got a severe stomachache and he's still sick.
글쎄 지난 밤 저녁을 먹는데 남편이 갑자기 복통을 심하게 일으켜 아직도 앓고 있어요.

527 back and forth
:: 왔다갔다

↳ first one way and then another way

Q Is your husband relaxing in the maternity ward waiting room?
네 남편은 분만 대기실에서 느긋하게 있니?

A No, I heard he was pacing back and forth and chainsmoking.
아니, 왔다갔다하면서 줄담배를 피우고 있대.

528 have a ball
:: 즐거운 시간을 보내다

↳ have a very good time

Q Are you enjoying the party?
파티가 즐거우십니까?

A Yes, and thanks for inviting us. We're having a ball.
네, 저희들을 초대해주셔서 고맙습니다. 즐거운 시간을 보내고 있어요.

529 go by the name of
:: ~라는 가명으로 통하다

↳ have another usually false name

Q Are you sure you can find out his real name?
자넨 그 자의 진짜 이름을 꼭 알아낼 수 있겠나?

A No, but whenever he's in Chicago he goes by the name of Big John.
아니오, 하지만 그 자는 시카고에 있을 때마다 Big John이란 가명으로 통합니다.

come natural   :: ~에게 쉽다

↳ to be born with the ability to do

Q You're a pretty good tennis player. Did you ever take lessons?
넌 아주 훌륭한 테니스 선수야. 레슨을 받은 적이 있니?

A No, I guess the sport just comes natural to me.
아니오, 그 운동은 제게 쉬운 것 같아요.

shoot straight from the shoulder :: 솔직하고 정직한

↳ be frank and honest

Q Does Joe usually express his frank opinions during staff meetings?
조는 중역회의 중 자기의 솔직한 의견을 표현합니까?

A Yes, he's one of the few who always shoots straight from the shoulder.
그럼요, 그는 언제나 솔직하게 대하는 몇 안 되는 사람들 중 하나예요.

run the show   :: 지배하다, 위압하다

↳ dominate

Q Is your mother the boss in your family, too?
네 어머니도 너희 집안에서 가장이시니?

A Yes, she's been running the show in my house ever since I can remember.
응, 내가 기억할 수 있는 때부터 쭉 우리 집을 좌지우지 해오셨지.

Day
18

go for broke   :: ~에 전부를 걸다

↳ try very hard to win

Q Are you going to give up trying to pass the entrance exam?
입학시험에 합격하려는 걸 포기할 참이야?

A No, this time I'm going for broke. I'm going to study for it 20 hours a day.
아니, 이번에 전력을 다해 볼 거야. 하루에 20시간씩 공부할 작정이야.

take a bow :: (갈채에) 답례하다

↳ accept the audience's applause or praise

Q Well, do you think the audience really liked my performance tonight?
오늘밤 청중들이 제 연주를 정말로 마음에 들어했나요?

A Yes, they're still applauding. Go back out on stage and take a bow.
그랬지, 아직도 박수를 보내고 있잖아. 무대로 나가서 답례를 하렴.

---

535 **to coin a phrase** :: 참신한 표현을 쓰자면

↳ to make a new verbal expression

Q You don't have a very high opinion of student radicals, do you?
넌 진보주의 학생을 좋게 생각하지 않지?

A No, I think most of them are, to coin a phrase, spoiled brats!
그래, 대부분은 새로운 표현을 쓰자면, 버르장머리 없는 선머슴들이야.

---

536 **come down with** :: 병에 걸리다

↳ get, usually a disease

Q Are you feeling okay today, Mary?
오늘 기분이 좋니, Mary?

A No, I think I'm coming down with the flu or something.
아니오, 감기나 뭐 그런 게 걸린 것 같아요.

---

537 **bound for** :: 향하다, ～쪽으로 나아가다

↳ headed for

Q Excuse me, sir, but is the train we're on going to Florida?
실례지만, 선생님, 우리가 탄 기차가 플로리다로 갑니까?

A No, it's bound for California. You'd better change trains real fast!

아니오, 캘리포니아 쪽으로 가는데요. 얼른 갈아타시는 게 좋겠군요.

538 get to the bottom of

:: 철저히 조사하다

↪ investigate thoroughly

Q Did you ever find out who started the false rumor about you?

너에 대해 누가 헛소문을 냈는지 알아 봤니?

A No, but I'm determined to get to the bottom of this whole matter.

아니, 하지만 이 문제를 전반적으로 철저히 조사하기로 결정했어.

539 not a bit

:: 절대로, 전혀

↪ not at all

Q Do you mind if I smoke in your car?

네 차에서 담배 좀 피워도 되겠니?

A No, not a bit.

응, 상관없어.

540 to blame

:: 탓할, 잘못을 저지른

↪ at fault

Q Did you scold the student who let the frog loose in your classroom?

교실에다 개구리를 풀어놓은 학생을 야단쳤습니까?

A No, because I still haven't found out who is to blame for the incident.

아니오, 그 사고를 탓할 학생을 아직 알아내지 못했기 때문에요.

103. In the early seventeenth century, the Iroquois Confederacy <u>comprised</u> the five nations of Mohawk, Oneida, Onondaga, Cayuga, and Seneca.

(A) undermined   (B) depended on
(C) revered   (D) consisted of

어휘 **comprise** ~로 구성되다(consist of) / **undermine** 약화시키다 / **revere** 공경하다

해석 17세기 초, 이러쿼이 연방은 Mohawk, Oneida, Onondaga, Cayuga, 그리고 Seneca라는 다섯 개의 부족으로 구성되어 있었다.

104. Bladder wrack, a tough, leathery brown seaweed, <u>clings to</u> rocks tenaciously.

(A) grows under   (B) hides under
(C) sticks to   (D) yields to

어휘 **wrack** 물가에 밀려온 해초 / **leathery** 가죽같은, 질긴 / **seaweed** 해초 / **cling to** 달라붙다(stick to) / **tenaciously** 단단히

해석 질긴 가죽 같은 갈색 바닷말인 Bladder 해초는 바위에 단단히 붙어 있다.

105. Topeka, Kansas, was settled in 1854 by people <u>opposed to</u> slavery.

(A) accustomed to   (B) acquainted with
(C) afraid of   (D) averse to

어휘 **be opposed to** ~에 반대하다(be averse to) / **be accustomed to** ~에 익숙하다 / **be acquainted with** ~와 잘 알다

해석 캔자스 주(州) Topeka에는 1854년 노예제도를 반대한 사람들이 정착했다.

106. I haven't got a can opener, but this knife will <u>serve my turn</u>.

(A) take the place of me   (B) suit my purpose

(C) help my turning   (D) protect me

> 어휘 **serve one's turn** ~의 소용에 닿다 / **take the place of** ~을 대신하다 / **suit** ~에 맞다, 적합하다
>
> 해석 깡통따개는 없지만, 이 칼이면 잘 들 것 같다.

---

107. <u>Drop me a ring</u> when you know your exam results.

(A) Send me a facsimile   (B) Give me a ring

(C) Send me telegram   (D) Write me a letter

(E) Visit me a moment

> 어휘 **drop[give] a ring** 전화걸다 / **a moment** (부사적으로) 잠깐 동안
>
> 해석 네 시험 결과를 알면 내게 전화하렴.

---

108. Korean students are <u>cutting a fine figure</u> at the finest schools in the US.

(A) living with no difficulty

(B) cutting the shortest way

(C) having their tests with ease

(D) getting good results in their studies

(E) making themselves changed differently

Day

18

> 어휘 **cut a fine figure** 두각을 나타내다 / **cut the shortest way** 질러가다
>
> 해석 한국 학생들은 미국에 있는 유수한 학교들에서 두각을 나타내고 있다.

19th Day

541 give a lift
:: 차에 태우다(태워주다)

↳ give a ride in a car

Q Do you need a ride anywhere?
어딘가 태워다 주길 바랍니까?

A Yes, I'd really appreciate you giving me a lift home.
네, 절 집에까지 태워다주시면 정말 감사하겠습니다.

542 speak at length about
:: ~에 관해 긴 시간 동안 말하다

↳ speak for a long time about

Q Did you learn much from Kissinger's lecture?
키신저의 강연에서 많은 걸 배웠니?

A Yes, because he spoke at length about my favorite subject : the Middle East.
그럼, 내가 좋아하는 주제인 중동 문제에 관해 오랜 시간 얘기했기 때문이야.

543 get the better of
:: 월등한 위치를 차지하다

↳ achieve a superior position

Q Janet's not very popular in the college dorm, is she?
Janet은 학교 기숙사에서 그다지 인기가 없지?

A No, because she always tries to get the better of her classmates.
그래, 그 앤 항상 자기 동료들을 이기려고 애쓰기 때문이야.

544 hold back
:: 감추다

↪ hide something

Q I've told you everything I know. So will you stop asking me questions?
내가 알고 있는 건 다 말씀드렸습니다. 그러니까 질문은 그만하시죠?

A No, I still think you're holding back something from me!
아니, 여전히 자네가 내게 뭔가 감추고 있는 것 같아.

545 in the face of
:: ~에 직면했을 때

↪ when confronted with

Q Do you think he'll make a good marine?
그가 해상 근무를 잘 해낼까요?

A No, I'm sure he'll be the first to run and hide in the face of danger.
아뇨, 위험에 직면하면 제일 먼저 도망쳐 숨을 걸요.

546 mark one's words
:: 내 말을 기억하다

↪ remember what one is saying to you

Q Do you think our son will ever become famous someday?
우리 아들이 언젠가는 꼭 유명해지겠죠?

A Yes, and you can mark my words on that prediction.
그럼, 당신은 그런 내 예언을 기억해두라구.

Day
19

547 touch up
:: 수정하다, 마무리하다

↪ put the finishing touches on

Q Is the portrait finished yet?
그 초상화는 이제 완성된 거니?

A No, I still have to touch it up in a few places.
아니오, 아직 몇 군데 마무리 손질을 해야 해요.

548 it's high time
:: 〜할 때다

↳ it's about time

Q Do you think I should lose some weight?
내가 몸무게 좀 빼야 할 것 같니?

A Yes, and it's high time you quit smoking, too.
응, 바야흐로 금연도 할 때야!

549 can't for the life of one
:: 아무리 해도 〜않다

↳ can't no matter how hard one try

Q Did you find your wallet yet?
네 지갑 아직 발견하지 못했니?

A No, and I can't for the life of me remember where I left it.
응, 그걸 어디다 뒀는지 아무리 해도 기억이 안나.

550 throw light on
:: 〜을 밝히다, 〜의 설명을 듣다

↳ enlighten

Q Did you conduct a thorough investigation of the matter?
그 사건을 철저히 조사했습니까?

A Yes, but strangely it didn't throw much light on the problem.
예, 하지만 이상하게도 그 문제를 밝힐 수가 없었습니다.

551 in all likelihood
:: 거의 〜할 것 같은

↳ it is likely

Q Do you think it'll rain tomorrow?
내일 비가 내릴 것 같니?

A Yes, in all likelihood.
그래, 그럴 것 같은데.

552 **at one's wit's end** :: 어찌해야 할 지 모르다

↳ one doesn't know what one should do

Q Have you found your lost puppy yet?
잃어버린 강아지 찾았니?

A No, and I'm at my wit's end! I've looked everywhere for it.
아니, 어찌해야 할 지 모르겠어! 샅샅이 다 찾아 봤는데 말야.

---

553 **feel for** :: ~에게 동정심을 느끼다

↳ sympathize with

Q Are you happy that you again got better grades than your brother?
네가 또 형보다 좋은 성적을 받아서 기쁘니?

A No, I really feel for him. He just happens to be my best friend.
아니오. 난 정말 형이 딱해요. 바로 제일 친한 친구이기도 하구요.

---

554 **in the event of** :: (만일) ~의 경우에는

↳ if it happens

Q Do you have a next of kin?
가까운 친척이 있어요?

A Yes, in the event of my death, please notify my uncle Jack.
네, 제가 죽게 된다면 Jack 삼촌께 알려주세요.

---

555 **hit the nail on the head** :: 핵심을 찌르다, 잘 알아맞히다

↳ do or say the right thing

Q Don't you think Bill's too independent to be a good husband and family man?
그는 너무 독립적이라 좋은 남편이나 가정적인 사람이 될 수 없을 것 같은데요.

A Yes, your observation about him has really hit the nail on the head.
그래요, 그에 대한 당신 관찰이 정말 옳아요.

Day

19

193

556 at loose ends

:: 혼란스러운

↳ restless and unsettled

Q Are you a little upset these days, Joe?
요새 마음이 좀 심란하니?

A Yes, frankly I've been at loose ends ever since I found out I'm going bald.
그래, 대머리가 돼가고 있는 걸 안 후로는 솔직히 마음이 혼란스러워.

557 ward off

:: 막다, 피하다

↳ keep away

Q Do you know why the natives wear those strange things around their necks?
원주민들이 왜 목에 우스꽝스러운 장식을 다는지 알아요?

A Yes, those are charms and they're supposed to ward off evil spirits.
네, 그것들은 부적이라 악령을 막아준다고 생각하죠.

558 shy away from

:: 피하다, 꺼리다

↳ avoid

Q Do you like rich desserts?
영양가가 풍부한 후식을 좋아하니?

A Yes, but I'm trying to shy away from sweets these days to lose some weight.
응, 하지만 요즘은 체중을 좀 줄이기 위해 단 것을 피하려고 애쓰고 있어.

559 top off

:: 마무리짓다, 끝내다

↳ complete

Q Are you a heavy smoker, George?
자네 골촌가, George?

A No, but sometimes I like to top off Sunday dinner with a Havana cigar.
아니, 하지만 가끔 일요일 정찬을 아바나 담배로 끝내는 걸 좋아하지.

on the wane
:: 쇠퇴하기(기울기) 시작하는

↳ declining

Q Is your record shop doing poorly these days?
근래 자네 레코드 가게 장사가 형편없나?

A Yes, thanks to the introduction of CDs, record sales are on the wane.
그렇다네, CD판 등장 덕분에 레코드 판매는 내리막이야.

for the most part
:: 대부분은, 대체로

↳ mostly

Q Are you satisfied with your new apartment?
새 아파트는 마음에 들어?

A Yes, for the most part.
응, 대체로.

get the picture
:: 알아듣다

↳ understand

Q Are you saying that I'm not good enough to marry your daughter?
제가 따님과 결혼할만하지 못하다고 말씀하시는 겁니까?

A Yes, so do you finally get the picture?
그러네, 자네 이해하겠나?

Day

19

all at once
:: 갑자기

↳ suddenly

Q How was your camping trip?
캠핑여행 어땠어?

A Terrible! As soon as we got to the camp site, all at once it began to snow.
말도 마. 야영지에 도착하자마자 갑자기 눈이 내려버렸어.

564 off the wall
:: 엉뚱한, 이상한

↳ strange

Q Did you see Woody Allen's new movie?
새로 나온 우디 앨런 영화 봤니?

A Yes, and it's off the wall like most of his others.
응, 그런데 대부분의 다른 작품들처럼 엉뚱해.

565 think nothing of it
:: 신경 쓰지 않다, 괜찮다

↳ it was nothing special

Q Is there anything I can do to repay your kindness?
베풀어주신 친절을 갚을 길이 있을까요?

A No, think nothing of it. It was my pleasure.
아뇨, 신경쓰지 마세요. 괜찮습니다.

566 pull out of
:: 철수하다

↳ withdraw

Q Is the U.S. a member of UNESCO?
미국은 유네스코 회원입니까?

A No, it pulled out of the organization a few years ago.
아니오, 몇 년 전에 그 기구에서 탈퇴했습니다.

567 wither on the vine
:: 말라죽다, 시들다

↳ die out

Q Are you sure that you'll soon have to close your pizza parlor?
틀림없이 피자가게를 곧 닫을 거니?

A Yes, because of a lack of customers it's starting to wither on the vine.
응, 손님이 없어서 가게가 안 되기 시작했어.

at times

:: 때때로, 가끔

↪ occasionally

Q Hey, Bill, could you baby-sit for my kids for two weeks this summer?

이봐요, Bill, 올 여름에 이 주일 동안 내 아이들 좀 봐줄 수 있겠어요?

A At times you can really be unreasonable. You don't expect me to say yes, do you?

때때로 당신은 정말 터무니 없군요. 승낙할 거라고 생각하는 건 아니죠?

---

run up a bill

:: (지출, 빚 따위를) 늘리다

↪ add many charges to your account

Q Do you want to go grocery shopping with me?

나하고 식품점에 쇼핑갈래?

A No, I'm going to stay home and watch TV. Don't run up a big bill, okay?

아니, 집에 있으면서 TV나 볼래. 많이 사지 마, 알았지?

---

well-rounded

:: 균형이 잡혀 완전한, 다방면의

↪ comprehensive

Q Is it that important for your daughter to attend an Ivy League college?

댁의 따님이 동부 명문 대학에 가는 게 그렇게 중요한가요?

A Yes, because I want her to get a well-rounded education.

네, 전 그 애가 가능한 다방면에서 완전한 교육을 받게 하고 싶어요.

Day

19

109. New developments in theoretical astronomy <u>took place</u> in the 1960's.

(A) began   (B) occurred
(C) were known   (D) were found

어휘 theoretical 이론상의 / astronomy 천문학 / take place 발생하다(occur)
해석 이론 천문학에서 새로운 발전이 1960년대에 일어났다.

110. We cannot <u>set at naught</u> what the lady said about it.

(A) tolerate   (B) ignore
(C) accept   (D) trust
(E) bring all for naught

어휘 set at naught 무시하다, 경멸하다 / bring all for naught 망치다, 무효로 만들다
해석 우리는 그 여인이 그것에 관해 말한 것을 무시할 수 없다.

111. They <u>set off</u> soon after daybreak.

(A) start   (B) stop
(C) keep   (D) set in

어휘 set off 출발하다 / daybreak 날이 샘 / set in 시작하다, 퍼지다
해석 그들은 해가 뜨자 곧 출발했다.

112. We must <u>set store by</u> his opinion that our country should be reunited in the long run.

(A) make widely known
(B) have a theoretical basis to

(C) make much of
(D) find fault with
(E) bear in our mind

어휘 set store by 중시하다 / in the long run 결국(finally) / make much
of ~을 중요하게 여기다 / find fault with ~를 헐뜯다(criticize) / bear in
mind 명심하다

해석 우리나라는 결국 통일되어야 한다는 그의 의견을 중요시해야 한다.

- -

113. Though he had no vote, the delegate from Hawaii was
allowed to <u>sit in on</u> the conferences.

(A) participate in   (B) interfere with
(C) contact with   (D) negotiate with
(E) break into

어휘 vote 선거권, 투표 / delegate 하원의원, 대의원(발언권은 있으나 투표권은
없음) / sit in on 참관하다, 견학하다 / interfere with 훼방놓다 / contact
with ~와 접촉하다 / negotiate with ~와 협상하다 / break into 침입하
다, 방해하다, 갑자기 ~하다

해석 투표권은 없었지만, 그 하와이 대표는 회의를 참관할 수 있도록 허락을 받았다.

- -

114. No one from this district was invited to <u>sit on</u> the jury
for the trial of the infamous kidnapper.

(A) defend   (B) denounce
(C) speak for   (D) be a member of
(E) question

어휘 sit on ~의 일원이다, 검사하다 / infamous 파렴치한 / kidnapper 유괴자
/ denounce 비난하다 / speak for 대변하다

해석 이 구역 출신 중 어느 누구도 그 파렴치한 유괴범의 재판에 배심원으로 초대되
지 않았다.

Answers ★ 109.(B) 110.(B) 111.(A) 112.(C) 113.(A) 114.(D)

---

571 **in a way**   :: 다소, 얼마간

↳ to a slight degree

Q Is your son's new girlfriend pretty?
댁의 아드님 새 여자 친구는 예쁜가요?

A Yes, in a way, especially if you compare her to his last one.
네, 어느 정도는요. 특히 지난번 애와 비교하면요.

---

572 **line up**   :: 조정하다, 일렬로 늘어서다

↳ schedule or arrange

Q Did you persuade any famous people to come to your charity ball?
자네 자선 파티에 유명인사들 누구라도 오기로 설득했나?

A Yes, I lined up three movie actresses, one anchorman and a few comedians.
그럼, 세 명의 여배우와 앵커맨 한 명하고 코미디언 몇 명을 조정해놨어.

---

573 **seeing that**   :: ~이므로, ~라는 걸로 볼 때

↳ because

Q Are you going to invite that jerk to your birthday party?
네 생일에 저 얼간이를 초대하려고 하니?

A Yes, seeing that he's rich he'll probably bring me a nice gift.
응, 그 사람은 부자니까 아마 나한테 근사한 선물을 가져올 거야.

concern oneself

:: 마음쓰다, 걱정하다

↳ worry about

Q Do you think I should have some cosmetic surgery done on my nose?
내 코가 성형수술을 받아야 할 것 같니?

A No, and why do you concern yourself so much about your physical appearance?
아니, 넌 왜 외모에 그렇게 마음을 많이 쓰니?

as best one can

:: 힘껏, 최선을 다해

↳ to the best of one's ability

Q Do you think you'll be able to fix this before Sunday?
일요일 전에 이걸 고칠 수 있을 것 같아요?

A Yes, I'll try as best I can to get it back to you by Saturday night.
그러죠, 최선을 다해서 토요일 밤까지 돌려드리겠습니다.

beyond dispute

:: 논쟁의 여지가 없는

↳ certain

Q Is your mayor an honest public official?
당신네 시장은 정직한 공무원입니까?

A Yes, his integrity is beyond dispute.
네, 그의 청렴결백은 논쟁할 여지가 없습니다.

ad lib

:: 즉흥적으로 하다, 즉석에서 하다

↳ improvise

Q Why isn't your after-dinner speech prepared yet?
왜 만찬 연설을 아직 준비하지 않으셨습니까?

A Because I've decided to ad lib it.
즉석에서 하려구요.

Day
20

trifle with :: 함부로 (가볍게) 사람을 다루다

↳ treat lightly or regard as of little importance

Q Is it easy to get a good grade in Prof. Jones' class?
Jones 교수님 수업에서 좋은 점수 받기가 쉬우니?

A No, he once gave a student an 'F' for trifling with him.
아니, 한번은 자기에게 함부로 구는 한 학생에게 F학점을 줬다니까.

---

579 **take precedence over** :: 우선하다, ~보다 낫다

↳ come first in importance

Q Will we be able to get any tickets for the concert tonight?
오늘밤 연주회 표를 구할 수 있을까?

A No, because college students take precedence over high school students like us.
아니, 대학생들이 우리 같은 고등학생들보다 우월권을 가지고 있기 때문이야.

---

580 **tear away from** :: 떼어내다

↳ stop from watching or doing

Q Did you let your kids watch all of the late movie last night?
어젯밤 아이들이 심야 영화를 다 보게 뒀니?

A No, but it was so interesting they could hardly tear themselves away from it.
아니, 하지만 너무 재미있어서 아이들을 보지 못하게 할 수 없었어.

---

581 **have the run of the place** :: 마음대로 사용하다

↳ have the freedom to do what one wants

Q Are your parents home?
부모님이 집에 계시니?

A No, they went to Mexico on vacation, so I have the run of the place.
아니, 멕시코에 휴가를 가셔서 내가 집을 마음대로 써.

202

to one's face

:: 면전에서

↳ directly and in person

Q Did you criticize your boss yesterday?
어제 자네 사장을 비판했나?

A Yes, to his face.
응, 그의 면전에서.

go wrong with

:: 고장나다, 잘못되다

↳ become broken

Q Did your car run out of gas?
자네 차에 기름이 떨어졌나?

A No, so I guess something must have gone wrong with the battery.
아니, 배터리에 무슨 이상이 있는 게 틀림없나봐.

all in a day's work

:: 예삿일

↳ it was really nothing at all

Q Did you write this report all by yourself? Very impressive!
이 리포트 자네 혼자 다 썼나? 아주 인상적인데!

A Yes, but it was just all in a day's work.
그럼요, 그건 예삿일이에요.

as easy as falling off a log

:: 거저 먹기

↳ very easy

Q Is bridge a difficult game to learn?
브릿지는 배우기 어려운 게임이니?

A No, for most people it's as easy as falling off a log.
아니, 대부분 사람들에게는 아주 쉽지.

Day
20

in the raw
:: 벌거벗고, 자연 그대로의

↪ naked

Q Do you think your husband would like a new pair of pajamas for his birthday?
당신 남편은 생일선물로 새 잠옷 한 벌을 갖고 싶어하시나요?

A No, because he always sleeps in the raw.
아니오, 그이는 언제나 벌거벗고 자거든요.

cutthroat
:: 목이 간댕거릴 만큼 치열하게 경쟁적인

↪ intensely competitive

Q Is your computer company doing well these days?
자네 컴퓨터 회사는 요즈음 잘 돼가나?

A Yes, but competition in the electronics industry is becoming too cutthroat.
응, 하지만 전자산업 경쟁이 점점 치열해지고 있어.

put to sleep
:: 안락사시키다

↪ kill, but out of mercy

Q Do you still have that old German Shepherd?
그 늙은 독일산 셰퍼드를 아직도 가지고 있니?

A No, we had to put Adolph to sleep last year.
아니, 작년에 아돌프를 안락사시켰어.

clam up
:: 입을 다물다, 묵비하다

↪ refuse to speak

Q Did you get any new information out of the suspect, sergeant?
경사, 용의자로부터 무슨 새로운 정보라도 얻었나?

A No, nothing. He clammed up during the entire interrogation.
아니오, 아무 것도 없었습니다. 심문하는 내내 입을 다물고 있었습니다.

590 be lousy with
:: 우글거리다

↳ crowded with

Q Were there many pickpockets around the train station?
기차역 근방에 소매치기가 많이 있었니?

A Yes, the place was lousy with them.
그럼, 거긴 그런 사람들로 북적였어.

591 as far as
:: ~하는 한

↳ to the degree that

Q Is Jim and his wife going to come to our party this Sunday?
Jim 부부가 이번 일요일 우리 파티에 올까요?

A Yeah, as far as I know.
그래요, 내가 아는 한에는.

592 feel like one's 10-feet tall
:: 의기충천하다

↳ feel very good

Q Did you get an A on your final exam?
학기말 시험에 A를 받았니?

A Yes, and I feel like I'm 10-feet tall.
응, 그래서 기분이 아주 좋아.

593 rub out
:: 죽이다, 제거하다

↳ kill

Q Was there another killing over the weekend?
주말동안 또 다른 살인이 있었습니까?

A Yes, a former gang member got rubbed out for informing to the police.
예, 경찰 보고상으로는 깡패 일원이었던 자가 피살됐습니다.

bring up

:: 화제에 올리다

↳ raise a subject

Q Do you always have to say only bad things about my cooking?
당신은 내 요리에 대해 언제나 나쁜 점만 말해야 해요?

A No, and I'm sorry I brought it up.
아니, 그런 얘기를 꺼내서 미안해.

595

stand one's ground

:: 자기 위치를 지키다

↳ hold your position without surrender or retreat

Q Do you think I should admit that maybe I'm wrong?
아마 내가 틀렸다고 인정해야 한다고 생각하니?

A No, stand your ground. People will respect you for that.
아니, 네 위치를 지켜. 사람들은 그것 때문에 널 존경할 거야.

596

get one's number

:: 의중을 간파하다

↳ understand one's motives

Q Bill's behavior is hard to understand sometimes, isn't it?
Bill의 행동은 가끔 이해하기 힘들지 않아?

A No, not really. I've got his number. He's just a little shy, that's all.
아니 그렇지 않아. 난 그의 마음을 알지. 그는 조금 부끄러워할 뿐이라구.

597

to say the least

:: 줄잡아 말하더라도

↳ that's for sure

Q Are you still angry with him because he got the job instead of you?
그가 네 대신 일자리를 차지해서 아직도 그에게 화가 나 있니?

A Yes, to say the least. In fact, I'd like to punch him!
줄잡아 말해도 그래. 사실은, 그를 한 대 갈기고 싶어!

hold one off   :: 얼씬하지 못하게 하다

↳ resist

Q Do you think we can resist their attacks much longer, General?

그들의 공격을 더이상 저지할 수 있다고 생각하십니까, 장군?

A No, I don't think we can hold them off more than a few hours.

아니오, 몇 시간밖에 더 막을 수 없을 것 같소.

make up   :: 꾸며내다

↳ invent

Q Did you really catch a shark when you went skindiving last weekend?

지난주에 스킨다이빙 갔을 때 정말로 상어를 잡았니?

A No, of course not! I only made up that story to impress my girlfriend.

아니, 물론 아니지! 내 여자친구가 감명받으라고 내가 지어냈을 뿐이야.

other than   :: 제외하고

↳ except

Q Did anyone else join your mountain climbing club last month?

지난달에 어떤 다른 사람이 네 산악회에 가입했니?

A No, other than Bill, who I had to beg to get him to join.

아니, Bill 외에는 없어, 그 애도 내가 가입하라고 졸라서 했다구.

Day

20

115. This piece of pure scientific work <u>gave rise to</u> the dynamo.

(A) denied   (B) evidenced
(C) returned   (D) caused

> 어휘 **a piece of work** 작품, 일 / **give rise to** 일으키다 / **dynamo** 발전기 / **evidence** 증명하다, 명시하다
>
> 해석 이 한 편의 순수 과학적인 작업이 발전기의 발명을 가져왔다.

- -

116. Ken swore he would <u>get even with</u> Terry one day.

(A) give his due to   (B) put the screws on
(C) run after   (D) take revenge on
(E) hand it to

> 어휘 **get even with** 복수하다 / **put the screws on** 압박하다 / **run after** 추적하다, 열중하다 / **take revenge on** 복수하다 / **hand it to** 경의를 표하다
>
> 해석 켄은 언젠가 테리에게 복수하겠다고 맹세했다.

- -

117. The mayor refused to <u>give in to</u> the demand of the group.

(A) acknowledge   (B) publicize
(C) reply to   (D) hand over
(E) yield to

> 어휘 **give in to** ~에게 굴복하다 / **hand over** 양도하다 / **yield to** 굴복하다
>
> 해석 시장은 그 단체의 요구를 들어줄 것을 거절했다.

118. I am going to <u>give up</u> the idea.

(A) contribute   (B) abandon

(C) surrender   (D) expand

어휘 give up 포기하다(abandon) / surrender 항복하다 / expand 확장하다

해석 나는 그 아이디어를 포기하려고 한다.

---

119. When the brave soldiers have gone from the earth and there is only their story among us, this battlefield will still <u>swarm with</u> their spirits.

(A) be inspired by   (B) take care of

(C) be full of   (D) be established by

어휘 swarm with ~로 가득차다, 운집하다 / inspire 영감을 주다 / take care of ~을 돌보다

해석 그 용감한 군인들이 지상에서 사라지고, 오직 그들에 대한 무용담만이 우리에게 남아 있을 때에도, 이 전장(戰場)은 여전히 그들의 정신으로 가득할 것이다.

---

120. I'd like to give him some advice, but I think he'd <u>take offence</u>.

(A) follow my advice   (B) do the opposite

(C) attack me   (D) be annoyed

어휘 give ~ an advice 충고하다 / take offence 성내다 / do the + 형용사 ~ 처럼 행동하다 / do the opposite 정반대인 체하다

해석 그에게 충고를 좀 하고 싶지만, 그가 화를 낼 것 같다.

Day

20

601 have no bearing (up)on

:: 관계가 없다

↳ have no relation with

Q Well, do you agree with what I just said?
저, 내가 방금 말한 것에 동의하니?

A No, because it doesn't really have any bearing upon what we're talking about.
아니, 왜냐하면 그건 우리가 얘기하는 것과는 정말 아무런 관계가 없어.

602 lead to

:: 이르다, 결과 ～이 되다

↳ result in

Q Is smoking marijuana dangerous?
마리화나를 피우는 게 위험하니?

A Yes, because it could lead to an addiction to more serious drugs.
그럼, 더 심한 마약 중독을 일으킬 수 있어.

603 out of commission

:: 사용불가

↳ not working properly

Q Is the cable car still out of order?
케이블카가 아직도 고장났니?

A Yes, it was put out of commission during the last rain storm.
응, 지난번 폭풍우 때 고장이 났어.

604 take one's mind off

:: 홀홀 털어버리다

↳ forget about

Q Do you have any hobbies?
취미 같은 게 있니?

A Yes, I sometimes play tennis to take my mind off all my troubles.
응, 골칫거리를 잊으려고 가끔 테니스를 치지.

605 as long as

:: ～하기만 하면

↳ if

Q Can I borrow your dictionary for a few minutes, Jim?
Jim, 사전 좀 잠깐 빌려줄 수 있니?

A Sure, as long as you return it before my next class.
다음 수업 시작하기 전에 돌려준다면, 빌려줄 수 있지.

606 beat to the draw

:: 앞지르다

↳ snatch victory from

Q Did you get a good seat?
좋은 자리 잡았어?

A No, too many other people beat us to the draw.
아니, 너무 많은 사람이 우리를 앞질렀어.

607 as it were

:: 즉, 말하자면

↳ so to speak

Q How was your trip to Hawaii?
하와이 여행은 어땠습니까?

A While we were there, it was, as it were, like being in Paradise.
말하자면 천국에 있는 기분이었어요.

608 make up for

:: 보상하다

↳ compensate for

Q Did you compensate him for breaking his vase?
그의 꽃병을 깬데 대한 보상을 했니?

A Yes, I made up for it by giving him one of mine.
응, 내 것 중에 하나를 주는 것으로 보상했어.

609 get a grip on oneself

:: 차근차근 해보다

↳ calm down and control oneself

Q Please, please, Sam, can't you help me just one more time?
제발, 제발, Sam, 한번만 더 도와줄 수 없겠니?

A No, and try to get a grip on yourself, okay!
아니, 네 스스로 잘 해봐, 알았지!

610 out of place

:: 격식에 벗어난

↳ not appropriate for the situation

Q Should I wear my blue jeans to the party tonight?
오늘밤 파티에 청바지를 입을까요?

A No, I think such clothing might be a little out of place.
안돼, 그런 복장은 장소에 좀 적합하지 않는 것 같아.

611 back off

:: 물러서다

↳ stop pressuring, move away

Q Aren't you going to quit wasting all your time and money gambling?
시간과 돈을 모두 낭비하는 짓은 그만두지 않을 거니?

A No, because it's the only fun I ever get. So just back off, okay!
그래, 그게 내가 갖는 유일한 재미야. 그러니까, 날 몰아붙이지마, 알았지!

612 tip one's hand

:: 실수로 의도를 알려주다

↳ reveal what you have or are going to do (show one's hand)

Q Should I show my classmates what my research has found so far?

내 연구 조사가 지금까지 뭘 알아냈는지 우리 반 친구들에게 보여줘야 하니?

A Yes, but be careful not to tip your hand. You want to get an A, don't you?

응, 하지만 네 능력이 드러나지 않게 조심해. 너 A를 받고 싶어 하잖니?

613 as yet

:: 아직은

↳ so far

Q Have you gotten any letters from your son?

아들한테서 편지 왔어요?

A As yet, I haven't, but I expect one any day now.

아직은 한 통도 없지만 곧 올 거예요.

614 know better than to

:: ～를 모를 정도로 어리석지 않다

↳ to be wise enough (not to)

Q Did Sam ever return the book he once borrowed from you?

전에 Sam이 네게서 빌려간 책 되돌려줬니?

A No, and I should have known better than to trust someone like him.

아니, 그와 같은 사람을 믿는 것이 어리석다는 걸 알았어야 했는데.

615 a couch potato

:: 게으름뱅이, 소파에 앉아 TV만 보며 많은 시간을 보내는 사람

↳ a lazy person (who spends most of his time watching TV)

Q Don't you think your dad needs to get some exercise?

너희 아빠는 운동을 좀 하셔야 한다고 생각지 않니?

A Yes, but he's been a couch potato ever since I can
   remember.
   그래, 하지만 아빠는 내가 기억할 수 있을 때부터 쭉 게으름뱅이셨어.

616 sit up and take notice   :: 예의주시하다

↳ pay close attention to

Q Conners really has a powerful serve, doesn't he?
   Conners 씨 서브는 정말 강력해, 그렇지?

A Yes, it really makes his opponents sit up and take notice.
   응, 상대로 하여금 정신을 바짝 차리게 하지.

617 larger than life   :: 인상적인, 감동을 주는

↳ impressive

Q Did you once meet Gen. Williams?
   윌리엄스 장군을 만나봤니?

A Yes, and I've never met anyone since who was more
   larger than life.
   응, 난 그렇게 인상적인 사람은 만난 적이 없어.

618 go places   :: 출세하다

↳ advance

Q Do you think he has any potential to become a
   successful businessman?
   그가 성공적인 비즈니스맨이 될 잠재력이 있다고 생각하십니까?

A Yes, I think he's a young man who is really going places.
   예, 그는 정말로 성공할 청년이라고 생각합니다.

619 settle an old score with   :: 쌓인 원한을 풀다

↳ get even with for a wrong done in the past

Q Did you finally have that meeting with your old English teacher?
너 드디어 옛날 영어선생님과 만났니?

A Yes, and I settled an old score with him over the F he once gave me.
응, 내게 준 F학점에 대해 쌓인 원한을 풀었지.

---

620 mow down :: 소탕하다, 쓸어버리다

↳ kill in great numbers

Q Was there another traffic accident at the intersection this morning?
오늘 아침 교차로에서 또 교통사고가 있었니?

A Yes, and this time a dump truck mowed down about 10 pedestrians.
응, 이번엔 덤프트럭이 열 명의 행인을 싹 쓸었다구.

---

621 give a free hand to :: 행동의 자유를 주다

↳ permit to make their own decisions

Q Do you know why the U.S. lost the war in Vietnam?
왜 미국이 베트남전쟁에서 패했는지 아니?

A Yes, President Johnson didn't give the military a free hand to do the job.
응, 존슨 대통령이 군에게 전쟁을 자유롭게 할 수 있는 권한을 안 줬기 때문이야.

---

622 in due course :: 때가 오면

↳ at the proper time in the future (in good time)

Q Are you ever going to do something about your overweight problem?
넌 너의 과다체중 문제에 대해 무슨 대책을 세울 작정이니?

A Yes, in due course, I hope.
응, 때가 오면 그러길 바래.

215

623 at a premium

:: 프리미엄을 붙여, 수요가 많은

↳ wanted very much

Q Are any more tickets available for the rock concert?
록 콘서트 티켓 더 있습니까?

A Yes, but they're very much at a premium right now.
예, 그런데 지금 프리미엄이 상당히 붙었어요.

624 pour over

:: 열심히 공부하다

↳ study earnestly

Q Did Sam decide to stay home tonight?
Sam은 오늘밤 집에 있기로 결정했니?

A Yes, he's pouring over his history text for a quiz tomorrow.
응, 내일 있을 퀴즈에 대비해 역사 교과서를 열심히 들여다보고 있어.

625 stay one's hand

:: 멈추다

↳ wait

Q Are you going to report him to the police?
그를 경찰에 신고할 작정이니?

A No, I'm staying my hand until I get more evidence.
아니, 증거를 더 확보할 때까지 기다릴 거야.

626 go straight

:: 착실해지다

↳ behave honestly (following a period of crime)

Q Do you have any plans for when you get out of prison?
감옥에서 나오면 무슨 계획이 있니?

A Yes, I'm going straight because I never want to come back here again.
응, 다시는 감옥에 오고 싶지 않으니 착실해지기로 했어.

627 **branch out**   :: 영역을 확장하다

↳ expand into

Q Do you have any special projects for next year?
우리 아이들이 특별한 프로젝트가 있습니까?

A Yes, my company is going to branch out into the computer business.
예, 저희 회사는 컴퓨터 사업으로 영역을 넓힐 거예요.

628 **a nine day wonder**   :: 반짝 스타

↳ a person whose fame doesn't last long

Q Do you think he'll still be a famous singer when our kids grow up?
우리 아이들이 클 때도 그가 여전히 유명한 가수가 되어 있을까?

A No, I'm sure he's just a nine day wonder.
아니, 확신하건대, 그는 반짝 스타야.

629 **no time to lose**   :: 시간이 얼마 남지 않다

↳ don't have much time left

Q What time does the store close tonight?
오늘 상점 문 몇 시에 닫지?

A In one hour, so we've got no time to lose if we want to finish shopping.
한 시간 후에, 그러니 쇼핑을 끝마치려면 시간이 얼마 안 남았다구.

630 **go broke**   :: 파산하다

↳ become penniless

Q Is your hobby still collecting expensive foreign sports cars?
네 취미는 아직도 비싼 외제 스포츠카를 수집하는 거니?

A No, my wife told me to quit before we all went broke.
아니, 내 아내가 말하길 우리가 파산하기 전에 그만두라는군.

영숙어 문제 단번에 공략하기

121. Residents in a city must <u>take precaution</u> not to pollute the air.

(A) have perception   (B) manage without waste
(C) take care beforehand (D) become precursor

어휘 **take precaution** 경계하다 / **perception** 지각(知覺), 인식 / **beforehand** 미리 / **precursor** 선구자, 전조

해석 도시 거주민들은 공기를 오염시키지 않도록 조심해야 한다.

---

122. In a dichotic listening test, two different auditory stimuli are presented <u>at the same time</u> to the subject, one to each ear.

(A) simultaneously   (B) from time to time
(C) intermittently   (D) suddenly

어휘 **dichotic** 소리의 세기가 다르게 들리는 / **auditory** 청각의, 귀의 / **stimuli** (pl.) 자극 **stimulus** (sg.) / **at the same time** 동시에 / **from time to time** 때때로 / **(at times) intermittently** 간헐적으로

해석 음차(音叉) 청력 검사에서는 서로 다른 두 개의 청각적 자극이 동시에 대상물인 각귀의 한쪽 귀에 주어진다.

---

123. You shouldn't <u>take</u> it <u>to heart</u>.

(A) complain severely   (B) endure trouble
(C) change your attitude (D) create a disturbance
(E) consider seriously

어휘 **take to heart** 서러워하다, 고민하다 / **disturbance** 소동

해석 심각하게 고민해서는 안 된다.

124. It's a criminal act to <u>tamper with</u> official documents for the purpose of fraud.

(A) tack away   (B) steal

Day

21

(C) alter   (D) make a copy of

(E) destroy

어휘 tamper with 참견하다, 원문을 바꾸다, 손을 대다 / fraud 기만, 사기 /
tack 진로를 바꾸다 / alter 개조하다 / make a copy of ~을 복사하다

해석 사기를 목적으로 공문서의 내용을 바꾸는 것은 범죄 행위다.

---

125. In early jazz pieces it was not uncommon for musicians to <u>play</u> the banjo.

(A) compose for   (B) sing with

(C) perform on   (D) do without

어휘 banjo 밴조 (현악기) / compose for ~를 위해 작곡하다 / perform on ~
으로 연주하다 / do without ~없이 지내다(dispense with)

해석 초기 재즈 작품들에서 음악가들이 밴조로 연주하는 것은 보기 드문 일이 아니
었다.

---

126. The bald eagle <u>is fond of</u> fish and prefers to live near water.

(A) likes   (B) finds

(C) hunts for   (D) dives for

어휘 bald eagle 흰머리독수리 / be fond of ~을 좋아하다 / hunt for ~을 찾
다, 사냥하다

해석 흰머리독수리는 물고기를 좋아하고, 물 근처에 사는 걸 더 좋아한다.

631 **much to one's relief**   :: 다행히

↳ luckily

Q Did the students decide to cancel the demonstration?
학생들은 시위를 취소하기로 결정했는가?

A Yes, much to our relief !
다행히도 그렇습니다.

632 **be Greek to one**   :: 일자무식인

↳ not understandable

Q Do you know much about English grammar?
영어 문법에 대해 잘 아니?

A No, I'm afraid most of it is just Greek to me.
아니, 유감스럽게 대부분 내가 모르는 것들이야.

633 **at large**   :: 범인 따위가 붙잡히지 않고

↳ not in jail

Q Have the police captured the escaped prisoner yet?
경찰에선 그 탈옥수를 아직 못 잡았습니까?

A No, he's still at large.
네, 아직 안 잡혔습니다.

634 play ball with

↳ cooperate

Q Do you finally get him to promise he'd cooperate in the investigation?

너 결국 그에게 투자하는 데 협조하겠다는 약속을 받아냈니?

A No, he still refuses to play ball with us.

아니, 그는 여전히 우리에게 협력하는 걸 거절하고 있어.

Day

22

635 win in a walk

↳ win easily

Q Are you sure your team will come in first place?

너희 팀이 일위로 나올 것이 확실하니?

A Yes, we'll win in a walk.

응, 우린 거뜬히 이길거야.

636 talk out of turn

:: 솔직하고 대담하게 말하다

↳ speak too frankly or boldly

Q Don't you think he's a little too frank sometimes?

그는 가끔 너무 솔직한 것 같지 않니?

A Yes, and I've warned him not to talk out of turn.

맞아, 그래서 너무 거리낌 없이 말하지 말라고 경고 좀 했지.

637 not have a clue

↳ not know anything about something (usually negative)

Q Do the police have any idea where the kidnappers are hiding?

유괴범이 어디에 숨어 있는지 경찰은 알고 있니?

A No, they don't have even a clue.

아니, 그들은 단서도 못 잡고 있는 걸.

638 all told

:: 전부 합해서

↳ including everything

Q How many telephone do you have in your apartment?
댁의 아파트에는 전화기가 몇 대나 있으시죠?

A All told, three.
모두 합해서 3대예요.

639 pull the plug on

:: 제동걸다

↳ stop or hinder

Q Did you cancel your trip to Europe this summer?
올 여름 유럽여행 가는 거 취소했어?

A Yes, because my father pulled the plug on it. He said it was too expensive.
응, 아빠가 못 가게 하셨어. 너무 비싸다고 하시더군.

640 take a shine to

:: 반하다, ~이 좋아하다

↳ start to like (take a fancy to)

Q Sally seems to like you a lot, doesn't she?
Sally가 널 많이 좋아하는 것 같지 않니?

A Yes, I think she's taken a real shine to me.
그래, 그녀가 내게 반한 것 같아.

641 on one's case

:: 귀찮게 하는

↳ paying close and irritating attention to (see get off my case)

Q Has your teacher been giving you extra homework?
선생님이 다른 숙제를 내주셨어?

A Yes, she's been on my case all semester.
응, 그녀는 학기 내내 날 귀찮게 해.

642 police up

:: 정돈하다

↳ make neat and orderly

Q Do you want me to cut the front lawn this weekend, dad?
제가 이번 주말에 앞쪽 잔디를 깎을까요, 아빠?

A Yes, and let's police up the back yard a little, too. We're having company Sunday.
그래, 뒤뜰도 좀 청소하자꾸나. 일요일에 손님이 오실거야.

Day

22

643 put away

:: 먹어치우다

↳ eat or drink, especially in large amounts

Q Are you hungry?
배고프니?

A Yes, and I think I could put away a 14-inch pizza all by myself.
응, 혼자서 14인치 피자 전부를 먹을 수 있을 것 같아.

644 at most

:: 기껏해야

↳ as the maximum

Q How much money can you lend me, Jim?
짐, 얼마나 꿔줄 수 있니?

A I'm afraid I can give you, at most, only $25.
기껏해야 25달러밖에 못 줄 거야.

645 scrape along

:: 근근히 먹고 살다

↳ survive (by)

Q Is your financial status getting any better these days?
요즘 재정 상태가 좀 나아지고 있니?

A Yes, a little because I'm managing to scrape along by working overtime.
응, 약간, 야근해서 겨우 근근이 살아가고 있거든.

223

646 the long and the short of it

:: 요컨대

↳ the general state of affairs

Q So it's your opinion that he shouldn't be entrusted with such an important job?
그에게 그런 중요한 일을 맡겨서는 안 된다는 게 네 의견이니?

A Yes, that's the long and the short of it.
응, 요컨대 그래.

647 out of a job

:: 실직하여

↳ unemployed

Q Is your company going to close?
너의 회사가 폐쇄되니?

A Yes, so that means I'm out of a job again.
응, 그건 내가 또 실직한다는 말이지.

648 the fault lies with

:: 잘못은 ~의 탓이다

↳ is to be blamed

Q Are you the one who caused the accident?
그 사고를 저지른 게 너니?

A No, the fault lies totally with the other driver.
아냐, 잘못은 완전히 다른 운전사에게 있다구.

649 junk mail

:: 광고물 등 수취인의 명시도 없는 귀찮은 우편물

↳ unasked for mail (usually advertising and the like)

Q Any mail for me this morning?
오늘 아침 내 앞으로 온 우편 있니?

A Yes, but it's just some junk mail I'm afraid.
응, 그런데 유감스럽게도 광고물뿐이야.

650 Achilles' heel :: 아킬레스건, 유일한 약점

↳ weakest point, especially in a person's character

Q Do you know where your political opponent is weakest?
당신 정적(政敵)의 최대 약점이 어디인지 아십니까?

A Yes, it's his recent divorce. It's his Achilles' heel.
예, 최근에 한 이혼이오. 그게 그의 유일한 약점이죠.

651 appeal to :: 호소하다

↳ resort to

Q Did you really get him to lend you $5,000?
정말로 그가 너에게 5,000달러를 빌려줬단 말이니?

A Yes, I appealed to his strong sense of compassion.
그래, 난 그의 강한 동정심에 호소했지.

652 pay good money for :: 비싼 값을 치르다

↳ pay a high price for

Q Are you going to give your cousin your old car?
네 사촌에게 그 낡은 차를 줄 셈이야?

A No, I paid good money for it, and besides, it's still in very good condition.
아니, 난 그 차에 비싼 값을 치렀다구. 게다가 그건 아직도 멀쩡하구.

653 pin one's hopes on :: 희망을 걸다

↳ depend on for help, a favor etc.

Q Are you sure he'll help you?
그가 널 도울 거라 믿어?

A Yes, and I'm pinning my hopes on him. He's the only friend I have left.
응, 난 그에게 희망을 걸고 있어. 그는 내게 남은 유일한 친구야.

in full swing

:: 한창 진행중인

↳ actively underway

Q Has the festival started yet?
축제가 벌써 시작했니?

A Yes, it's now in full swing.
응, 지금 한창 진행중이야.

roll back

:: 물가를 예전 수준으로 되돌리다

↳ cause (prices, wages, interest rates) to return to a lower level

Q Do you think we'll get a salary increase this year?
올해 봉급이 인상될 것 같니?

A No, because the government is trying to get companies like ours to roll back wages.
아니, 정부가 우리 같은 회사들의 임금을 예전 수준으로 되돌리려 하고 있어서.

rustle up

:: 준비하다

↳ gather or find

Q Do you eat dinner yet?
저녁 먹었니?

A No, so why don't you go into the kitchen and rustle me up some dinner?
아니, 부엌에 들어가서 저녁밥 좀 준비해 줄래?

take the pledge

:: 금주(禁酒)를 맹세하다

↳ promise not to drink alcohol anymore (or sign the pledge)

Q Did your husband come home drunk again last night?
어제 밤에 네 남편 또 술 취해서 집에 왔니?

A Yes, but he promised me he'd take the pledge on January 1 next year.
응, 하지만 내년 1월 1일부터는 금주하겠다고 맹세했어.

658 **ride out**

↳ withstand (hopefully) without suffering great damage

Q Is Hurricane Andrew expected to pass through our town this afternoon?
허리케인 앤드류가 오늘 오후 우리 마을을 통과하지?

A Yes, so all we can do is go down into the basement and just try to ride out the storm.
응, 우리가 할 수 있는 일이라곤 지하실에 내려가 그 폭풍을 견디는 것뿐이야.

659 **pride and joy** :: 자랑거리

↳ a person or possession that makes one very proud and happy

Q Is this a picture of your daughter? What a beautiful young woman!
이게 네 딸 사진이야? 너무나 아름다운 여자애로구나!

A Yes, she's my pride and joy.
응, 그녀는 내 자랑거리야.

660 **for certain** :: 확실히

↳ undoubtedly true or accurate

Q Do you know his name?
그의 이름을 아니?

A I don't know for certain the name of the man.
나는 그 사람의 이름을 확실히 알지 못해.

127. We have <u>used up</u> the paste. Let's try this new one.

(A) tried   (B) abandoned

(C) tested   (D) consumed

어휘 **use up** 다 써버리다, 지치게 하다 / **paste** 치약 / **abandon** 단념하다, 버리다 / **consume** 소모하다

해석 치약을 다 썼다. 새 치약을 쓰도록 하자.

---

128. The <u>weeding out</u> of the weak members of animal populations in nature appeared to some Victorians a sufficient excuse for imperialism and sweatshops.

(A) selection   (B) conversion

(C) elimination   (D) separation

어휘 **weed out** 잡초를 제거하다 / **population** (일정한 지역의) 개체군, 모집단 / **excuse** 구실, 핑계 / **imperialism** 제국주의 / **sweatshop** 노동 착취 공장 / **conversion** 전환, 개조

해석 자연의 세계에서 나약한 동물 개체군을 제거하는 것은 몇몇 빅토리아조 사람들에게는 제국주의와 노동력을 착취하는 공장을 설명해주는 충분한 변명거리로 비쳐졌다.

---

129. He <u>went down with</u> gastric flu when he was in London away from home.

(A) subdued   (B) treated

(C) contracted   (D) diagnosed

어휘 **gastric** 위(胃)의 / **subdue** 억누르다, 완화시키다 / **contract** 병에 걸리다, 수축시키다 / **diagnose** 진단하다

해석 집에서 떨어져 런던에서 사는 동안 그는 유행성 위염에 걸렸다.

130. Americans are apt to <u>wind up</u> a question with a lift of the hand, a tilt of the chin or widening of the eyes.

(A) finish   (B) begin
(C) suggest   (D) guess

어휘 **be apt to** ~하기 쉽다 / **wind up** 끝맺다 / **tilt** 경사, 기울기 / **widen** 둥그래지다

해석 미국인들은 질문을 끝맺을 때 손가락을 들어올리거나 턱을 비스듬히 하거나 혹은 눈을 둥그렇게 뜨는 경향이 있다.

Day 22

---

131. We have trouble in our relationship, but I feel we can <u>work</u> it <u>out</u> for ourselves.

(A) resolve   (B) discuss
(C) discard   (D) alter

어휘 **work out** 해결하다 / **discard** 버리다, 해고하다 / **alter** 바꾸다, 개조하다

해석 우리들 관계에 갈등이 있긴 하지만, 우리 스스로의 힘으로 잘 해결할 수 있으리라는 느낌이 든다.

---

132. The Freedom of Information Act gives private citizen _____ government files.

(A) access to   (B) excess of
(C) redress of   (D) release from

어휘 **information** 보도, 교시, 자료 / **give access to** ~에의 접근을 허용하다 / **excess of** ~의 과잉, 초과 / **redress of** ~의 교정, 시정

해석 보도 자료 자유 이용 법령은 개개 시민들이 정부 문서에 접근하는 것을 허용한다.

661 **cut loose**
:: 흥청망청 놀다

↳ party without restraint, go wild

Q Do you have any plans for this weekend?
이번 주말에 무슨 계획 있니?

A Yes, my girlfriend and I are going to go downtown and cut loose.
응, 내 여자친구랑 시내에 가서 신나게 놀거야.

662 **pry into**
:: 캐묻다

↳ ask too many questions about

Q Did you ask Jane what's bothering her these days?
너 제인에게 요즘 뭐 때문에 괴로운지 물어 봤니?

A No, I don't want to pry into her personal affairs.
아니, 그녀의 사적인 일을 캐묻고 싶진 않아.

663 **for nothing**
:: 헛되이

↳ free; without some good reason

Q Wow! Your swimming pool must be the biggest in town.
와우! 네 수영장이 마을에서 가장 클 거야.

A Yes, it is ! I wasn't born in Texas for nothing. Everything big there.
응, 그렇지! 과연 텍사스에서 태어날만했어. 모든 게 다 크거든.

664 **strain every nerve**   :: 사력을 다하다

↳ try very hard

Q Did you lose again to your intercity rival?
너희 또 도시별 라이벌에게 졌니?

A Yes, even though we strained every nerve to defeat him.
응, 우린 그를 물리치려고 안간힘을 썼는데도 졌어.

665 **know the ins and outs of**   :: 이면을 훤히 알다

↳ know the details of something

Q Do you think she will be able to handle her new assignment in Tokyo?
그녀가 동경에서의 새 업무를 잘 해낼 수 있을까?

A Yes, because she knows the ins and outs of Japanese culture.
응, 일본 문화의 이면을 잘 알고 있으니까.

666 **come of age**   :: 물이 오르다

↳ reach full development

Q Is Bill still spending a lot of time at the health club?
Bill은 아직도 많은 시간을 헬스클럽에서 보내니?

A Yes, and he's really coming of age as an amateur weight lifter.
응, 아마추어 역도선수로서 정말 완숙했어.

667 **wait up for**   :: 자지 않고 기다리다

↳ postpone going to bed until someone returns back home

Q Will you be back home early tonight?
오늘 일찍 들어오실 거예요?

A No, so don't wait up for me, Honey. I'll see you in the morning.
아니, 나 때문에 안 자고 기다리지 마, 여보. 아침에 보자구.

668 look for trouble
:: 사서 고생하다

↳ seek problems or difficulties

Q Don't you know this part of town is very dangerous?
넌 이 시내 지역이 위험하다는 거 몰라?

A No, I didn't, and I'm certainly not looking for trouble.
몰랐어, 절대 사서 고생하고 싶진 않아.

669 bear out
:: 뒷받침하다

↳ support the truth of

Q Are you worried the new computer data after analysis will disprove your theory?
분석 후에 새로운 컴퓨터 데이터가 너의 이론을 반증할까 걱정되니?

A No, I'm sure it will bear it out.
아니, 난 그게 내 이론을 뒷받침할 거라 확신해.

670 if anything
:: 어느 정도냐 하면

↳ rather

Q Is Mrs. Smith a good teacher?
Smith 부인은 좋은 선생님입니까?

A Good! If anything, she's probably the best one on campus.
훌륭하세요! 어느 정도냐 하면, 그녀는 캠퍼스에서 아마 최고일 거예요.

671 rain cats and dogs
:: 비가 억수같이 오다

↳ rain very hard

Q Have you looked out the window yet this morning?
오늘 아침 창 밖에 내다봤니?

A Yes, and it's raining cats and dogs now.
응, 지금 비가 억수같이 오고 있어.

672 on account of

:: ~때문에

↳ because of

Q Was the baseball game canceled?
야구경기 취소됐니?

A Yes, on account of rain.
응, 비 때문에.

673 for a rainy day

:: 궂은 날을 대비해

↳ for a time when it will be needed

Q Do you still put most of your paycheck in the bank?
아직도 너의 월급 대부분을 은행에 저금하니?

A Yes, because I'm saving my money for a rainy day.
만일의 경우를 대비해서 저축하는 거야.

674 on the average

:: 평균적으로

↳ usually

Q Do you call your mother frequently?
엄마한테 자주 전화하니?

A Yes, I call her on the average about three times a week.
응, 평균적으로 일주일에 세 번쯤 전화해.

675 once and for all

:: 한 번만에, 분명히

↳ definitely

Q Are you sending your dog to obedience school?
너 개를 훈련 학교에 보낼 거니?

A Yes, and I'm going to get him to obey me once and for all.
응, 난 틀림없이 그 개가 내 말에 복종하게 할거야.

676 **ease off** :: 쉬엄쉬엄 하다

↳ work less hard

Q Did your doctor give you any advice?
의사 선생님이 조언 좀 해주셨나요?

A Yes, he told me to ease off my busy schedule at the office and find a hobby.
예, 사무실에서의 바쁜 일정을 좀 완화시키고 취미를 가지래요.

677 **wear and tear** :: 소모, 닳아 없어짐

↳ damage and aging due to the passage of time

Q Do you want to buy my computer?
컴퓨터 살래?

A Yes, but you'll have to give me a discount for all the wear and tear.
예, 하지만 오래되고 낡았으니까 깎아주셔야 해요.

678 **the last straw** :: 인내의 한계를 넘게 하는 것

↳ no more can be endured

Q Did the new waitress spoil coffee on another customer?
새 여 종업원이 또 손님에게 커피를 엎질렀니?

A Yes, and that's the last straw. I'm going to fire her tomorrow.
응, 이건 참는 데도 한도가 있어. 내일 그녀를 해고할 거야.

679 **opt for** :: 선택하다

↳ choose

Q Are you going to try to enter Law School?
로스쿨에 들어갈 작정이야?

A No, I'll opt for Business School because my grades aren't very good.
아니, 성적이 좋지 않아서 비즈니스 스쿨을 선택할 거야.

680 **on the rise** :: 증가하는

↳ increasing

Q Are you going to move out of New York?
뉴욕에서 이사 나올 거니?

A Yes, unfortunately crime is on the rise again.
응, 불행하게도 범죄가 다시 늘어나고 있어서.

681 **tack on** :: 부가하다

↳ add

Q Did the union members finally sign the contract?
노조원들이 결국 그 계약에 서명했니?

A No, but they said they might if management would tack on a few more benefits.
아니, 하지만 경영자가 몇 가지 이익을 더 추가한다면 서명할지도 모른다고 말했어.

682 **it's one's job** :: 당연히 할 일이다

↳ it's one's work which one should do

Q Can I ever thank you enough?
어떻게 감사해야 좋을까?

A No, don't thank me. It's my job.
아냐, 감사하지 않아도 돼. 당연히 내가 할 일이야.

683 **stuck in** :: 막히다

↳ trapped in

Q Want to go shopping with me this afternoon?
오늘 오후에 나랑 쇼핑갈래?

A No, I'd rather stay home than get stuck in city traffic.
아니, 시내 교통 체증 속에 빠져 있느니 집에 있을래.

684

by dint of
:: 덕택으로

↳ because of much effort

Q Jack's only 32 and did you say he got promoted to manager already?

Jack은 겨우 32살인데, 벌써 경영자로 승진했다는 거니?

A Yes, by dint of hard work, but also because his uncle is the company president!

그래, 열심히 일한 덕택이지, 하지만 역시 그의 숙부가 회사 사장이니까!

685

a close call
:: 위기일발, 구사일생

↳ a narrow escape from danger

Q Did your wife hit the pedestrian?

당신 부인이 행인을 치었소?

A No, but she missed him by about three inches. What a close call!

아니오, 하지만 거의 3인치 빗나갔어요. 위기일발이었죠!

686

get along well with
:: ~와 잘 지내다

↳ cooperate well with

Q Do you know why he transferred to another section?

그가 왜 다른 부서로 옮겼는지 아니?

A Yes, because he just couldn't get along very well with his co-workers here.

응, 그는 자기 동료들과 잘 지낼 수 없었어.

687

by nature
:: 날 때부터

↳ naturally

Q Do you know very much about him?

그에 대해 많은 걸 아니?

A Yes, he seems to be by nature very kind and gentle.

응, 그는 원래가 친절하고 상냥해.

688 carry on

:: 칭얼거리다

↳ react too emotionally, cry

Q Is Jane still crying?
Jane이 아직도 울고 있니?

A Yes, she's been carrying on now for almost two hours!
응, 지금 거의 두 시간 동안이나 칭얼대고 있어.

689 next to nothing

:: 거의 공짜인

↳ almost for nothing

Q Was your new refrigerator expensive?
네 새 냉장고 비쌌니?

A No, with the trade-in it costed next to nothing.
아니, 보상판매로 사서 거의 공짜였어.

690 be obliged to

:: 어쩔 수 없이 ~하다

↳ have to

Q Did you have to invite him to the party?
그를 파티에 초대해야 했니?

A Yes, I was obliged to because he's my wife's uncle.
응, 아내의 숙부라서 어쩔 수 없었어.

133. She spoke <u>straight from the shoulder</u> when she told me what she thought.

(A) clearly (B) naturally
(C) frankly (D) commonly
(E) generously

어휘 **speak straight from the shoulder** 서슴없이 말하다 / **generously** 관대하게

해석 그녀는 자신이 생각하는 바를 내게 말할 때면 서슴없이 솔직하게 이야기했다.

---

134. I decided to go to party <u>on the spur of the moment</u>.

(A) after careful thought
(B) for only a short time
(C) without previous thought
(D) at the earliest possible moment

어휘 **on the spur of the moment** 즉석에서, 순간적인 충동에서 / **spur** 박차, 자극

해석 즉시 파티에 가기로 마음먹었다.

---

135. It would not be accurate to way that Lee's general staff were glorified clerks, but the statement would not be <u>too wide of the mark</u>.

(A) very relevant (B) too irrelevant
(C) out of question (D) pointed
(E) unverifiable

어휘 **accurate** 정확한 / **general staff** 참모부 / **glorify** 찬미하다 / **clerk** 서기관 / **too wide of the mark** 크게 빗나간 / **relevant** 관련된 ↔ **irrelevant** 엉뚱한 / **out of question** 틀림없이, 물론 / **pointed** 신랄한 / **unverifiable** 입증할 수 없는

해석 이 사단장의 참모부가 칭송받는 서기들이라는 건 정확한 표현은 아니지만, 그 런 말이 아주 엉뚱하지는 않을 것이다.

---

136. Before I go to Paris I must <u>brush up on</u> my French.

(A) review
(B) try out for
(C) feel up to
(D) catch up with

어휘 **brush up on** 복습하다 / **try out for** 출전하다 / **feel up to** 해낼 수 있을 것 같다 / **catch up with** ~을 따라잡다

해석 파리로 가기 전에 불어를 복습해야겠다.

Day 23

---

137. The house was turned <u>upside-down</u> by the burglars.

(A) into pieces
(B) in disorder
(C) in good order
(D) in good condition
(E) to a factory

어휘 **upside-down** 거꾸로, 혼란스러운 / **burglar** 강도 / **into pieces** 산산조 각이 난 / **in disorder** 혼란한

해석 도둑이 집을 엉망으로 만들어 놓았다.

---

138. What's wrong with Ben? He seems to be <u>on edge</u> about something this morning.

(A) nearby
(B) bored
(C) nervous
(D) serious
(E) secret

어휘 **be on edge about** ~에 초조해 하다 / **secret about** 입이 무거운

해석 벤한테 무슨 일이 있는 거야? 오늘 아침 뭔가 불안해하는 기색이더라.

Answers ★ 133.(C) 134.(C) 135.(B) 136.(A) 137.(B) 138.(C)

239

691 keep an eye on
:: 눈을 떼지 않다

↳ watch carefully

Q Do you want me to do anything while you're on vacation?
당신 휴가 동안 제가 뭔가 해드릴까요?

A Yes, could you keep an eye on our house while we're gone?
예, 우리가 여행가고 없는 동안 집 좀 봐 주실래요?

692 off the record
:: 비공개로

↳ not officially recorded (see on the record)

Q Did the Senator agree to an interview with your newspaper?
그 상원의원이 당신 신문사와의 인터뷰에 동의했습니까?

A Yes, but he insisted that all his remarks must be off the record.
예, 하지만 자신의 말이 모두 공개돼서는 안 된다고 주장했어요.

693 shortcut
:: 지름길

↳ a quicker, more direct route

Q How did you get here so quickly? Did you take a taxi?
어떻게 이렇게 빨리 왔어? 택시 탔어?

A Yes, and the driver knew a very good shortcut.
운전기사가 좋은 지름길을 알았어.

694 **make noises** :: 의견이나 감상을 말하다

↳ express his feelings or intentions

Q Your husband seems a little unhappy with his job these days, doesn't he?
네 남편 요즘 직장 일로 좀 안 좋아 보이는데, 그렇지 않니?

A Yes, he's starting to make noises about looking for another place to work.
맞아, 그는 다른 직장을 구하겠다고 말하기 시작했어.

695 **take a whack at** :: 시도하다

↳ attempt (take a try at)

Q Would you like to go bowling with us tonight?
오늘밤 우리랑 볼링치러 갈래요?

A Yes, I'd like to take a whack at learning how to bowl.
예, 볼링치는 법을 한번 배워보고 싶어요.

696 **with bells on** :: 흔쾌히

↳ for sure, willingly

Q Are you coming to my party next Saturday night?
다음주 토요일 밤 파티에 오시겠습니까?

A Yes, I'll be there with bells on.
예, 기꺼이 참석하지요.

697 **a dry run** :: 예행 연습

↳ a rehearsal or practice

Q Are you going to test the new model soon?
곧 새로운 모델 대회에 나갈 거니?

A Yes, we're going to give it a dry run tomorrow.
응, 우린 내일 리허설을 할 예정이야.

698 **farm out**   :: 하청 주다, 맡기다

↳ send work to other people to do

Q Could you help me type some of these letters?
이 편지 입력하는 것 좀 도와줄래요?

A No, I'm busy right now. Why don't you farm out the
work to some of the other secretaries?
안돼요, 지금 바빠요. 다른 비서에게 그 일을 맡기시지 그래요?

699 **can't get over**   :: 못 알아볼 정도다

↳ be very surprised at

Q You didn't recognize me, did you?
너 나 못 알아보았지?

A No, I didn't. I can't get over how much you've changed.
응, 얼마나 변했는지 못 알아보겠다.

700 **as plain as the nose on one's face**
                                      :: 얼굴에 붙은 코만큼이나 명확한

↳ it is very clear

Q Are you sure that's the right answer to question six?
너는 문제 6번 답이 그게 맞다고 확신해?

A Yes, it's as plain as the nose on your face.
응, 그건 너무 확실해.

701 **at the end of one's tether**   :: 한계에 이른

↳ unable to suffer any more

Q Are you going to take your vacation early this year?
올해는 일찍 휴가를 낼 생각이니?

A Yes, I'm really at the end of my tether in the office these
days. I need some rest.
응, 요즘 사무실에서 한계에 달했어. 휴식이 필요해.

242

702 **worlds apart** :: 정반대인

↳ very different (see poles apart)

Q Are there many differences between the two candidates?
두 후보 사이에 다른 점이 많이 있나요?

A No, except for one thing: their ideas on Russia are
worlds apart.
아뇨, 하나만 제외하고요. 러시아에 대한 그들의 생각은 정반대예요.

703 **scurry off** :: 허둥지둥 가다

↳ hurry away toward

Q Where are the children? Isn't it time to study the Bible?
아이들이 어디 있죠? 성경공부 할 시간이잖아요?

A Yes, but they went scurrying off for the living room to
watch cartoons.
그래요. 하지만 만화보려고 거실로 급히 갔어요.

704 **at one's service** :: 원하는 대로

↳ I'm ready to do whatever you want

Q Could you help me lift this heavy box?
이 무거운 박스 드는 것 좀 도와주시겠어요?

A Yes, of course. I'm at your service.
예, 물론이죠. 무엇이든 분부만 하십시오.

705 **in short** :: 요컨대, 결국

↳ briefly

Q Do you know what the movie is about?
그 영화 무슨 내용인지 아니?

A Yes, in short it's about a young boy and his dog.
응, 결국 소년과 개에 대한 얘기지.

706 attach importance to

:: ~을 중요시 하다

↳ consider important

Q Do you know why the boss spoke to me so unkindly this morning?

오늘 아침 사장이 왜 내게 그렇게 불친절하게 말했지?

A No, but don't attach any importance to it. He's usually unkind to everyone.

신경쓰지 마. 누구에게나 그래.

707 go through

:: 완수하다, 끝내다, 견디다

↳ complete, often with difficulty

Q Do you like your new job?

네 새 직장이 마음에 드니?

A Yes, but to get promoted I'll have to go through with a lot of training.

응, 하지만 승진되려면 많은 훈련을 완수해야 돼.

708 in the main

:: 대개는

↳ on the whole

Q Are you satisfied with your courses this semester?

이번 학기 수업이 만족스럽니?

A Yes, in the main. But I just wish our teachers wouldn't give us so much homework.

응, 대체로. 하지만 선생님들이 숙제 좀 많이 안 내줬으면 좋겠어.

709 needless to say

:: 말할 필요도 없이

↳ it goes without saying

Q Is your new boss good to you?

새로 온 사장님이 네게 잘해주니?

A No, and needless to say I miss my old boss very much.

아니, 말할 필요도 없이 난 옛날 사장님이 그리워.

710 roly-poly

:: 토실토실 살찐

↳ fat and round

Q Can I have some more dessert?
후식 좀 더 먹어도 돼요?

A No, you don't want to become too roly-poly, do you?
안돼, 토실토실 살찌는 건 원치 않잖아?

711 ten to one

:: 십중팔구

↳ very likely

Q Do you think we have a good chance to buy our own house someday?
언젠가 우리 집을 살 좋은 기회가 있을까요?

A Yes, ten to one we'll buy one before we're in our thirties.
응, 틀림없이 우린 30대 이전에 집을 살 거야.

712 give one a freehand

:: 재량에 맡기다

↳ give one unlimited freedom of action

Q Is he still the owner of the company?
그가 아직 그 회사의 오너예요?

A Yes, but he gave his son a freehand in managing it.
예, 하지만 그는 경영을 아들의 재량에 맡겼어요.

713 line up behind

:: 지지하다

↳ support

Q Are you going to vote for him?
그에게 표를 던질 거니?

A Yes, let's all line up behind him because he's from our hometown.
응, 그는 우리 고향출신이니까 모두 그를 지지하자.

Day

24

or what   :: 안 그런가?

↳ an emphasis on the preceding word or words

Q Do you think he's handsome?
그가 잘 생겼다고 생각해?

A Yes, and is he rich or what?
응, 그리고 부자이든지, 안 그런가?

rush into   :: 서둘러 해치우다

↳ do too quickly without enough preparation

Q Did you hear that they're getting married next Sunday?
그들이 다음주 일요일에 결혼한다는 소식 들었어?

A No, and it's a big surprise. Aren't they rushing into
marriage a little too soon?
아니, 정말 놀라운데. 그들이 너무 빨리 결혼을 해치우는 거 아니니?

loosen up   :: 몸을 풀다

↳ do warming-up exercises

Q Are you ready to play?
운동할 준비 됐어?

A No, just let me loosen up a few more minutes.
아니, 몇 분만 더 몸 좀 풀고.

relate to   :: 사이좋게 잘 지내다

↳ understand or appreciate, get along well with

Q Do you think he become a good minister?
그가 훌륭한 성직자가 될까?

A Yes, because he's very good at relating to all kinds of
people.
응, 그는 모든 종류의 사람과 잘 알고 지내니까.

first of all   :: 첫째로, 무엇보다도

↳ in the first place (or first off)

Q Is there something wrong, Mom?
뭐 잘못됐어요, 엄마?

A Yes, first of all, why didn't you clean your room like I told you?
그래, 무엇보다도 왜 내가 말한대로 네 방 청소를 하지 않았니?

all for it   :: 전적으로 동감하여

↳ supporting it

Q Do you think I'm making a mistake to postpone my marriage?
내가 결혼을 연기하는 게 실수하는 거라고 생각해?

A No, I'm all for it. You're still too young to get married.
아니, 전적으로 동감해. 넌 결혼하기엔 너무 어려.

Day
24

at one's own risk   :: 위험을 감수하고

↳ bear full responsibility for any loss or injury

Q Is this part of the beach open in the mornings?
해변의 일부가 아침에 개방됩니까?

A Yes, but you'll have to swim at your own risk. The lifeguards arrive after lunch.
예, 하지만 불상사에 대해서는 자신이 책임지고 수영해야 됩니다. 구조원이 점심 후에나 오니까요.

139. He was late for work so many times that the boss had no _____ but to fire him.

(A) alternative (B) plan
(C) trouble (D) verdict

어휘 **have no alternative[choice] but to** ~외에는 다른 대안이 없다 / **verdict** 판단, 판정

해석 그는 아주 여러 번 지각했기 때문에 사장은 그를 해고하지 않을 수 없었다.

---

140. The new chairman on the board had absolutely no power, he was just a _____.

(A) figurehead (B) blackleg
(C) bottleneck (D) footman

어휘 **board** 평의회, 회의 / **absolutely** 전혀 (부정을 강조) / **figurehead** 표면상의 대표 / **blackleg** 사기꾼 / **bottleneck** 교통 체증, 애로 사항 / **footman** 하인

해석 그 위원회의 새 의장은 전혀 힘이 없었다. 그는 다만 명목상의 대표에 불과했다.

---

141. I am at loss which way to go as I am a stranger here. = I have no _____ which way to go as I am a stranger here.

(A) time (B) idea
(C) chance (D) talk

어휘 **be at loss** 어찌할 바를 모르다(have no idea)

해석 초행길이라 어느 길로 가야할지 모르겠군요.

142. My grandmother was _____ social class, but in her stories she told me about poor people, unfortunate people, and people who were better off.

(A) obsessed by   (B) sensitive to

(C) sympathetic to   (D) indifferent to

(E) dependent on

어휘 be obsessed by ~에 얽매이다, 사로잡히다 / be better off 더 잘 살다, 형편이 좋다 / sensitive to ~에 민감한 / sympathetic to ~에 호소하는 / indifferent to ~에 무관심한

해석 우리 할머니는 사회 계급에 무관심하셨지만, 내게 말씀하실 때 보면 가난한 사람들과 불행한 사람들, 그리고 잘 사는 사람들에 관한 이야기를 하셨다.

Day

24

143. Their ideas are <u>alien</u> to our way of thinking.

(A) fit   (B) familiar

(C) similar   (D) opposed

어휘 be alien to ~와 다르다

해석 그들의 생각은 우리가 생각하는 방식과 다르다.

144. Sandy was <u>astounded</u> at her brother's news.

(A) amazed   (B) happy

(C) perplexed   (D) bothered

어휘 be astounded at ~에 놀라다 / perplexed 난처한, 당황한

해석 샌디는 오빠 소식을 듣고 놀랐다.

---

721 **be keen about**   :: 매우 좋아하다

↳ enthusiastic about

Q Are you going to watch the Clint Eastwood movie on TV tonight?
오늘밤 TV에서 하는 클린트 이스트우드 영화 볼거니?

A No, because frankly I'm not very keen about violent westerns.
아니, 솔직히 난 폭력 서부영화는 별로 좋아하지 않거든.

---

722 **nip in the bud**   :: 미연에 방지하다

↳ stop in the early stages

Q Mr. Mayor, do you know what you're going to do about inflation?
시장님, 인플레에 대해 시장님이 하실 일이 뭔지 아십니까?

A Yes, I'm going to nip it in the bud through wage-price controls.
예, 임금 조절을 통해 인플레를 미연에 방지할 예정입니다.

---

723 **much to one's dismay**   :: 우울하게도

↳ unhappily

Q Did you have a good weekend?
주말 즐겁게 보냈습니까?

A No, much to my dismay it rained all Sunday.
아뇨, 우울하게도 일요일 내내 비가 왔어요.

---

724 look out!

:: 조심해!

↳ be careful!

Q Let's eat lunch in that restaurant across the street, okay?
길 건너 식당에서 점심먹자, 좋지?

A Yes, and… hey, look out! There's an open manhole right in front of you!
응, 이것 봐, 조심해! 바로 네 앞에 맨홀이 열려 있어!

725 at length

:: 장황하게

↳ in considerable detail

Q What was the lecturer's speech about?
강사가 뭐에 대해 연설했죠?

A He spoke at length about the Middle East situation.
중동정세에 대해서 장황하게 말했습니다.

726 pore over

:: 정신 집중하다

↳ study or give close attention to

Q Do you know where he is?
그가 어디 있는지 아세요?

A Yes, he's in the library poring over his books for the test tomorrow.
예, 내일 시험에 대비해 도서관에서 책을 숙독하고 있습니다.

727 portion out

:: 분배하다

↳ share or divide

Q Do you know what happened to the ice cream that was in the icebox?
얼음 상자 안에 있던 아이스크림이 어떻게 됐는지 아십니까?

A Yes, mom portioned it out to me and my friends after lunch today.
예, 어머니께서 오늘 점심 뒤에 저와 친구들에게 나눠주셨습니다.

728 go without saying :: 말할 것도 없다

↳ it is needless to say

Q Is Johnny a good student?
Johnny는 훌륭한 학생입니까?

A Yes, and it goes without saying that he's popular with his teachers.
예, 말할 필요도 없이 그는 선생님들에게 인기가 있습니다.

729 get hold of :: 연락을 취하다

↳ find a person so you can speak with him

Q Are you still using the telephone?
아직도 전화를 쓰고 있니?

A Yes, I'm trying to get hold of my dentist. I've got a bad toothache.
응, 치과의사와 연락을 하려고 해. 치통이 심하거든.

730 call the roll :: 출석부르다

↳ call the names on a certain list

Q Am I late?
내가 늦었니?

A No, the teacher is just starting to call the roll.
아니, 선생님이 이제 막 출석을 부르기 시작했어.

731 get at :: 의도하다

↳ try to say

Q Do you understand what I'm trying to say?
내가 무슨 말하려는 건지 알겠니?

A No, I'm not quite sure what you are getting at.
아니, 무슨 말하는 건지 전혀 모르겠어.

732 keep company

:: 함께하다

↳ stay with me so I won't be lonely

Q Are you going out tonight?
오늘밤 외출하십니까?

A No, I'm going to stay home and watch TV. Want to come over and keep me company?
아뇨, 집에서 TV시청할 겁니다. 오셔서 저와 함께 계실래요?

733 call to mind

:: 회상시키다

↳ cause one to remember

Q Did you attend your daughter's play?
따님의 연극에 참석하셨습니까?

A Yes, and it called to mind my youth when I had to perform in a school play.
예, 학교 연극 공연하던 젊은 시절 생각이 나더군요.

Day 25

734 take heart

:: 용기를 내다

↳ be encouraged by the fact

Q I can't wait until summer vacation, can you?
여름방학까지 기다릴 수 없어, 넌?

A No, but take heart: there're only a few more weeks until June.
아냐, 용기를 내, 6월까진 몇 주 안 남았어.

735 no doubt

:: 분명히

↳ very likely

Q Did Annie get into college?
Annie는 대학에 들어갔나요?

A Yes, and her parents no doubt are very proud of her.
예, 그녀의 부모님도 분명히 그녀를 자랑으로 여길 겁니다.

736 sum up   :: 판단하다

↳ judge

Q Do you think he'll be a good employee?
그가 좋은 일꾼이 되리라 생각하세요?

A Yes, I'd sum him up as honest and hardworking.
예, 저는 그를 정직하고 근면하다고 판단합니다.

737 get the upper hand   :: 우세하다

↳ get control or power over

Q Do you have a secret for keeping your class under control?
당신 학급을 통제하는 비결이 있습니까?

A Yes, I never let them get the upper hand.
예, 저는 그들이 결코 날뛰도록 놔두지 않습니다.

738 for good measure   :: 덤으로

↳ as an extra

Q Is this tape recorder on sale?
이 녹음기 할인 판매중이니?

A Yes, and if you buy it I'll give you 2 tapes for good measure.
그래, 네가 산다면 테이프 2개를 덤으로 줄게.

739 at the top of one's lungs   :: 목청껏

↳ very loudly

Q Why didn't you warn me that the other car was approaching?
너 왜 나한테 다른 차가 접근하고 있다고 말해주지 않았니?

A I did at the top of my lungs, but you didn't hear me.
제가 목청껏 소리질렀지만 당신이 듣지 못했잖아요.

740 take sides

:: 편들다

↳ support one side over the other

Q Do you support Jack in the election?
선거에서 잭을 지지하니?

A No, I've decided not to take sides with either candidate since they're both friends.
아니, 후보들이 친구니까 어느 쪽도 편들지 않기로 했어.

741 talk down to

:: 깔보고 말하다

↳ speak to in a condescending way

Q Since you can't seem to get your work done on time, would you like us to help you?
제때에 일을 마칠 수 없을 것 같으니 우리가 도와줄까?

A No, and don't talk down to me, okay? I can do the job by myself!
아니, 날 깔보고 말하지마. 알았지? 나 혼자 할 수 있어.

742 give rise to

:: 일으키다

↳ cause

Q Do you think the drinking age should be lowered to 18?
음주 연령을 18세로 낮춰야 한다고 생각하니?

A No, because that would give rise to many problems.
아니, 그러면 많은 문제가 야기될 거야.

743 rile up

:: 짜증나게 하다

↳ bother or upset (also rile)

Q Do you know why the boss is in such a bad mood this morning?
오늘 아침 사장 기분이 왜 안 좋은지 아니?

A Yes, he's all riled up because his secretary didn't come to work again today.
비서가 오늘도 출근하지 않아서 몹시 화났어.

744 come in for :: 받다

↳ be subject to

Q Did the New York Times criticize the President in today's editorial?
뉴욕타임스가 오늘 사설에서 대통령을 비난했니?

A Yes, and recently he's been coming in for a lot of criticism.
그래, 최근 그는 많은 비난을 받고 있어.

745 talk one's ear off :: 지루하게 하다

↳ bore

Q Bill's boring, isn't he?
Bill은 지루하지 않니?

A Yes, he really knows how to talk your ear off.
그래, 그는 너를 지루하게 하는 법을 아나봐.

746 dress one down :: 야단치다

↳ scold

Q Did mom scold you for coming home with another bad report card?
성적이 나쁘다고 엄마에게 또 야단맞았니?

A Yes, she really dressed me down this time.
그래, 이번엔 엄마가 정말로 야단쳤어.

747 earn one's keep :: 제 밥벌이를 하다

↳ support oneself

Q Is it okay if my friend stays with me this semester?
제 친구가 이번 학기에 저와 있어도 되나요?

A Yes, if he earns his keep.
그래, 그가 제 밥벌이를 한다면.

748 take one by surprise

:: 놀라게 하다

↳ surprise one

Q Did you expect Sen. Casey to lose?
Casey 상원의원이 패하리라 예상했니?

A No, his defeat really took me by surprise.
아니, 그의 패배에 정말 놀랐어.

749 on deck

:: 다음 차례

↳ waiting to be next, especially a baseball batter

Q Is it my turn to bat?
내가 칠 차례니?

A Yes, get ready. You're on deck.
그래, 준비해. 다음은 네 차례야.

Day
25

750 die hard

:: 좀처럼 없어지지 않다

↳ persist despite opposition

Q Do you still smoke?
아직도 담배 피우나?

A Yes, and I've been smoking for 20 years. Old habits die hard.
그래, 20년이나 피웠는데 좀처럼 끊을 수가 없어.

145. When you read a novel, get a quick, <u>overall</u> view.

    (A) important   (B) normal

    (C) impressive   (D) clear

    (E) comprehensive

> 어휘 **get a view** 한번 보다 / **overall** 전부의, 종합적인 / **comprehensive** 포괄적인, 넓은
>
> 해석 소설을 읽을 때는 전체적으로 한번 빨리 보아라.

146. Nothing can be more thrilling than the years of youth when every possibility is wide open. It is such a tragedy that many people pass through their youth without ever trying to satisfy the _____ for adventure that they must surely have somewhere inside them.

    (A) claim   (B) aspiring

    (C) hope   (D) craving

> 어휘 **have a craving for** ~을 갈망하다 / **aspire** 열망하다 / **claim for** ~에 대한 요구
>
> 해석 모든 기회가 활짝 열린 젊은 시절만큼 피를 끓게 하는 것은 없다. 많은 사람들이 분명 자신의 내면 어딘가에서 갈망하고 있을 모험에 대한 욕구를 충족시키지 않고 지나친다는 것은 매우 비극적인 일이다.

147. When a man is faced with a choice difficult to make between two courses of action, both undesirable, he is said to be in a _____.

    (A) contradiction   (B) antinomy

    (C) dilemma   (D) antithesis

어휘 **be faced with** ~에 직면하다 / **undesirable** 달갑잖은, 바람직스럽지 않은 / **be said to** ~라고 말들 한다 / **be in a dilemma** 진퇴양난에 빠지다 / **contradiction** 모순 / **antinomy** 이율배반, 자가당착 / **antithesis** 정반대

해석 둘 다 탐탁지 않지만 두 행로 중 하나를 골라야 하는 어려운 선택에 직면했을 때, 진퇴양난에 빠졌다고 말한다.

---

148. He was as <u>deft</u> at handling complaints as he was at tennis.

(A) intelligent   (B) angry
(C) skillful   (D) crude

어휘 **be deft at** ~에 능숙하다 / **handle** 처리하다, 다루다 / **crude** 가공하지 않은, 조잡한

해석 그는 테니스를 치는 솜씨만큼 불만을 처리하는 데도 능숙하다.

---

149. These houses are <u>exempt</u> from paying rates.

(A) closely inspected   (B) not liable
(C) going to be demolished   (D) to sell

어휘 **be exempt from** ~이 면제되다 / **rates** (pl.) 지방세 / **liable** 책임져야 할, 자칫하면 ~해야 하는 / **demolish** 파괴하다

해석 이 주택들은 지방세를 내지 않아도 된다.

---

150. He had taken a pair of white rats into the church and had let them <u>loose</u> on the floor.

(A) tight   (B) dead
(C) careless   (D) free

어휘 **let one loose** ~을 도망치게 놓아주다

해석 그는 흰 쥐 한 쌍을 교회 안으로 데리고 와서 마룻바닥에 풀어놓았다.

Answers ★ 145.(E) 146.(D) 147.(C) 148.(C) 149.(B) 150.(D)

26th Day

---

751 **nest egg** :: 비상금

↳ money stored to be used when in need

Q Do you know what she does with all her money?
그녀가 가진 돈으로 뭘 하는지 아니?

A No, but she's got almost $10,000 in her nest egg.
몰라, 하지만 그녀는 비상금이 거의 1만달러야.

---

752 **nothing to speak of** :: 별로 없는

↳ not much

Q Did he leave his widow a lot of money?
그는 미망인에게 거액을 남겼니?

A No, nothing to speak of.
아니, 별로 없어.

---

753 **hit-and-run** :: 뺑소니치는

↳ the guilty person escaped from the scene of the accident

Q Do you know who hit your car?
누가 네 차를 받았는지 아니?

A No, it was a hit-and-run accident.
몰라, 뺑소니 사고였어.

---

754 **in honor of** :: 기념하여

↳ out of respect for (or in his honor)

Q Do you know the name of this beautiful park?
이 아름다운 공원 이름을 아니?

A Yes, it's called the Eisenhower Park. It was named in honor of the American president.
그래, 아이젠하워 공원이야. 미국 대통령을 기려서 이름지은 거야.

---

755 trot out   :: 선보이다

↳ bring out for other to see

Q Did you go to the computer show?
컴퓨터 쇼에 갔니?

A Yes, and most of the major companies trotted out their new models.
그래, 큰 회사 대부분이 신 모델을 내보였어.

---

756 live down   :: 씻다, 잊어버리다

↳ enable people to forget some past failure by good conduct

Q Did you really make a speech before 2,000 people with your zipper down?
정말 지퍼를 내린 채 2천명 앞에서 연설했어요?

A Yes, and I don't think I will ever be able to live down such an embarrassment.
그래, 이런 망신을 씻을 수 없을 것 같아.

---

757 break wide open   :: 결정적으로 승기를 잡다

↳ start winning decisively

Q Did he score 45 points?
그가 45점을 득점했니?

A Yes, and he broke the game wide open in the fourth quarter.
그래, 4쿼터에서 결정적으로 이기기 시작했어.

261

758 have (or get) nothing on

:: 증거가 없다

↳ they can't find any evidence of any guilt

Q Did the FBI arrest the Congressman?
FBI가 그 의원을 체포했니?

A Yes, but he insists they've got nothing on him.
그래, 하지만 그는 증거가 없다고 주장해.

759 fend for oneself

:: 자립하다

↳ do it on his own

Q Are you going to pay for your son's college education?
아들 대학 교육비를 부담할 거니?

A No, I want him to learn to fend for himself.
아니, 그가 혼자서 벌 수 있기를 바래.

760 hands-on

:: 실제적인

↳ applied and not theoretical

Q Is this institute better than the old one you attended?
이 학원이 네가 다니던 옛 학원보다 더 좋니?

A Yes, because it gives its students much hands-on training
with computers.
그래, 컴퓨터로 학생들에게 실제적인 훈련을 많이 시키니까.

761 the likes of one

:: ~같은 사람

↳ such a one as

Q Are you going to vote against Mayor Jones?
존스 시장에 반대 투표할 거니?

A Yes, because I hope our city never sees the likes of a
man again.
그래, 우리 시에서 이런 사람을 다시는 보기 싫어서야.

be shy of
:: 부족하다

↳ be lacking

Q Do you need to borrow some more money?
돈을 더 빌릴 필요가 있니?

A Yes, I'm still shy of the $2,000 I need to repay my debt.
그래, 아직도 부채를 갚으려면 2천 달러가 부족해.

pass up
:: 놓치다

↳ miss

Q Did Miss Jones reject him, too?
Jones 양이 그 역시 퇴짜 놓았니?

A Yes, and I think she passed up her best chance to get married.
그래, 그녀가 결혼할 가장 좋은 기회를 놓친 것 같아.

take offense at
:: 버럭 화내다

Day
26

↳ become angry or upset because of the criticism

Q Did you make him angry again?
그를 또 화나게 했니?

A Yes, but I didn't know he would take offense at such a small criticism.
그래, 그가 이런 사소한 비판에도 화낼 줄 몰랐어.

hit home
:: 정곡을 찌르다

↳ go directly to the mark

Q Did you watch the TV special last night about parent children problems?
부모와 자녀 문제에 관한 TV 특별 프로 봤니?

A Yes, and it really hit home because my family has some of the same problems, too.
그래, 정말 핵심을 찔렀어. 우리 집에도 그런 문제가 있으니까.

shove off :: 자리를 털다

↳ leave

Q Do you have time for another drink?
또 한 잔 할 시간 있어?

A No, I'd better shove off and get home before my wife starts worrying.
없어, 마누라가 걱정하기 전에 일어나 집에 가는 게 좋겠다.

traipse around :: 정처 없이 돌아다니다

↳ walk around (aimlessly)

Q Does your daughter have to be home before midnight?
자네 딸은 자정 전에 귀가해야 하나?

A Yes, I don't want her traipsing around town with those friends of hers.
그래, 친구들과 싸돌아다니는 걸 원치 않아.

up to scratch :: 성능이 좋은

↳ in good condition (see up to snuff)

Q Are you taking your car to the repair shop this afternoon?
오후에 네 차를 수리업소에 가져갈 거니?

A Yes, the engine is not up to scratch.
그래, 엔진이 좋지 않아.

how come :: 왜

↳ why

Q Could I borrow your car tonight?
네 차를 빌릴 수 있니?

A No, and how come you always ask me and not your brother?
안돼, 너는 왜 항상 형에게는 안하고 내게만 부탁하니?

wallow in :: 빠지다

↳ roll about (usually feeling sorry for oneself)

Q Is she crying again?
그녀는 또 우니?

A Yes, and I wish she'd stop wallowing in her own unhappiness.
그래, 불행하다는 생각에 그만 빠졌으면 좋겠어.

---

771 **wish on** :: 떠맡기다

↳ force to receive or accept

Q Do you enjoy working as a truck driver?
트럭 운전사로 일하는 것에 만족하니?

A No, and I would wish this kind of job on my worst enemy.
아니, 이런 일을 내가 가장 싫어하는 원수에게 떠맡기고 싶어.

---

772 **rest up** :: 쉬다

↳ take a rest

Q Are you ready for another set?
다른 차림이 준비 됐습니까?

A No, let me rest up a few more minutes.
아뇨, 몇 분만 더 쉬게 해주세요.

Day
26

---

773 **go into particulars** :: 상세히 설명하다

↳ give the details

Q Do you go to church every sunday?
매주 일요일에 교회가니?

A No, and I don't want to go into any particulars about why I don't.
아니, 안 가는 이유를 상세히 설명하고 싶진 않아.

774 case-by-case
:: 경우에 따라

↳ depending on the circumstances

Q Do you think every student should receive a scholarship?
모든 학생이 장학금을 받아야 한다고 생각하니?

A No, financial aid should be given on a case-by-case basis.
아니, 재정적인 지원은 하나하나 심사해서 주어져야 해.

775 make a go at
:: 성공하다

↳ get it to work or be successful

Q Are you going to sell your store?
가게를 팔거니?

A Yes, I just couldn't make a go at it.
응, 도저히 성공할 수 없어.

776 twiddle one's thumbs
:: 손가락만 만지작거리다

↳ do nothing

Q Are you going somewhere this weekend?
이번 주말에 어디 가니?

A No, I'm just going to stay home and twiddle my thumbs.
아니, 집에서 손가락만 빨거야.

777 a cut above
:: 보다 조금 좋은

↳ (a little) better than the others

Q Is this brand of coffee much better than the others?
이 커피가 다른 것보다 좋니?

A Yes, I think it's a cut above the rest.
그래, 조금 더 좋은 것 같다.

778 a pat on the back
:: 칭찬

↳ praise

Q Did he really adopt two orphans?
그는 정말 고아 두 명을 양자로 삼았니?

A Yes, and he deserves a pat on the back.
응, 그는 찬사를 받을 만해.

779 that'll do
:: 그것으로 족하다

↳ enough of that

Q Mom, do I have to clean my room every day?
엄마, 매일 내 방을 청소해야 되나요?

A Yes, and that'll do! I don't want to hear any more complaining.
그래, 그러면 돼. 더이상 불평을 듣고 싶진 않아.

780 keep away from
:: 멀리하다

↳ avoid (see shy away from)

Q Did your doctor give you any good advice?
의사가 유익한 충고를 했니?

A Yes, he told me to keep away from greasy food.
그래, 기름기 있는 음식을 피하라고 했어.

Day
26

151. James was <u>oblivious to</u> the noise around him.

(A) nervous about   (B) furious about

(C) unaware of   (D) irritated by

어휘 be oblivious to ~에 몰두하여 의식하지 못하다, 잘 잊어먹다 / furious 펄펄 뛰는, 격노한 / be unaware of ~을 모르다

해석 제임스는 주변의 시끄러움을 의식하지 못했다.

---

152. The traditional goal of science has been to discover how things are, not how they ought to be, but can a <u>clean-cut</u> distinction between fact and value in the interaction of science and society be sustained any longer?

(A) sanitary   (B) vivid

(C) sharp   (D) theoretical

(E) understandable

어휘 clean-cut 단정한, 명확한 / distinction between ~사이의 구별, 차이 cf. among을 쓰지 않음. / interaction 상호작용 / sustain 뒷받침하다, 지지하다 / sanitary 위생적인 / sharp 뚜렷한, 선명한 / understandable 알만한

해석 과학의 전통적인 목표는 물체들이 어떻게 존재해야 하는가가 아니라, 어떻게 존재하느냐를 밝히는 것이 었지만, 과학과 사회의 상호작용 속에서 사실과 가치 사이의 분명한 차이를 더이상 확증할 수 있는가?

---

153. It is part of the duty of school janitors to check the fire extinguishers regularly, and make sure that they will be ready in a(an) _____.

(A) escape   (B) situation

(C) emergency   (D) hour

해석 학교 수위의 의무 중 일부는 정기적으로 소화기를 점검하고 소화기가 비상시에 확실히 잘 준비되도록 하는 것이다.

---

154. Frank is a very good bowler, but Jane is just <u>run-of-the-mill</u>.

(A) unsatisfactory   (B) ordinary
(C) outstanding   (D) extraordinary
(E) under average

어휘 bowler 볼링 선수 / run-of-the-mill 보통의, 평범한 / outstanding 뛰어난

해석 프랭크는 매우 훌륭한 볼링 선수지만, 제인은 그저 그렇다.

---

155. I am afraid that she will <u>get sore</u> and move away if she catches me watching her.

(A) get angry   (B) have a sore throat
(C) become frustrated   (D) be sullen
(E) be flattered

어휘 get sore 화를 내다 / catch 발견하다 / have a sore throat 목이 아프다 / frustrate 좌절시키다 / sullen 부루퉁한, 언짢은 / be flattered 우쭐하다

해석 내가 그녀를 지켜보고 있다는 걸 발견하고 그녀가 화가 나서 가버릴까봐 두렵다.

---

156. Top executives <u>cut their teeth</u> on selling ice cream.

(A) learn in young age   (B) hush up
(C) feel for   (D) look into

어휘 learn in young age 어린 나이에 배우다 / hush up 은폐하다 / feel for 동정심을 느끼다 / look into 조사하다

해석 정상급 중역들은 어린 나이에 아이스크림 판매를 배웠다.

Answers ★ 151.(C) 152.(C) 153.(C) 154.(B) 155.(A) 156.(A)

---

781 **get in**

:: 공급받다

↳ get the supply of

Q Does your store have any leather gloves?
네 상점에 가죽장갑 있니?

A Yes, we got in a shipment of them this morning.
응, 오늘 아침 공급받았어.

---

782 **be faced with**

:: 당면하다

↳ be confronted with

Q Did you vote in the last election?
지난 선거에 투표했니?

A Yes, I felt I had to because of all the problems we're faced with these days.
그래, 요즘 우리의 당면 문제 때문에 투표해야 한다고 생각했어.

---

783 **the rank-and-file**

:: 노동자층

↳ the workers

Q Do you think the union president will be reelected?
그 노조 위원장이 재선될 것 같니?

A Yes, because he still has strong support from the rank-and-file.
응, 그는 아직도 노동자의 강력한 지지를 받고 있어.

amount to　　　　　　　　　:: 총계가 ~에 이르다

↳ add up to

Q How much change do you have, Jim?
Jim, 잔돈이 얼마나 있니?

A Not enough to amount to buying even a cup of coffee.
커피 한 잔 살 돈도 안 돼.

cut one's teeth on　　　　　　:: 어려서 배우다

↳ learn or do as a beginner

Q Did you learn how to ski when you were young?
어렸을 때 스키를 배웠니?

A Yes, and I cut my teeth on ski jumping when I was only 13 years old.
그래, 13살 때 스키 점프를 배웠어.

go down the tubes　　　　　　:: 몰락하다

↳ collapse

Q Did the crime rate increase again this month?
이 달에 또 범죄율이 증가했니?

A Yes, and our city is really going down the tubes.
응, 우리 도시는 정말 몰락하나봐.

Day

27

in nine cases out of ten　　　:: 십중팔구

↳ in almost all cases

Q Do most people get divorced because of money problems?
대부분의 사람들은 돈 문제로 이혼하니?

A Yes, in nine cases out of ten.
응, 십중팔구는 그래.

burn one up

:: 화나게 하다

↳ make one angry

Q Did your husband make you angry again?
남편이 또 널 화나게 했니?

A Yes, his constant complaining about my cooking really burns me up.
응, 내 요리를 자꾸 불평하는 게 정말 화가나.

pan out

:: 실현되다

↳ materialize

Q Did you visit Europe on your vacation?
휴가 중 유럽을 방문했니?

A Yes, but our travel plans to see Rome didn't pan out because of bad weather.
그래, 하지만 로마를 보려던 계획은 날씨가 나빠 실현되지 못했어.

go figure

:: 헤아려 보다

↳ see if you can understand that!

Q Do you know why the economy is in such terrible shape?
경제가 왜 이렇게 엉망인지 아니?

A No, and none of the economists know either. Go figure.
아니, 경제학자들도 몰라. 헤아려 보라구.

as is often the case

:: 흔히 그러듯

↳ as it is often true

Q Did both of his children get in trouble with the police?
그의 자녀 둘 모두 경찰과 문제가 있었나요?

A Yes, as is often the case in families with alcoholic father.
예, 가족 중 술만 퍼마시는 아버지가 종종 일으키는 경우처럼요.

bed of Procrustes   :: 매우 엄격한 것

↳ something very restrictive

Q Do you agree with the new government regulations?
새 정부 법안에 동의하십니까?

A No, I think they are a bed of Procrustes that will block
progress.
아뇨, 발전을 저해하는 엄격한 것이라고 생각합니다.

---

keep it in mind   :: 명심하다

↳ remember

Q Don't forget to write home when you arrive at the
University.
대학교에 도착하면 집에 편지쓰는 걸 잊지 마라.

A No, I won't forget, Mom. I'll keep it in mind.
예, 안 잊을게요, 엄마. 명심할게요.

---

take st. in stride   :: 차분히 받아들이다

↳ accept calmly

Day
27

Q Are you upset because you didn't pass tour driver's
license test again?
운전면허 시험에 또 불합격해 화났니?

A No, I always try to take disappointments in stride.
아니, 실망을 차분히 받아들이려고 노력해.

---

only on condition that   :: ∼하기만 한다면

↳ only if (also only on the condition that)

Q Can I buy a motorcycle, Mom?
오토바이 사도 되나요, 엄마?

A Yes, but only on condition that you always wear a
helmet.
응, 하지만 항상 헬멧을 써야해.

796 take it easy
:: 서둘지 않다

↳ go slowly and carefully

Q Are the roads still very icy?
길이 아직도 빙판인가요?

A Yes, so take it easy driving to work this morning.
예, 그러니 오늘 아침은 회사까지 운전 주의하세요.

797 nerves are on edge
:: 초조하다

↳ be very nervous

Q Have you smoked one pack of cigarettes already?
벌써 담배 한 갑을 다 피웠나요?

A Yes, my nerves are really on edge today.
예, 오늘은 무척 초조하군요.

798 take at one's word
:: 말을 믿다

↳ believe

Q Are you sure he'll return the money you lent him?
당신이 빌려준 돈을 그가 갚으리라 확신합니까?

A Yes, he promised me, so I have to take him at his word.
제게 약속했으니까 그를 믿어야겠죠.

799 odds and ends
:: 잡동사니

↳ assorted items

Q Is there anything important in this box?
이 상자 안에 중요한 게 들었나요?

A No, just some odds and ends I've collected over the years.
아뇨, 단지 수년간 수집한 잡동사니들이 약간 있어요.

by sight but not by name

:: 얼굴은 알지만 이름은 모르는

↳ I've seen one before but I don't know one's name

Q Do you recognize the person in this picture?
이 사진의 사람을 알아볼 수 있니?

A Yes, I know her by sight but not by name.
응, 얼굴은 아는데 이름은 몰라.

get it

:: 이해하다

↳ understand

Q Have you ever heard that joke before?
그 농담을 들은 적 있니?

A No, and frankly I didn't get it.
아니, 사실 이해 못했어.

carry out

:: 수행하다

↳ perform

Day

27

Q Do you want to see me, Captain?
부르셨나요, 선장님?

A Yes, why haven't you carried out my orders for the barracks to be cleaned?
그래, 막사를 청소하라는 내 지시를 왜 수행하지 않았나?

take care of

:: 처리하다

↳ do

Q Do you mail the letters yet?
편지 부쳤니?

A No, but I'll take care of them this afternoon.
아뇨, 하지만 오늘 오후에 하겠습니다.

804 get by
:: 그럭저럭 꾸려나가다

↳ manage

Q Are you going to ask the boss for more money?
사장에게 돈을 더 요구할 겁니까?

A Yes, because my salary is not enough for me to get by.
예, 제 급여로는 먹고살기에 충분치 않아서요.

805 get across to
:: 이해시키다

↳ cause to understand

Q Is Bill going to quit college?
Bill은 대학을 그만둘 건가요?

A Yes, I wasn't able to get across to him how important a
college education is.
예, 대학 교육이 얼마나 중요한지 그를 이해시킬 수가 없었어요.

806 take cover
:: 몸을 피하다

↳ seek shelter or protection

Q Is it starting to rain?
비가 오기 시작하나요?

A Yes, so let's take cover under that tree over there.
예, 저쪽 나무 밑으로 몸을 피합시다.

807 gain ground
:: 진전되다

↳ make progresss

Q Do you think the Democrats will win the White House
this election?
민주당이 이번 선거에서 백악관을 차지할 거라고 생각하니?

A No, but I expect them to gain enough ground to control
the Senate.
아니, 하지만 충분히 상원을 지배할 만큼 진전될 거야.

808 **take a turn for the worse** :: 악화되다

↳ become worse

Q Do you still have a cold?
아직도 감기 기운이 있니?

A Yes, and I think it's taking a turn for the worse.
응, 악화되나봐.

809 **hang a left** :: 좌회전하다

↳ go or turn left (see hang a right)

Q Should I turn left at the next stoplight?
다음 신호등에서 좌회전합니까?

A No, hang a left at the next intersection.
아뇨, 다음 교차로에서 좌회전하세요.

810 **take effect** :: 효과를 보다

↳ become operating or show results

Q Do you still have a headache?
아직도 두통이 있습니까?

Day
27

A Yes, and it sure is taking a long time for this aspirin to take effect.
예, 이 아스피린 효과가 나타나는데 확실히 시간이 많이 걸리는군요.

영숙어 문제 단번에 공략하기

157. <u>As is often the case</u>, whenever a change is made to the line of a car manufacturer, the new models come in for a fair amount of criticism-and sometimes the criticism comes from those who haven't really experienced the cars.

(A) as it were   (B) as often as not
(C) as thing are   (D) as it is often true

어휘 **as it were** 말하자면 / **as often as not** 종종 / **as thing are** 현 상태로는 / **as it is often true** 흔히 있는 일이지만

해석 흔히 그렇듯이 자동차 메이커에 변화의 바람이 불 때마다 새 모델이 상당한 비난을 받게 된다. 그리고 그 차를 전혀 타본 적도 없는 사람들이 비난을 하기도 한다.

---

158. President George Bush says jogging helped him quit drinking years ago and now helps him <u>take</u> the war on terrorism <u>in stride</u>.

(A) take seriously   (B) accept calmly
(C) rake in   (D) take one's mind off

어휘 **take seriously** 심각하게 받아들이다 / **accept calmly** 차분히 받아들이다 / **rake in** 긁어들이다 / **take one's mind off** 훌훌 털어버리다

해석 부시 대통령은 조깅이 예전에 술을 끊는데 도움이 되었으며 지금은 테러와의 전쟁을 느긋하게 생각하는데 도움이 된다고 말한다.

---

159. There are strong signs that my views are <u>gaining ground</u>.

(A) bear up   (B) hit the bottle
(C) become popular   (D) steal away

어휘 **bear up** 어려움을 참아내다 / **hit the bottle** 술을 많이 마시다 / **become popular** 인기가 올라가다 / **steal away** 은밀한 곳으로 가다

해석 내 견해들이 점차 유력해지는 강력한 징후가 보인다.

160. Granny's been collecting things for a very long time and of course over the years she's picked up some very unique items that don't really fall into a "specific category". We've decided to bunch them all up in this group we call <u>Odds & Ends</u>!

(A) couch potato   (B) dead ringer
(C) fossil   (D) assorted items

어휘 **couch potato** 빈둥빈둥 TV만 보는 사람 / **dead ringer** 꼭 닮은 물건 /
fossil 화석, 시대에 뒤떨어진 사람

해석 할머니는 오랜 동안 여러 가지를 수집하셨다. 물론 수년 동안 그녀는 아주 진
귀한 것도 모았는데 이것들은 세부항목에 속하지 않는 것들이다. 우리는 그것
들을 뭉뚱그려 잡동사니라는 그룹으로 부르기로 했다.

---

161. Within half an hour, though, the Botox began to <u>take effect</u>, and she was ultimately pleased with the treatment.

(A) come into operation   (B) burn out
(C) jazz up   (D) carry away

어휘 **come into operation** 효과를 내다 / **burn out** 지치다 / **jazz up** 화려하게
장식하다 / **carry away** 과민반응하다

해석 반시간 안에 보톡스가 효과를 나타냈다. 그리고 그녀는 치료가 너무나도 기뻤다.

---

162. The teacher's <u>fair-haired boy</u> always do well on tests.

(A) battle-ax   (B) black sheep
(C) favored person   (D) carbon copy

어휘 **battle-ax** 앙칼지고 드센 여자 / **black sheep** 어떤 집단에서 수치스런 사
람, 말썽꾼 / **favored person** 총애받는 사람 / **carbon copy** (외모나 행동
이) 똑같은 사람

해석 그 교사의 총애받는 학생은 시험 성적이 늘 좋다.

Answers ★ 157.(D) 158.(B) 159.(C) 160.(D) 161.(A) 162.(C)

811 keep one's head

:: 침착하다

↳ keep calm (see lose one's head)

Q Is it starting to snow?
눈이 오기 시작하니?

A Yes, but let's keep our heads and try to find a place to stay tonight.
응, 침착하고 오늘밤 머물 곳을 찾기나 하자.

812 name after

:: 이름을 따서 짓다

↳ give a name to someone in honor of a person

Q Have you found a good name for your baby yet?
좋은 아기 이름을 찾았나요?

A No, but I'm thinking of naming her after my grandfather.
아뇨, 조부 존함을 따서 지을까 해요.

813 take one for a fool (or an idiot)

:: 바보로 보다

↳ think one is a fool

Q Could you lend me $1,000?
천 달러 빌려 줄래?

A No, of course not. What do you take me for a fool?
물론 안 되지. 날 바보로 보니?

natural-born

:: 타고난

↳ born to be

Q Do you think he should play in the outfield?
그가 외야를 맡아야 한다고 생각하세요?

A No, I think he's a natural-born shortstop.
아뇨, 그는 타고난 유격수라고 생각해요.

take for granted

:: 당연하게 생각하다

↳ assume something as a matter of course

Q Did you take your kids with you to the party?
애들을 파티에 데려갔나요?

A Yes, because I took it for granted that they were invited, too.
예, 그들도 역시 초대받아 당연하다고 생각했어요.

keep track of

:: 가까이 따르다

↳ follow closely

Q Did she buy another computer magazine?
그녀는 다른 컴퓨터 잡지를 샀나요?

A Yes, she's really trying hard to keep track of new software.
예, 그녀는 새로운 소프트웨어에 접근하려고 무척 애쓰고 있어요.

Day
28

come out for

:: 지지를 표시하다

↳ express support for

Q Did the New York Times decide to support Sen. Jones?
뉴욕 타임즈는 Jones 상원의원을 지지하기로 했나요?

A No, the newspaper came out for his opponent.
아뇨, 그의 적에 대해 지지를 표했어요.

818 **set one's mind on**   :: 굳게 마음먹다

↳ be strongly determined to do

Q Were you surprised to hear that Bill graduated first in his class?
Bill이 1등으로 졸업한 것에 놀랐나요?

A No, because I always knew he could do whatever he set his mind on.
아뇨, 그는 마음먹은 것은 뭐든지 할 수 있다는 것을 알고 있었어요.

819 **be geared up for**   :: 준비하다

↳ be prepared for some activity

Q Sam seems very excited these days, doesn't he?
Sam이 요즘 흥분하는 것 같지 않아요?

A Yes, he's all geared up for his big date this weekend.
예, 그는 이번 주말 중요한 데이트에 만반의 준비를 하고 있어요.

820 **for the best part of**   :: 대부분

↳ for most of

Q Did you watch the football game Sunday?
일요일 축구 경기를 시청했니?

A No, I haven't watched sports on TV for the best part of a month.
아니, 거의 한 달간 TV 스포츠 시청은 안 했어.

821 **go easy on**   :: 가혹하지 않게 하다

↳ don't be extreme or too strict

Q Do you think Johnny should be punished for what he did?
Johnny는 그가 한 짓에 대해 처벌받아야 한다고 생각하니?

A Yes, but go easy on him. He's just a child, remember.
응, 하지만 너무 가혹하지 않게. 그는 어린애라구, 잊지 마.

be bent on
:: ~할 결심인

↳ be determined to do

Q Was Sen. Smith on another news program this weekend?
Smith 상원의원은 이번 주말 다른 뉴스 프로에 출연했니?

A Yes, he must be bent on running for president someday.
응, 그는 언젠가는 대통령에 출마할 결심인 게 틀림없어.

roll in the aisles
:: 파안대소하다

↳ laugh uncontrollably

Q Did you enjoy the comedy?
그 코미디 재미있었나요?

A Yes, it had most of the audience rolling in the aisles.
예, 청중 대부분은 파안대소했어요.

make the most of
:: 최대한 이용하다

↳ get the best use or greatest gain from

Q Is he going to enter politics?
그가 정치에 입문할거니?

A Yes, and he'll try to make the most of his handsome face.
응, 그는 잘생긴 얼굴을 최대한 이용하려고 해.

Day 28

crow over
:: 자랑하다

↳ boast

Q Did he win another bowling tournament?
그가 볼링 토너먼트에서 또 이겼니?

A Yes, and I wish he wouldn't always crow over how good he is.
응, 그가 얼마나 잘하는지 항상 자랑하지 않았으면 좋겠어.

826 make peace
:: 화해하다

↳ reconcile

Q Did you say you haven't seen your father in ten years?
10년간 네 아버지를 보지 못했다고 했니?

A Yes, and I think it's time we made our peace.
응, 이제 우리는 화해할 때가 된 것 같아.

827 come off second-best
:: 패배하다

↳ be defeated

Q Did you win the contest?
콘테스트에서 상을 탔니?

A No, unfortunately we came off second-best.
아니, 불행히도 우린 졌어.

828 pay back
:: 갚다

↳ repay

Q Did you repay your college loan yet?
대학 등록금 대출을 갚았니?

A Yes, I paid it all back last year.
응, 작년에 모두 갚았어.

829 go for it
:: 이루려고 노력하다

↳ try hard to get it

Q Do you think I'm tall enough to get on the basketball team?
내가 농구팀에 낄 만큼 키가 크다고 생각하니?

A Yes, so go for it.
응, 그러니 열심히 해 봐!

take to task :: 꾸중하다

↳ scold

Q Did the boss yell at you this morning?
사장이 오늘 아침에 자네에게 소리쳤나?

A Yes, she took me to task for coming late again.
응, 또 지각했다고 꾸중했어.

to one's taste :: 기호에 맞는

↳ pleasing or acceptable

Q Would you like to listen to some classical music tonight?
오늘밤 고전음악을 들을래?

A No, I think rap music is more to my taste.
아니, 내 기호엔 랩 음악이 더 맞아.

tattle on :: 고자질하다

↳ tell or inform on

Q Are you going to tell mom you saw him eat the last
piece of cake?
그가 마지막 남은 케이크를 먹는 것을 봤다고 엄마에게 말할거니?

A No, because it's not good to tattle on one's brother.
아니, 형제를 고자질하는 건 나쁜 거니까.

Day 28

the salt of the earth :: 소금과 같은 존재

↳ the best people

Q Do you like the people in this part of Europe?
유럽의 이 지역 사람들이 마음에 드니?

A Yes, they seem to be the salt of the earth.
예, 그들은 최고인 것 같아요.

834 phase out

:: 차츰 중단되다

↳ discontinue or end gradually

Q Do you think our state will still have passenger trains 10 years from now?
우리 주가 이제부터 10년간 객차를 보유하리라 생각하니?

A No, they're already being phased out because of money problems.
아니, 그들은 이미 재정 문제로 점차 중단되고 있으니까.

835 for the sake of

:: ~를 위해

↳ in order to help or please

Q Do you know why Sam works so hard?
Sam이 왜 그리 열심히 일하는지 아니?

A Yes, for the sake of his family. He loves them very much.
응, 그의 가족을 위해서야. 그는 가족을 매우 사랑하거든.

836 armed to the teeth

:: 중무장한

↳ armed completely

Q Are the robbers in this part of the city dangerous?
이 도시 지역의 강도들은 위험합니까?

A Yes, because they're armed to the teeth.
예, 그들은 중무장했거든요.

837 queer

:: 동성애자

↳ homosexual

Q Is he married?
그는 결혼했나요?

A No, and one of his friends told me he's queer.
아뇨, 그의 친구 중 하나가 그는 동성애자라고 했어요.

838 **without question** :: 분명히

↳ certainly

Q Is this the man who stole your wallet, sir?
이 사람이 당신 지갑을 훔친 사람인가요, 선생님?

A Yes, he's the one, without question.
예, 분명히 그 사람입니다.

839 **pitch in** :: 뛰어들어 돕다

↳ join or help others with a job they are doing

Q Was your friend's house damaged in the flood last month?
지난달 홍수로 친구집이 파손되었니?

A Yes, so let's pitch in and help him rebuild it.
응, 그러니 뛰어들어 그가 집을 다시 짓도록 도와주자.

840 **tell on** :: 일러바치다

↳ inform on

Q Did your mother say we have to end our relationship?
너희 어머니께서 우리 관계를 끝내야 한다고 하셨니?

A Yes, because my little brother told on her that you taught me how to smoke.
응, 네가 담배 피우는 방법을 내게 가르쳐 주었다고 내 어린 동생이 고자질 했어.

Day

28

영숙어 문제 단번에 공략하기

163. Tell me what you think, and don't <u>mince your words</u>.

(A) blow one's own horn   (B) dry out

(C) have a way with   (D) soften one's words

어휘 **blow one's own horn** 자화자찬하다 / **dry out** 술을 끊다 / **have a way with** ~을 잘 다루다 / **soften one's words** 완곡하게 표현하다

해석 네 생각을 그대로 말해봐. 완곡하게 표현하지 말고.

---

164. Because of his <u>high-handed</u> attitude, he can't sell cars.

(A) hyper   (B) offbeat

(C) overly proud   (D) pigheaded

어휘 **hyper** 흥분하기 쉬운 / **offbeat** 색다른 / **overly proud** 지나치게 고자세인 / **pigheaded** 고집센

해석 그는 지나치게 고자세라서 자동차를 팔 수 없다.

---

165. I felt a <u>nip in the air</u> when I opened the window.

(A) cold feeling   (B) sea leg

(C) skinflint   (D) wet noodle

어휘 **sea leg** 생활력 / **skinflint** 구두쇠 / **wet noodle** 약골

해석 내가 창문을 열었을 때 한기를 느꼈다.

166. She's never serious. She's always <u>cracking jokes</u>.

(A) tell a joke   (B) crack one's jaw
(C) belt down   (D) pal around

어휘 **crack one's jaw** 허풍떨다 / **belt down** 들이마시다 / **pal around** 친구들
과 어울리다

해석 그녀는 진지할 때가 없어. 늘 농담만 한다니까.

---

167. I am a tone deaf so I can't <u>carry a tune</u>.

(A) have a crush on   (B) sing well
(C) chow down   (D) ask out

어휘 **have a crush on** ~에게 반하다 / **chow down** 왕창 먹다 / **ask out** 데이
트 신청을 하다

해석 나는 음치라서 노래를 잘하지 못해요.

---

168. There is a lot of <u>hustle and bustle</u> in this office at the
end of the fiscal year.

(A) wishy-washy   (B) very busy activity
(C) half-wit   (D) simpleton

Day
28

어휘 **wishy-washy** 우유부단한 / **half-wit** 모자란 사람 / **simpleton** 단순한 것
을 좋아하는 사람

해석 매년 회계연도 말 사무실에는 엄청나게 바쁘고 북적거린다.

29th Day

841 run out on

:: 버리다

↳ abandon

Q Do you know why he looks so sad these days?
요즘 그가 왜 침울해 보이는지 아니?

A Yes, his wife finally ran out on him.
응, 그의 아내가 결국 그를 버렸어.

842 tootle off

:: 떠나다

↳ leave

Q Would you like to stay for dinner tonight?
오늘밤 저녁식사 하실래요?

A No, thanks. My family is waiting for me at home so I'd better tootle off.
아뇨, 집에서 가족이 기다려서 떠나는 게 좋겠네요.

843 under the table

:: 몰래

↳ secretly

Q Is our mayor a millionaire?
시장님은 백만장자인가?

A Yes, and like many politicians he's received a lot of money under the table.
응, 많은 정치인들처럼 그도 몰래 많은 돈을 받았어.

no sooner ~ than   :: ~하자마자

↳ as soon as

  Q Did you and Joe have another fight?
    너와 조는 또 싸웠니?

  A Yes, because no sooner had I entered the room than he
    started to criticize me.
    응, 방에 들어가자마자 내 욕을 하기 시작했어.

uncalled for   :: 지나친

↳ not justified or appropriate

  Q Don't you think his criticisms of your paintings were too
    strong?
    네 그림에 대한 그의 비평이 너무 심하지 않니?

  A Yes, they were completely uncalled for.
    응, 너무 지나쳐.

up to   :: ~에게 달린

↳ it's all one's decision

  Q Do you want me to quit smoking?
    내가 담배 끊길 바라니?

  A Yes, of course, but it's all up to you.
    응, 물론이지. 하지만 그건 네게 달렸어.

Day

29

I'll catch you later   :: 나중에 보자!

↳ I'll take or see you later

  Q Do you have to go home already?
    벌써 집에 가야 하니?

  A Yes, so I'll catch you later.
    응, 나중에 보자.

848 | under the wire
:: 마감 바로 전

↳ just before the time when something must be finished

Q Did you pay your income taxes yet?
소득세를 벌써 냈니?

A Yes, and just under the wire.
응, 마감 바로 전에.

849 | take under one's wing
:: 보호하다

↳ protect

Q Do you have time to introduce the new student to her new school?
새로 온 학생을 학교에 소개할 시간이 있니?

A Yes, I'll be happy to take her under my wing for a few days.
응, 며칠간 그녀를 보호하는 게 기뻐.

850 | up and around
:: 건강을 되찾은

↳ in good health again after an illness

Q Did the doctor give you some good news?
의사 선생님이 좋은 소식을 주셨나요?

A Yes, she said my husband should be up and around in a few weeks.
예, 그녀는 제 남편이 몇 주 안에 건강을 되찾을 거라고 했어요.

851 | face up to
:: 마지못해 받아들이다

↳ accept, though it may be unpleasant to do so

Q Did you tell dad you're thinking about not going to college?
대학에 갈 생각이 없다는 것을 아버지께 말씀드렸니?

A Yes, and he'll just have to face up to the fact that I don't like to study.
응, 아버지는 내가 공부하기 싫어한다는 사실을 마지못해 받아들여야 하실 거야.

day by day
:: 나날이

↳ gradually

Q Do you still have a backache?
아직도 등이 아프니?

A Yes, but day by day it's getting better.
응, 하지만 점차 낫고 있어.

fair and square
:: 정정당당하게

↳ honestly

Q Did the other team try to cheat?
다른 팀이 반칙을 하려고 했니?

A Yes, but we won fair and square.
응, 하지만 우린 정정당당하게 이겼어.

under one's breath
:: 귓속말로

↳ in a whisper

Q Do you have something to tell me?
내게 할 말 있니?

A Yes, but because it's personal, I'll have to tell it to you under my breath.
응, 하지만 개인적인 얘기라 조용히 귓속말로 해야겠어.

Day
29

die off
:: 멸종되다

↳ become extinct

Q Are you against whale hunting?
고래 사냥에 반대하니?

A Yes, because the species is very close to dying off.
응, 그 종은 거의 멸종되고 있잖아.

856 up-to-date
:: 최신식의

↳ modern

Q Are you going to have your operation done in this hospital?
이 병원에서 당신 수술을 마칠 겁니까?

A Yes, because the equipment here is all up-to-date.
예, 여기 장비가 모두 현대적이거든요.

857 have an ear for
:: 소질이 있다

↳ be very good at

Q Did you decide to change your college major?
대학 전공을 바꾸기로 했니?

A Yes, because I discovered I don't have an ear for music.
응, 음악엔 소질이 없다는 것을 알았어.

858 make believe
:: ~인 척하다

↳ pretend (see make-believe)

Q Do you want to play Cowboys and Indians?
카우보이스와 인디언스 놀이를 하고 싶니?

A No, let's make believe we're pirates looking for buried treasure.
아니, 숨겨진 보물을 찾는 해적놀이를 하자.

859 on one's own
:: 독립적인

↳ independent

Q Does your son still live with you?
아드님은 아직 함께 사나요?

A No, he moved out and is now living on his own.
아뇨, 그는 이사해서 지금은 독립해 살아요.

860 turn over   :: 시동걸다

↳ begin to start (regarding a motor)

Q Do you know why your engine won't start?
당신 엔진이 왜 시동이 걸리지 않는지 아세요?

A Yes, it won't turn over because I forgot to put antifreeze in the radiator.
예, 라디에이터에 부동액 넣는 걸 잊었기 때문에 시동이 안 걸려요.

861 have someone's ear   :: 신임을 받다

↳ have access to, get one to listen to you

Q Is the Secretary of State the most influential cabinet member these days?
요즘 국무장관은 가장 영향력 있는 내각 인사니?

A Yes, he always seems to have the President's ear.
응, 그는 항상 대통령의 신임을 받는 것 같아.

862 make a scene   :: 소란 피우다

↳ create a disturbance

Q Why is your son crying and screaming like that? Is he sick?
아드님이 왜 저렇게 울며 소리치는 겁니까? 아픈가요?

A No, he's making a scene because I won't buy him some ice cream.
아뇨, 아이스크림을 안 사주니까 소란을 피우는 겁니다.

Day 29

863 on end   :: 끊임없이

↳ continuously

Q Did you have a good time on your skiing vacation?
스키 휴가는 즐거웠니?

A Yes, and especially because it seemed to snow for days on end.
응, 특히 며칠간 눈이 계속 온 것 같아.

864 make a point of
:: 꼭 ~하다

↳ give importance to (make it a point to do)

Q Do you have many friends?
친구가 많니?

A Yes, and I always make a point of helping them when
they're in trouble.
응, 그들이 어려울 때 항상 돕거든.

865 get within earshot
:: (소리가) 들리는 거리에 있다

↳ get within hearing distance

Q Did you hear what they were talking about?
그들이 무슨 얘길 하는지 들었어요?

A No, I couldn't get within earshot.
아뇨, 가청거리에 없었어요.

866 make certain
:: 확실한

↳ be sure (see make sure)

Q Do you want me to turn off the air conditioner?
제가 에어컨을 끌까요?

A Yes, and make certain you turn off the lights too before
you leave.
예, 떠나기 전에 불도 확실히 끄세요.

867 edge out
:: 근소한 차이로 이기다

↳ win by a small margin

Q Are the New York Yankees still in third place?
뉴욕 양키즈는 아직도 3위니?

A No, they edged out the Chicago White Sox and are now
in second place.
아니, 시카고 화이트 삭스를 근소한 차이로 이기고 이제 2위야.

868 make a face

:: 싫어하는 표정을 짓다

↪ make an expression on one's face showing dislike

Q Did your mother scold you for bringing home another kitten?
어머니께서 네가 집에 다른 고양이를 데리고 온 걸 꾸중하셨니?

A Yes, she just made a face when I showed it to her.
예, 고양이를 보여드리자 곧 싫어하는 표정을 지으셨어요.

869 be on one's back

:: 귀찮게 시키다

↪ annoy one to do it (see get off one's back)

Q Are you finally going to start looking for a job?
새 일자리 구하는 것을 시작할 겁니까?

A Yes, because my father has been on my back to do so for weeks.
예, 아버지께서 수주간 그렇게 하도록 귀찮게 시켰어요.

870 hard feelings

:: 원한, 증오, 악감정

↪ resentment

Q Did you apologize to her?
그녀에게 사과했니?

A Yes, and she said she has no hard feelings to me.
응, 그녀는 내게 악감정이 없대.

169. He <u>huffed and puffed</u> and finally got up the steep hill.

   (A) doll up   (B) get a grip
   (C) breath very hard   (D) egg on

   어휘 **doll up** 잘 차려입다 / **get a grip** 자제하다 / **egg on** 부추기다

   해석 그는 숨을 헐떡이며 마침내 가파른 언덕을 올라갔다.

---

170. She is good looking piece of <u>cheese cake</u>.

   (A) beefcake   (B) wild card
   (C) beer belly   (D) pin-up girl

   어휘 **cheese cake** 매력적인 여자 / **beefcake** 근육질의 남자 / **wild card** 예측
     할 수 없는 사람 / **beer belly** 불룩 나온 배 / **pin-up girl** 매력적인 여자

   해석 그녀는 멋진 외모를 가진 벽걸이 모델 같은 여자다.

---

171. Tom can repair car engines. He knows the <u>tricks of the trade</u>.

   (A) all the skills   (B) at pains
   (C) bad apple   (D) poker face

   어휘 **tricks of the trade** 필요한 모든 기술과 지식 / **at pains** ~를 위해 애쓰는
    / **bad apple** 눈엣가시 / **poker face** 무표정한 얼굴

   해석 탐은 자동차 엔진을 고칠 줄 안다. 그는 필요한 기술과 지식을 갖추고 있다.

172. It's about time we looked at the crux of the matter.

(A) brown noser   (B) channel surf

(C) ball of fire   (D) central issue

어휘 **brown noser** 아첨꾼 / **channel surf** TV채널을 계속 바꾸기 / **ball of fire** 적극적이고 능력 있는 사람

해석 이제 우리가 중심 안건을 다룰 때가 되었다.

---

173. She can't live without her parents. She is a clinging vine.

(A) cock of the walk   (B) deadbeat

(C) dependent person   (D) cold fish

어휘 **cock of the walk** 자기가 제일 잘났다고 여기는 사람 / **deadbeat** 게으름뱅이 / **cold fish** 쌀쌀 맞은 사람

해석 그녀는 부모 없이 살아갈 수 없다. 그녀는 아주 의존적인 사람이다.

---

174. My mom thinks my boy friend has a good company manners.

(A) common manners   (B) best manner

(C) singular manner   (D) cold manner

어휘 **common manners** 버릇없는 매너 / **best manner** 훌륭한 매너 / **singular manner** 독특한 방식 / **cold manner** 차가운 매너

해석 우리 엄마는 내 남자친구가 훌륭한 매너를 가졌다고 생각한다.

Day
29

871 weak as a kitten

:: 기력이 전혀 없는

↳ extremely weak

Q Was Jane good at hiking?
제인은 등산을 잘했니?

A No, after an hour, she was as weak as a kitten.
아니, 한 시간 지나니까 맥이 하나도 없어보였어.

872 play the field

:: 여러 다리 걸치다

↳ date many different persons

Q What do you think of that guy at the bar who asked me out?
바에서 내게 데이트 신청한 사람 어떻게 생각하니?

A I don't think he cares for you, I think he's playing the fields.
난 그가 너를 좋아한다고 생각지 않아. 그는 여러 사람을 만나고 있는 것 같아.

873 beat it

:: 나가! 꺼져!

↳ get out; go away

Q Sorry. I broke your camera.
미안해요. 제가 당신 카메라를 망가뜨렸어요.

A Get out of here! Beat it!
나가버려! 꺼져!

between jobs :: 실직 중인

↳ unemployed

Q Tell me about your current position.
당신의 현재 처지를 말해보세요.

A I'm between jobs right now.
현재 실직 중입니다.

pop the question :: 청혼하다

↳ propose to marry

Q When are you going to ask her to marry you?
너 언제 그녀에게 결혼하자고 말할거야?

A I will pop the question tonight.
오늘밤에 청혼할거야.

potluck :: 각자 음식을 준비하여 먹는

↳ with dishes of food brought by different people

Q What are we going to eat at the church dinner?
교회 저녁식사 때 뭘 먹지?

A It's potluck, you can eat whatever you find.
각자 음식을 준비하는 파티야. 뭐든 있는 대로 먹을 수 있어.

mountain dew :: 밀주

↳ illegal liquor

Q Frank, do you want to come over and try some mountain dew?
프랭크, 놀러 와서 밀주 맛 좀 볼래?

A Did you really make your own liquor?
네가 정말 밀주를 빚었니?

Day
30

878 **at arm's length**   :: 거리를 두고

↳ at a distance

Q Do you still keep in touch with your friend, Jack?
너 여전히 친구 잭과 연락하니?

A Occasionally, I am trying to keep him at arm's length.
가끔이야, 그와 거리를 두려고 해.

879 **beef up**   :: 강화하다

↳ strengthen

Q What do you think of my proposal?
넌 내 제안에 대해 어떻게 생각하니?

A I think you should beef up the cost benefit discussion.
내 생각엔 네가 비용상의 이점을 강조해야해.

880 **cold shoulder**   :: 차갑게 대함

↳ intentionally ignore someone

Q Did you talk to Julie this morning?
너 오늘 아침에 줄리와 얘기했니?

A No. I tried but she gave me the cold shoulder.
아니. 그러고 싶었는데 내게 아는 척도 안하더라.

881 **shot in the arm**   :: 활력제

↳ something motivational

Q After the injured player ran back onto the field, the team played great.
부상 선수가 경기장에 복귀하고 나서 그 팀이 선전했어.

A His return was a shot in the arm.
그의 복귀가 활력소가 된거야.

walk on air :: 날아갈 듯한 기분

↳ self-contented

Q She seems very happy.
그녀는 매우 행복해 보여.

A Ever since her marriage she has been walking on air.
결혼한 이후론 날아갈 듯한 기분이잖아.

charley horse :: 쥐, 근육경련

↳ severe pain where the muscle becomes tight

Q Why are you limping?
왜 다리를 저니?

A I have a charley horse.
쥐가 났어.

go south :: 악화되다

↳ become worse

Q How did he react to losing his wife?
부인을 잃은 후 그는 어떠니?

A His health went steadily south.
건강이 점점 악화되고 있어.

cry uncle :: 항복하다

↳ admit defeat

Q Do you want to continue playing chess?
체스 계속 둘 거니?

A No, I don't think I can win. I'm crying uncle now.
아니, 승산이 없어. 이제 졌다.

Day

30

886 have a big mouth

:: 말이 많은, 입이 가벼운

↳ talkative, unable to keep a secret

Q Does he always talk this much?
그는 항상 말이 많니?

A Yes, he has a big mouth.
응, 아주 수다스러워.

887 hotdog

:: 잘난 체하는 사람

↳ one who acts to impress others

Q Why does he like such dangerous sports?
그는 왜 위험한 그런 스포츠를 좋아하지?

A He's a hotdog and wants to show off.
잘난 체하는 사람이라서 과시하고 싶어해.

888 on the level

:: 정직한

↳ honest or legitimate

Q Are they on the level?
그들은 정직하니?

A Yes, they've always been trustworthy.
응, 항상 믿을만 했어.

889 stick something out

:: 끝까지 참고 견디다

↳ endure something unpleasant

Q I don't want to learn how to swim. I'm going to cancel the remaining classes.
난 수영 배우기 싫어. 남은 강의를 취소할 거야.

A You will be glad if you stick it out.
끝까지 견디면 만족할 거야.

birthday suit

:: 알몸

↳ naked

Q Why didn't you open the door quickly?
왜 문을 빨리 안 열었니?

A I was in my birthday suit when you knocked.
네가 노크할 때 내가 알몸이었거든.

good Samaritan

:: 자선을 행하는 사람

↳ one who helps others

Q Did you have to change your car's flat tire?
펑크난 타이어를 바꿔야 했니?

A No, a good Samaritan stopped and did it for me.
아니, 고마운 분이 멈춰서 대신 해줬어.

fair weather friend

:: 잘 나갈 때만 친구인 사람

↳ a friend only in good times

Q Do you still keep in touch with Paul?
여전히 폴과 연락하니?

A No, not after he ignored me when I needed his help. He
is a fair weather friend.
아니, 내가 필요할 때 모른 척 한 이후론 안 해. 좋을 때만 친구인 놈이야.

man of the hour

:: 이 순간 가장 중요한 사람

↳ the most important person at this time

Q They are about to announce the new President.
곧 신임 대통령을 발표할 거야.

A Who do you think will be the man of the hour?
넌 누가 가장 중요한 인물이 될 거라고 생각하니?

Day

30

hot shot :: 매우 성공한 사람

↳ one who is very successful

Q I gather Scott gets promoted faster than most employees.
난 스콧이 대부분의 사원들보다 빨리 승진했다고 생각해.

A He is a hot shot in our company.
그는 회사에서 크게 성공한 사람이야.

beat a dead horse :: 끝난 일로 시간을 낭비하다

↳ waste one's time on an issue that has been decided

Q Mary has been complaining about the court decision.
메리는 법정판결에 계속 불평하고 있어.

A Doesn't she know she is beating a dead horse?
죽은 말 채찍질하기라는 걸 왜 모를까?

cuckoo :: 정신 나간, 멍청이

↳ crazy, stupid

Q Did you see his pierced tongue?
그의 혀에 한 피어스 봤니?

A I think he is cuckoo.
내 생각에 그는 미쳤어.

fit as a fiddle :: 건강이 아주 좋은

↳ very healthy

Q How was your operation? Successful?
수술은 어땠니? 성공적이야?

A Yep. I am fit as a fiddle.
응. 아주 상태가 좋아.

898 on cloud nine

:: 날아갈 듯 행복한

↳ very happy

Q How did you feel when you first saw your baby?
첫 애를 봤을 때 기분이 어땠어?

A I was on cloud nine.
구름 위에 뜬 기분이었지.

899 matter of fact

:: 사무적인 태도

↳ showing little emotion

Q Was he happy to win?
그가 이겨서 행복해하던?

A No. He was matter of fact when he told me.
아니. 내게 말할 때 무덤덤한 태도였어.

900 have the guts

:: 배짱이 있다

↳ have the courage to do something

Q Why don't you go rock-climbing with us?
우리하고 암벽등반 갈래?

A I don't have the guts to do that.
난 그럴 배짱이 없어.

Day

30

307

175. Bill can be regarded stupid but in fact he is <u>crazy like a fox</u>.
 (A) finicky　　　　　(B) very angry
 (C) very cunning　　(D) beside oneself

 어휘 finicky 까다로운 / angry 화가 난 / cunning 교활한, 영리한 / beside oneself 이성을 잃은
 해석 빌은 어리석다고 여겨질 수도 있지만 실은 매우 영리하다.

176. Where do you <u>hail from</u>?
 (A) come originally from　(B) come on strong
 (C) carry away　　　　　(D) change one's tune

 어휘 hail from 본래 ~출신이다 / come on strong 공격적인, 고집센 / carry away 과민반응하다 / change one's tune 의견을 바꾸다
 해석 어디 출신이세요?

177. She always <u>bows and scrapes</u> to him.
 (A) blow one's own horn　(B) last long
 (C) behave obediently　　(D) act foolishly

 어휘 blow one's own horn 자화자찬하다 / last long 오래 지속되다 / behave obediently 순종적으로 행동하다 / act foolishly 어리석게 굴다
 해석 그녀는 언제나 그에게 순종적이다.

178. She has a <u>heart of gold</u> and is always helping people.

(A) heart of stone   (B) high-handed

(C) hotheaded   (D) generous

어휘 **heart of stone** 냉혹한 사람 / **high-handed** 거만한 / **hotheaded** 성마른 / **generous** 관대한

해석 그녀는 인정이 많아서 늘 남을 도와준다.

---

179. She <u>chickened out</u> just before getting on the plane.

(A) cheer up   (B) charge up

(C) withdraw due to fear   (D) cheese off

어휘 **cheer up** 기운나게 하다 / **charge up** 격려하다 / **withdraw due to fear** 두려워서 포기하다 / **cheese off** 화나게 하다

해석 그녀는 비행기에 올라타기 전에 무서워서 포기하고 말았다.

---

180. For a year I was so bored I was <u>climbing the walls</u>.

(A) calm down   (B) choke up

(C) crazy out   (D) extremely bored

어휘 **calm down** 진정하다 / **choke up** 목이 메게 하다 / **crazy out** ~을 너무 좋아하는 / **climb the walls** 극도로 심심한, 흥분된

해석 1년 동안 너무 심심해서 죽는 줄 알았다.

Answers ★ 175.(C) 176.(A) 177.(C) 178.(D) 179.(C) 180.(D)

PART 2

각종 시험 대비
기출 숙어 사전

□ **abandon** [əbǽndən]　　★ ★ ★ ★ ★

● abandon A for B B를 위해 A를 포기하다

He *abandoned* law *for* art.

그는 예술을 위해 법학을 포기하였다.

A

● abandon A to B A를 B에게 의탁하다

He *abandoned* her *to* the control of his mother.

그는 그녀를 그의 어머니 관리에 내맡겼다.

● abandon oneself to ~에 빠지다

He *abandoned himself to* drinking.

그는 술에 빠져버렸다.

□ **abbreviate** [əbríːvièit]　　★ ☆ ☆ ☆ ☆

● abbreviate A to B A를 B로 줄여 쓰다

They *abbreviate* "United Nations" *to* "UN".

'국제연합'은 'UN'으로 줄여 쓴다.

□ **abide** [əbáid]　　★ ☆ ☆ ☆ ☆

● abide by ~을 준수하다, 지키다(=keep)

You must *abide by* your promise.

약속은 반드시 지켜야 한다.

□ **accommodate** [əkάmədèit]　　★ ★ ☆ ☆ ☆

● accommodate oneself to ~에 순응하다

You must *accommodate yourself to* your new circumstances.

당신은 새로운 환경에 적응해야 한다.

● accommodate ~ with 친절을 베풀다, 공급하다

He kindly *accommodate* us *with* a night's lodging.

그는 고맙게도 우리에게 하루의 숙박을 제공해주었다.

☐ **accord** [əkɔ́ːrd] ★ ★ ★ ☆ ☆

- accord A to B B(사람)에게 A(사물)를 수여하다, 주다

  They *accorded* a warm welcome *to* the traveler.
  그들은 여행자를 따뜻하게 맞아들였다.

☐ **account** [əkáunt] ★ ★ ★ ☆ ☆

- account for 해명하다, 설명하다(=explain)

  That *accounts for* his absence.
  그것으로 그의 결석 이유를 알았다.

  There is no *accounting for* tastes.
  좋고 싫은 데는 이유가 없다.(각인각색)

☐ **accuse** [əkjúːz] ★ ★ ★ ☆ ☆

- accuse A of B A(사람)를 B(사물)로 고발하다, 비난하다

  She *accused* him *of* theft.
  그녀는 그 사내를 절도죄로 고발하였다.

  They *accused* him *of* cowardice.
  사람들은 그를 겁쟁이라고 비난하였다.

☐ **accustom** [əkʌ́stəm] ★ ★ ★ ★ ☆

- accustom A to B A(사람)를 B(사물)에 익숙하게 하다

  He *accustomed* his children *to* the cold in the land.
  그는 자식들을 그곳의 추위에 익숙하게 하였다.

- accustom oneself to A A에 익숙해지다

  Accustom yourself to getting up early.
  일찍 기상하는 습관을 들여라.

□ **ache** [eik] ★☆☆☆☆

- **ache for** 갈망하다(=be eager for)

  They *ache for* freedom.

  그들은 자유를 갈망한다.

□ **acquaint** [əkwéint] ★★★☆☆

- **acquaint A with B** A(사람)에게 B(사물)를 알리다

  Acquaint him *with* your intention.

  네 의향을 그에게 알려주어라.

- **acquaint oneself with A** A에 정통하다

  You must *acquaint yourself with* your job.

  자기 일에 정통하여야 한다.

□ **acquit** [əkwít] ★☆☆☆☆

- **acquit ~ of** 무죄로 하다, 방면하다, 해제하다

  The jury *acquitted* him *of* any guilt in the matter.

  배심원은 그를 그 일에 있어 무죄라고 석방했다.

□ **act** [ækt] ★★★★☆

- **act on(upon)** 작용하다(약이 듣다), ~에 따르다(=follow)

  This drug *act on* the stomach.

  이 약은 위장에 잘 듣는다.

  He *acted on* his own belief.

  그는 자신의 신념에 따라 행동하였다.

□ **adapt** [ədǽpt]   ★ ★ ★ ★ ☆

- adapt A from B B를 A로 개조하다

  He *adapted* the play *from* a novel.

  그는 소설을 희곡으로 개작하였다.

- adapt oneself to A A에 적응하다

  He quickly *adapted himself to* the new circumstances.

  그는 재빨리 새로운 환경에 적응하였다.

- adapt A to B A를 B에 적응시키다

  He *adapted* his plan *to* the new situations.

  그는 자신의 계획을 새로운 상황에 맞추었다.

□ **add** [æd]   ★ ★ ★ ★ ☆

- add A to B A를 B에 덧붙이다, 부가하다

  The teacher *added* another example *to* his explanation.

  선생님께서는 그의 설명에 다른 보기를 덧붙였다.

- add up to 결국 ~이 되다, ~을 뜻하다(=mean)

  That's all that this *adds up to*.

  요컨대 그렇게 된다.

□ **address** [ədrés]   ★ ★ ☆ ☆ ☆

- address oneself to A A에게 말을 걸다

  He *addressed himself to* the chairman.

  그는 의장에게 발언하였다.

□ **adhere** [ædhíər, ədhíər]   ★ ★ ☆ ☆ ☆

- adhere to 들러붙다, 집착(신봉)하다

  I *adhere to* my resolution.

  나는 결심을 굽히지 않는다.

314

□ **adjust** [ədʒʌ́st] ★★★☆☆

• **adjust oneself to A** A에 순응하다

The body *adjusts itself to* changes of temperature.
인체는 온도의 변화에 순응한다.

• **adjust A to B** A를 B에 맞추다, 조정하다

She *adjusted* the seat *to* the height of her child.
그녀는 아이의 키에 맞도록 의자를 조절해 주었다.

□ **admonish** [ædmɑ́niʃ] ★☆☆☆☆

• **admonish A of B** A(사람)에게 B(사물)를 알리다

I *admonished* him *of* the danger.
나는 그에게 그 위험성을 경고하였다.

Teacher *admonished* him *of* his fault.
선생님은 그의 잘못을 일깨웠다.

□ **adore** [ədɔ́ːr] ★☆☆☆☆

• **adore A as B** A를 B로 받들다

They *adored* her *as* a living goddess.
그들은 그녀를 살아 있는 여신으로 경모했다.

□ **advance** [ædvǽns] ★★★☆☆

• **advance A to B** A를 B에 빌려주다, 선불하다

They seldom *advance* wages *to* any of the workers.
회사에서는 종업원에게 임금 가불을 좀처럼 해주지 않는다.

A

□ **advise** [ædváiz] ★★★☆☆

· ● advise A of B A(사람)에게 B(사물)를 통지하다
Please *advise* us *of* the date.
그 날짜를 통지해 주십시오.

□ **afflict** [əflíkt] ★☆☆☆☆

● afflict ~ with 괴롭히다(=distress)
I don't want to *afflict* you *with* my trouble.
나는 나의 문제로 당신을 괴롭히기는 싫다.

□ **agree** [əgríː] ★★★★★

● agree to A A(사물)에 동의하다
I *agreed to* the proposal.
나는 그 제안에 동의하였다.

● agree with A A(사람)와 의견이 일치하다
I *agree with* you in all your views.
당신의 모든 의견에 찬성합니다.

□ **allow** [əláu] ★★★★☆

● allow A B A(사람)에게 B를 주다
He *allowed* her 100 dollars a week.
그는 그녀에게 매주 100달러를 주었다.

● allow A to+V A가 ~하도록 허락하다
I can't *allow* you *to* behave like that.
나는 네가 그렇게 행동하는 걸 허락할 수 없다.

□ **alternate** [ɔ́ːltərnèit]   ★ ★ ☆ ☆ ☆

- **alternate with** ~와 교대되다
  Days *alternate with* nights.
  낮과 밤은 번갈아 온다.

□ **amount** [əmáunt]   ★ ★ ☆ ☆ ☆

- **amount to A** A에 달하다, A가 되다
  His debts *amounted to* a thousand dollars.
  그의 빚은 천 달러에 달했다.

  This answer *amounts to* a refusal.
  이 답변은 거절이나 다름없다.

□ **annoy** [ənɔ́i]   ★ ★ ★ ☆ ☆

- **annoy ~ with** 귀찮게 굴다, 애타게 하다, 괴롭히다
  Pardon me for *annoying* you *with* such a trifle.
  이런 사소한 일로 당신을 괴롭힌 것을 용서 바랍니다.

□ **announce** [ənáuns]   ★ ★ ☆ ☆ ☆

- **announce A to B** A(사물)를 B(사람)에게 알리다
  They *announced* his death *to* only some friends.
  그들은 그의 죽음을 몇몇 친구에게만 알렸다.

□ **answer** [ǽnsər]   ★ ★ ★ ★ ☆

- **answer for A** A를 책임지다, 보증하다
  I *answered for* his honesty.
  나는 그의 정직함을 보증하였다.

- **answer to A** A에 부합하다

  The features *answered to* the description.

  얼굴 생김새가 묘사와 부합했다.

☐ **appeal** [əpíːl] ★☆☆☆☆

- **appeal to A for B** A(사람)에게 B를 간청하다

  He *appealed to* us *for* support.

  그는 우리에게 후원을 간청했다.

☐ **apply** [əplái] ★★★★★

- **apply for** 신청하다, 응모하다

  Many persons *applied for* the job.

  상당수가 그 직종에 응모했다.

- **apply oneself to** ~에 전념하다

  He *applied himself to* learning English.

  그는 영어 학습에 열중하였다.

- **apply A to B** A를 B에 적용·응용하다

  They *apply* atomic energy *to* navigation.

  사람들은 원자력을 항해에 응용한다.

  This rule does not *apply to* children.

  이 규칙은 어린이들에게 해당되지 않는다.

☐ **approximate** [əpráksəmət] ★★☆☆☆

- **approximate to** ~에 가깝다

  His account for that affair *approximated to* the truth.

  사건에 대한 그의 설명은 사실에 가까웠다.

□ **argue** [ɑ́ːrgjuː] ★★☆☆☆

• **argue ~ into** 남을 설득하여 ~을 시키다, 단념시키다

I *argued* him *into* going abroad.

나는 그를 설득하여 외국에 가게 했다.

□ **arise** [əráiz] ★☆☆☆☆

• **arise from** ~로부터 일어나다

Accidents *arise from* carelessness.

사고는 부주의에서 생긴다.

□ **ascribe** [əskráib] ★★★☆☆

• **ascribe A to B** A를 B의 탓으로 돌리다

He *ascribed* his failure *to* bad luck.

그는 자신의 실패를 불운 탓으로 돌렸다.

□ **ask** [æsk] ★★★★★

• **ask after** ~의 안부를 묻다(=inquire after)

He *asked after* her.

그는 그녀에게 안부를 물었다.

• **ask A for B** A에게 B를 청하다

He *asked* her *for* some money.

그는 그녀에게 약간의 돈을 요구했다.

• **ask A of B** B에게 A를 묻다, 부탁하다

I *asked* a question *of* him.

나는 그에게 질문을 했다.

I wish to *ask* a favor *of* you.

자네에게 부탁이 하나 있네.

319

- **ask A to B** A를 B에 초대하다

  I *asked* them *to* the party.

  나는 그들을 파티에 초대했다.

- **for the asking** 소원대로

  You can have the sample *for the asking*.

  신청하시는 대로 견본을 가져가실 수 있습니다.

☐ **assent** [əsént]   ★ ★ ☆ ☆ ☆

- **assent to** ~에 동의·찬성하다

  He *assented to* my proposal.

  그는 내 제안에 찬성했다.

☐ **assign** [əsáin]   ★ ★ ☆ ☆ ☆

- **assign A B** A에게 B를 할당하다

  They *assigned* him the work.

  그들은 그에게 작업을 할당했다.

- **assign A to B** A를 B에 임명, 발령하다

  He was *assigned to* the laboratory.

  그는 실험실로 발령받았다.

☐ **associate** [əsóuʃièit]   ★ ★ ★ ☆ ☆

- **associate A with B** A로 B를 연상하다

  We *associate* giving presents *with* Christmas.

  선물주기하면 크리스마스를 연상하게 된다.

- **associate with** ~와 관계·제휴하다

  Then I was *associated with* him.

  당시 나는 그와 제휴하고 있었다.

☐ **assure** [əʃúər]　　　　　　　　★ ★ ☆ ☆ ☆

- assure A of B A(사람)에게 B를 보증·확약하다
  He *assured* me *of* his assistance.
  그는 나를 돕겠다고 확약했다.

☐ **atone** [ətóun]　　　　　　　　★ ☆ ☆ ☆ ☆

- atone for 보상·배상하다, 속죄하다
  He *atoned for* the wrong he had done.
  그는 자신이 저지른 잘못의 대가를 치렀다.

☐ **attach** [ətǽtʃ]　　　　　　　　★ ☆ ☆ ☆ ☆

- attach oneself to ~에 소속·배속시키다
  He first *attached himself to* the Liberals.
  그는 처음엔 민주당원이었다.

☐ **attain** [ətéin]　　　　　　　　★ ★ ☆ ☆ ☆

- attain to ~에 도달하다, ~이 되다
  At last he *attained to* a position of great influence.
  드디어 그는 크게 영향력 있는 위치에 이르렀다.

☐ **attend** [əténd]　　　　　　　　★ ★ ★ ★ ☆

- attend 참석·출석하다(=be present at)
  He *attends* school regularly.
  그는 학교에 어김없이 출석한다.

- attend on 시중들다, 간호하다(=wait on)
  She had three servants *attending on* her.
  그녀는 하인 세 사람의 시중을 받고 있었다.

- **attend to** 주의하다, 힘쓰다(=pay attention to)
  Attend to your teacher.
  선생님 말씀을 잘 들어라.

☐ **attribute** [ətríbjuːt]   ★ ★ ★ ☆ ☆

- **attribute A to B** A를 B에 돌리다(=ascribe A to B)
  He *attributed* his success *to* hard work.
  그는 자신의 성공을 노력 탓으로 돌렸다.

☐ **avail** [əvéil]   ★ ☆ ☆ ☆ ☆

- **avail oneself of** ~을 이용하다
  We should *avail ourselves of* this opportunity.
  우리는 이 기회를 이용하여야 한다.

☐ **avenge** [əvéndʒ]   ★ ★ ☆ ☆ ☆

- **avenge ~ on** 복수하다, 원수를 갚다, 앙갚음을 하다
  I *avenged* an insult *on* him.
  나는 그의 모욕에 대해 복수했다.

☐ **banish** [bǽniʃ]   ★ ★ ☆ ☆ ☆

- **banish A from B** A를 B에서 추방하다
  The king *banished* him *from* his country.
  왕은 그를 국외로 추방하였다.

☐ **bargain** [báːrgən]   ★ ☆ ☆ ☆ ☆

- **bargain for** 예상하다, 기대하다
  I didn't *bargain for* that.
  그것은 뜻밖의 일이었다.

□ **base** [beis] ★ ★ ★ ☆ ☆

• base A on(upon) B A의 근거·기초를 B에 두다, 입각하다

He *based* his opinion *on* facts.
그는 자기 견해의 근거를 사실에 두었다.

□ **be** [bi;/bi] ★ ★ ★ ★ ☆ **A / B**

• be above ~ing ~를 넘어서다, 초월하다

He *is above telling* lies.
그는 거짓말할 사람이 아니다.

• be for ~에 찬성하다(↔be against)

He must *be for* my plan.
그는 반드시 내 계획에 찬성할 것이다.

• be up to ~에 책임이 있다

It'*s up to* you.
너에게 달렸다.

□ **bear** [bɛər] ★ ★ ★ ★ ★

• bear in mind 명심하다, 유의하다

Bear in mind what I said.
내가 한 말을 명심해라.

• bear oneself 행동하다(=behave)

He *bears himself* well under difficult circumstances.
그는 어려운 상황 아래 훌륭하게 행동하고 있다.

□ **beat** [biːt] ★ ★ ☆ ☆ ☆

• beat about(around) the bush 핵심을 벗어나다

Please don't *beat about the bush*, telling me the exact point.
핵심을 벗어나지 말고, 요점만 말해주시오.

□ **become** [bikʌm] ★★★☆☆

- become 어울리다, 잘 맞다(=fit well)

  It does not *become* you to complain.

  불평을 다 하다니, 너답지 않구나.

- become of (의문사 what이 주어) ~이 어떻게 되다

  What has *become of* him?

  그는 어떻게 되었을까?

□ **beg** [beg] ★★☆☆☆

- beg for 간청하다, 애원하다(=ask for)

  He *begged for* mercy.

  그는 자비를 간청했다.

□ **begin** [bigín] ★★★★☆

- begin with ~로 시작되다(=start with)

  The concert *began with* a piano solo.

  그 음악회는 피아노 독주로 시작되었다.

□ **beguile** [bigáil] ★☆☆☆☆

- beguile~with (어린애 따위를) 즐겁게 하다, 지루함을 달래다

  We *beguiled* the children *with* fairy tales.

  우리는 옛날 이야기로 애들을 즐겁게 해주었다.

□ **behave** [bihéiv] ★☆☆☆☆

- behave oneself 얌전하게 행동하다

  Behave yourself.

  얌전하게 굴어라.

□ **believe** [bilíːv]　　　　　　　★★★☆☆

- **believe in** 존재·인격·가치를 신뢰하다

  I *believe in* you.
  난 네 인격을 믿는다.

□ **bell** [bel]　　　　　　　★☆☆☆☆

- **bell the cat** 고양이 목에 방울을 달다, 위험한 일을 떠맡다

  Who will *bell the cat*?
  과연 누가 위험을 무릅쓰고 나서겠는가?

□ **belong** [bilɔ́ːŋ]　　　　　　　★★★☆☆

- **belong to** ~의 소유이다, ~에 속하다(=be the property of)

  Man *belongs to* the great group of animals called "mammals."
  인간은 '포유동물'이라는 대집단에 속한다.

□ **bestow** [bistóu]　　　　　　　★★☆☆☆

- **bestow A on B** B(사람)에게 A(사물)를 주다, 수여하다

  He *bestowed* many favors *on* me.
  그는 내게 많은 호의를 베풀었다.

  He *bestowed* millions *on* many charities.
  그는 수백만을 자선사업에 증여하였다.

□ **bet** [bet]　　　　　　　★★☆☆☆

- **bet A on B** B에 A를 걸다

  He has *bet* 20 dollars *on* the horse.
  그는 20달러를 그 말에 걸었다.

□ **betray** [bitréi]   ★☆☆☆☆

- **betray A to B** A를 B에게 팔다
  The traitor *betrayed* his country *to* the enemy.
  반역자는 조국을 적에게 팔아넘겼다.

□ **beware** [biwέər]   ★★☆☆☆

- **beware of** ~을 조심하다, 경계하다
  Beware of the dog.
  개조심.

□ **bind** [baind]   ★☆☆☆☆

- **bind oneself to + V** ~할 것을 맹세하다, 보증하다
  He has *bound himself to* keep the secret.
  그는 비밀을 지키겠다고 맹세하였다.

□ **blame** [bleim]   ★★★★☆

- **blame A for B** A를 B로 비난하다
  He will *blame* you *for* neglecting your duty.
  그는 직무태만이라고 너를 책할 것이다.

- **blame ~ on** (죄과를 남에게) 돌리다, ~의 탓으로 하다
  He *blamed* his failure *on* his teacher.
  그는 그의 잘못을 선생 때문이라고 비난했다.

□ **bless** [bles]   ★★☆☆☆

- **bless ~ with** 은총을 베풀다, 축복하다, 구하다
  God *blessed* him *with* good health.
  신은 그에게 좋은 건강을 베풀었다.

□ **border** [bɔ́ːrdər]   ★ ☆ ☆ ☆ ☆

• **border on** ~에 인접하다

  Wales *borders on* England.
  웨일즈는 잉글랜드와 인접하고 있다.

  His humor *borders on* the farcical.
  그의 유머는 어릿광대극 같다.

□ **break** [breik]   ★ ★ ★ ★ ★

• **break one's word(promise)** 약속을 어기다

  He never *breaks his promise*.
  그는 결코 약속을 어기지 않는다.

• **break out** 일어나다(=occur suddenly)

  I hope war will not *break out*.
  전쟁이 일어나지 않기를 바란다.

• **break up** 해산시키다(=disperse, scatter)

  The police *broke up* the meeting.
  경찰은 집회를 해산시켰다.

□ **bring** [briŋ]   ★ ★ ★ ★ ★

• **bring about** 야기하다, 초래하다(=cause to happen)

  Misunderstanding will often *bring about* a quarrel.
  오해는 종종 싸움을 불러일으킨다.

• **bring back** 회상시키다, 회복시키다

  The picture *brought back* a lot of memories to me.
  그 사진은 나에게 여러 가지 추억을 회상시켰다.

  The change of air *brought* him *back* to health.
  전지 요양으로 그는 건강을 회복하였다.

- **bring down** 내리다, 쓰러뜨리다

  The good harvest *brought down* the price of rice.

  풍작은 쌀값을 하락시켰다.

- **bring forth** 낳다, 생기게 하다

  March winds and April showers *bring forth* May flowers.

  3월의 바람과 4월의 비는 5월의 꽃을 피게 한다.

- **bring forward** 제출하다(=present)

  Bring forward a case for comparison.

  비교를 위하여 일례를 들라.

- **bring home to** 절실히 느끼게 하다

  Her death *brought home to* me the very sorrow of life.

  그녀의 죽음은 인생의 슬픔을 절실히 느끼게 했다.

- **bring in** 가져오다, 초래하다(=produce)

  The disposal of the property will *bring* him *in* several thousand dollars.

  재산을 처분하면 그에게는 수천 달러의 돈이 들어올 것이다.

- **bring off** 딴 데로 옮기다, 구출하다(=rescue)

  They *brought off* the passengers on the wrecked ship.

  그들은 난파선으로부터 승객을 구출했다.

- **bring out** 내놓다, 세상에 내세우다(=cause to appear)

  He is going to *bring out* a translation of a Korean tale.

  그는 한국의 설화를 번역 출판하려 하고 있다.

- **bring to** 정신차리다(=bring around), 정지시키다

  He tried to *bring* me *to* myself by several means.

  그는 나를 정신차리게 하려고 여러 가지 방법을 다했다.

- **bring oneself to** ~하고픈 기분이 나다

  He could not *bring himself to* tell a lie.

  그는 거짓말할 기분이 아니었다.

- **bring up** 기르다, 양육하다(=raise, rear)

  She has *brought up* seven children.

  그녀는 일곱 자녀를 키웠다.

☐ **build** [bild] ★★☆☆☆

- **build up** 확립하다, 만들다

  The firm has *built up* a wide reputation for fair dealings.

  그 회사는 양심적인 거래로 좋은 평을 널리 얻고 있다.

☐ **bump** [bʌmp] ★☆☆☆☆

- **bump into** 우연히 만나다(=come across)

  I *bumped into* an old friend on my way home.

  나는 귀가길에 옛 친구와 마주쳤다.

☐ **burden** [bə́ːrdn] ★★☆☆☆

- **burden A with B** A(사람)에게 B(사물)를 지게 하다

  He *burdened* himself *with* many packages.

  그는 짐을 잔뜩 가지고 있었다.

☐ **burst** [bəːrst] ★☆☆☆☆

- **burst into** 갑자기 ~하기 시작하다

  She *burst into* tears at the news.

  그녀는 그 소식에 갑자기 울음을 터뜨렸다.

☐ **cake** [keik]   ★ ☆ ☆ ☆ ☆

- **cake with** ~로 굳히다
  The car was *caked with* snow.
  그 자동차에는 눈이 얼어붙어 있었다.

☐ **calculate** [kǽlkjulèit]   ★ ★ ☆ ☆ ☆

- **calculate on** ~을 예상·기대하다
  We can't *calculate on* his help.
  우리는 그의 도움을 기대할 수 없다.

☐ **call** [kɔ:l]   ★ ★ ★ ★ ★

- **call after** ~을 따서 이름 짓다
  He was *called* Henry *after* his grandfather.
  그는 조부의 이름을 따서 헨리라고 불렸다.

- **call at** 방문하다
  I will *call at* his office tomorrow.
  내일 그의 사무실로 방문할 생각이다.

- **call down** 꾸짖다(=reprimand, scold)
  He was *called down* by his boss for coming late.
  그는 지각한 탓으로 사장에게 꾸지람을 들었다.

- **call for** 요구하다(=demand, require), 큰 소리로 부르다
  He *called for* a cup of tea.
  그는 큰 소리로 홍차를 한 잔 달라고 말했다.

- **call forth** (용기 따위를) 불러일으키다(=summon)
  This picture *called forth* her reminiscences.
  이 사진은 그녀에게 여러 가지 추억을 불러 일으켰다.

- **call in** 불러들이다, 거둬들이다
  The gold coins have been *called in* by the government.
  금화는 정부에 의해 회수되었다.

- **call it a day** 일과를 끝마치다

  Call it a day!

  일과 끝!

- **call on** 방문하다(사람), cf. call at + 장소

  I'll *call on* you tomorrow.

  나는 내일 너를 방문할 것이다.

- **call off** 취소하다(=cancel)

  The party was *called off* because of the rain.

  파티는 우천으로 취소되었다.

- **call to mind** 상기하다(=remember)

  I cannot *call* it *to mind* now.

  지금 그것을 생각해 낼 수가 없다.

☐ **can** [kən; kǽn]   ★ ★ ★ ★ ★

- **can but + V** 오직 ~할뿐이다

  I *can but* try.

  아무튼 해보기나 하자.

- **can not but + V** ~하지 않을 수 없다

  I *can not but* laugh.

  웃을 수밖에 없다.

- **can not ~ too** 아무리 ~해도 지나치지 않다

  You *can not* be *too* diligent.

  아무리 부지런해도 지나치지 않다.

☐ **care** [kεər]   ★ ★ ★ ★ ☆

- **care** 걱정하다

  Although he says nothing, he *cares* a great deal.

  말은 않지만 늘 걱정하고 있다.

- **care for** 좋아하다, 돌보다

  She seemed to *care for* nothing but music.
  그녀는 음악만 좋아하는 것 같았다.

  She *cares for* the sick.
  그녀는 병자를 돌본다.

- **care to do** ~하고파 하다, 탐내다(=like, want)

  I *don't care to* run the risk.
  그 위험한 일을 하고 싶지는 않다.

□ **carry** [kǽri]   ★ ★ ★ ☆ ☆

- **carry on** 계속하다(=continue), 경영하다(=conduct)

  All you have to do is to *carry on* your study.
  당신이 해야 할 전부는 연구를 지속하는 것이다.

  It is not easy to *carry on* business here.
  여기서 장사하기란 쉽지 않다.

- **carry out** 수행하다, 실행하다(=accomplish, execute)

  You must *carry out* your first plan.
  당신은 첫 번째 계획을 수행해야 한다.

□ **catch** [kætʃ]   ★ ★ ★ ★ ★

- **catch at** 달라붙다, 환영하다

  A drowning man will *catch at* a straw.
  물에 빠진 사람은 지푸라기라도 붙잡는다.

- **catch hold of** ~을 붙들다(=seize)

  He *caught hold of* a man by the neck.
  그는 한 사내의 목덜미를 붙들었다.

- **catch in** (폭풍우 등이) 몰려오다

  We were *caught in* a shower.
  우리는 소나기를 만났다.

- **catch on** 히트치다, 인기를 얻다(=take)

  The play caught on well.

  연극은 인기를 얻었다.

- **catch sight of** ~을 발견하다

  I caught sight of him near the school in the morning.

  아침에 학교 근처에서 그를 봤다.

- **catch up with** 따라가다(=come up with)

  He worked hard to catch up with the rest of the class.

  그는 나머지 급우들을 따라잡으려고 열심히 공부했다.

C

□ **center** [séntər]　　★☆☆☆☆

- **center on** ~에 집중시키다

  The hope of his parents was centered on their son.

  양친의 희망은 오로지 아들에게 집중되어 있었다.

□ **certify** [sə́ːrtəfài]　　★☆☆☆☆

- **certify A of B** A(사람)에게 B(사물)를 보증하다

  This does not certify us of the truth of any event in the future.

  이것이 미래의 어떠한 일도 진실임을 우리에게 보증하는 것은 아니다.

□ **chance** [tʃæns]　　★★★☆☆

- **chance on** 우연히 만나다, 발견하다

  There he chanced on a real treasure — a first edition.

  거기서 그는 뜻하지 않게 정말 횡재라고 할 수 있는 초판본을 발견하였다.

□ change [tʃeindʒ] ★★★★☆

- **change A for B** A를 B로 바꾸다
  He *changed* a dollar bill *for* ten dimes.
  그는 1달러 짜리 지폐를 10센트 짜리 은화 10개로 바꾸었다.

- **change for the better(worse)** 호전(악화)되다
  The matter has *changed for the better*.
  사태가 호전되었다.

- **change A into B** A를 B로 변화시키다
  Heat *changes* water *into* steam.
  열은 물을 수증기로 변화시킨다.

- **change A with B** A를 B와 바꾸다
  He *changed* places *with* me.
  그는 나와 자리를 바꿨다.

□ challenge [tʃǽlindʒ] ★☆☆☆☆

- **challenge ~ to** 도전하다, 걸다, 결투를 요구하다
  He *challenged* me *to* a duel.
  그는 나에게 결투하자고 도전하였다.

□ charge [tʃɑːrdʒ] ★★★★☆

- **charge ~ for** (지불을) 부담시키다, 청구하다, 값을 매기다
  I *charged* 2,000 won *for* driving to Seoul station.
  나는 서울역까지 차 삯 2,000원을 요구했다.

- **charge oneself with** ~를 인수하다(=undertake)
  He *charged* himself *with* the task.
  그는 그 일을 인수했다.

☐ **chew** [tʃuː] ★☆☆☆☆

- **chew on(over)** 심사숙고하다(=meditate)

You'd better *chew on* your future.

네 장래에 대해 심사숙고하는 게 좋을게다.

☐ **cling** [kliŋ] ★☆☆☆☆

- **cling to** ~에 밀착하다(=stick to)

Wet clothes *cling to* the body.

젖은 옷은 몸에 착 달라붙는다.

☐ **coincide** [kòuinsáid] ★★☆☆☆

- **coincide with** ~와 일치하다

Her ideas *coincide with* mine.

그녀의 생각은 내 생각과 같다.

☐ **collide** [kəláid] ★☆☆☆☆

- **collide with** ~와 충돌하다

The bus *collided with* a truck.

버스는 트럭과 충돌했다.

☐ **combat** [kəmbǽt, kúmbæt] ★☆☆☆☆

- **combat with** ~와 싸우다, 투쟁하다

We *combated with* the enemy for our rights.

우리는 우리의 권리를 위해 적과 투쟁하였다.

C

□ **come** [kʌm]   ★ ★ ★ ★ ★

- **come about** 일어나다(=happen)

    A great change has *come about* after the revolution.
    혁명 후 커다란 변화가 일어났다.

- **come across** 우연히 만나다, 발견하다

    I've never *come across* such a strange event.
    나는 여태껏 이처럼 이상한 사건을 겪어 본 적이 없다.

- **come after** ~에 뒤따르다(=follow)

    Come after me. (= Follow me.)
    나를 따라오세요.

- **come along** 찾아오다

    Come along with me, please.
    따라오세요.

- **come and go** 왔다갔다하다, 변천하다

    Money will *come and go*.
    돈이란 있다가도 없는 것.

- **come around** (계절이) 돌아오다

    The leap year *comes around* once in four years.
    윤년은 4년에 한 번씩 돌아온다.

- **come at** 얻다(=get), ~에 다다르다(=arrive at)

    We prize most those which are hardest to *come at*.
    우리들은 가장 얻기 어려운 것을 가장 소중히 한다.

- **come by** 수중에 넣다(=obtain)

    How did you *come by* such a lot of money?
    그렇게 많은 돈을 어떻게 얻었니?

- **come down** 내리다, 전해지다, 병들다(=become ill)

    He *came down* with malaria while staying in
    Sumatra.
    그는 수마트라 체재 중 말라리아에 걸렸다.

- **come down on** 덤벼들다(=attack),불호령 하다(=scold)

  The enemy *came down on* a sleeping village.

  적은 잠든 마을을 공격했다.

- **come forward** 앞으로 나아가다, 지원하다

  No one *came forward* to help her.

  누구도 그녀를 도와주겠다고 나서는 사람이 없었다.

- **come in** 들어가다, 유행하다(=become fashionable)

  Nylon garments did not *come in* till late.

  나일론 의류는 근래까지 쓰이지 않았다.

  Let us wait here till the train *come in*.

  기차가 닿을 때까지 여기서 기다립시다.

- **come in contact with** ~와 접촉하다

  We must always *come in contact with* new books.

  우리는 늘 새로운 책을 접해야 한다.

- **come from** 원인은 ~이다, 태어난 곳은 ~이다

  I *come from* California.

  나는 캘리포니아 출신이다.

- **come in for** 상속받다

  He will *come in for* a large fortune when his uncle dies.

  그는 아저씨가 돌아가시면 막대한 재산을 상속받게 될 것이다.

- **come into** (장소, 상태에) 들어가다

  A new country *came into* being.

  새로운 국가가 생겼다.

- **come near ~ing** 얼마 안 있어 ~할 참이다

  The boy *came near being* drowned.

  소년은 익사할 뻔했다.

- **come of** ~에서 생기다(=be caused by)

  She *comes of* a good family.

  그녀는 양가의 출신이다.

- **come off** 멀어지다(=leave), 개최되다(=be held)

  The examination *came off* yesterday.
  시험은 어제 실시되었다.

  Won't the color *come off*?
  빛깔이 퇴색하지 않을까?

- **come on** 몰려오다

  A typhoon is *coming on*.
  태풍이 다가온다.

- **come out** 나타나다, ~이 되다

  His new novel will *come out* next month.
  그의 신소설이 다음달 나온다.

  Things have *come out* against us.
  결국 사태는 우리에게 불리하게 되었다.

- **come over** 뒤덮다, 지배하다

  A deep darkness *came over* the land.
  짙은 암흑이 대지를 뒤덮었다.

- **come round** 돌아오다, 회복하다(=recover)

  My birthday will *come round* next Monday.
  내 생일은 내주 월요일에 돌아온다.

- **come through** ~을 뚫고 나아가다(=get over)

  He *came* successful *through* the difficulty.
  훌륭하게 난관을 뚫고 나아갔다.

- **come to nothing** 수포로 돌아가다

  Those efforts have *come to nothing*.
  그런 노력은 허사가 되었다.

- **come to the point** 핵심(본론)으로 들어가다

  Let us now *come to the point* in hand.
  이제 직접 본론으로 들어갑시다.

- **come under** ~의 항목에 들다, 영향(지배)을 받다

  Tea and sugar *come under* the head of groceries.
  차와 설탕은 식품의 부류에 들어간다.

The country *came under* the influence of U.S.S.R.
그 나라는 소련의 영향권에 들어갔다.

- **come up to** ~에 다다르다(=reach)

  He did not *come up to* my expectation.
  내 기대에 어긋났다.

☐ **command** [kəmǽnd]   ★ ☆ ☆ ☆ ☆

- **command a fine view** 전망이 좋다

  This window *commands a fine view*.
  이 창문은 전망이 좋다.

☐ **commend** [kəménd]   ★ ★ ☆ ☆ ☆

- **commend A to B** A를 B에 맡기다, 위탁하다

  He *commended* his children *to* his uncle.
  그는 자식들을 아저씨에게 맡겼다.

☐ **comment** [kάment]   ★ ★ ★ ☆ ☆

- **comment on** ~에 대해 비평·논평하다

  Everyone *commented on* his new poem.
  누구나 입을 모아 그의 신작시를 평했다.

☐ **commit** [kəmít]   ★ ☆ ☆ ☆ ☆

- **commit oneself to** 전력하다

  He *committed himself to* the belief in God.
  그는 신앙에 전념하였다.

□ **communicate** [kəmjúːnəkèit] ★★☆☆☆

- **communicate with** ~와 통신하다, 통하다

  They *communicated with* each other for years.
  그는 수년 동안 서로 연락했다.

  The hall *communicates with* the dining room.
  홀은 식당과 통해 있다.

□ **compare** [kəmpέər] ★★★★☆

- **compare A to B** A를 B에 비유하다, ~에 비기다

  Life is often *compared to* a voyage.
  인생은 흔히 항해에 비유된다.

  Shakespeare *compares* a man's life *to* a brief candle.
  셰익스피어는 인생을 간들거리는 촛불로 비유했다.

- **compare A with B** A를 B와 비교·대조하다

  He *compared* the copy *with* the original.
  그는 사본을 원본과 대조하였다.

□ **compel** [kəmpél] ★★☆☆☆

- **compel A to + V** A를 (강제로) ~하게 하다

  The rain *compelled* us *to* stop the game.
  비 때문에 시합을 중지하지 않을 수 없었다.

□ **compete** [kəmpíːt] ★★☆☆☆

- **compete with** ~와 경쟁하다

  They *competed with* each other for the prize.
  그들은 상을 차지하려고 경쟁했다.

☐ **complain** [kəmpléin]   ★★★☆☆

- complain of ~을 불평·비난하다
  You must not *complain of* your food.
  음식 투정하지 마라.

☐ **compliment** [kάmpləmənt]   ★★☆☆☆

- compliment ~ on 경의를 표하다, 칭찬하다, 알랑거리다
  The academic circles *complimented* him *on* his achievements.
  학계는 그의 공적을 찬양했다.

C

☐ **compromise** [kάmprəmàiz]   ★★★☆☆

- compromise with ~와 타협·화해하다
  We *compromised with* them on the matter.
  우리는 그 일에 대해 그들과 타협하였다.

☐ **confer** [kənfə́:r]   ★★★☆☆

- confer ~ on 수여하다, 주다(=give, grant)
  The university *conferred* an honorary degree *on* the president.
  대학은 대통령에게 명예박사 학위를 수여했다.

☐ **confine** [kənfáin]   ★★☆☆☆

- confine A to B A를 B에 제한하다
  I will *confine* myself *to* making a few remarks.
  몇 마디만 더하고 저는 마치겠습니다.

congratulate [kəngrǽtʃulèit]　★★☆☆☆

- **congratulate A on B** A(사람)에게 B(사물)를 축하하다
  I *congratulate* you *on* your marriage.
  결혼 축하해.

connect [kənékt]　★★★☆☆

- **connect A with B** A를 B와 연결하다
  Doctors *connect* crime *with* insanity.
  의사들은 범죄를 정신병과 연관시킨다.

consent [kənsént]　★★★☆☆

- **consent to** ~을 동의하다, 승낙하다
  Her mother will not *consent to* her going there alone.
  그녀가 거기에 혼자 가는 건 그녀 엄마가 승낙하지 않을 거야.

consist [kənsíst]　★★★★☆

- **consist in** ~에 놓여 있다, 존재하다(=lie in)
  Happiness *consists in* contentment.
  행복은 만족함에 있다.

- **consist of** ~로 구성되다
  Water *consists of* hydrogen and oxygen.
  물은 수소와 산소로 구성된다.

- **consist with** ~와 양립하다, 일치하다
  The story does not *consist with* the evidence.
  이야기는 증거와 부합되지 않는다.

□ **consult** [kənsʌ́lt]　　　　　　　★★★☆☆

● **consult with** ~와 협의하다

You must *consult with* them about the matter.

너는 그 문제에 대해 그들과 협의해야 한다.

□ **contrast** [kəntrǽst]　　　　　　★★☆☆☆

● **contrast with** ~와 대조를 이루다

The white peaks *contrast* finely *with* the blue sky.

흰 봉우리들은 파란 하늘과 좋은 대조를 이루고 있다.

□ **contribute** [kəntríbjuːt]　　　　★★★☆☆

● **contribute A to B** A를 B에게 기증·기부하다

She *contributed* lots of money *to* the hospital.

그녀는 병원에 막대한 돈을 기부했다.

□ **convince** [kənvíns]　　　　　　★★☆☆☆

● **convince A of B** A(사람)에게 B(사물)를 확신시키다

I cannot *convince* him *of* its truth.

나는 그것이 사실이라는 점을 그에게 확신시킬 수 없었다.

● **convince oneself of** ~을 확신하다

He *convinced himself of* her honesty.

그는 그녀의 정직성을 확신했다.

□ **cope** [koup]　　　　　　　　　★☆☆☆☆

● **cope with** ~에 대처하다(=meet)

We cannot *cope with* the present difficulties.

우리는 현 난관을 감당할 수 없다.

□ **count** [kaunt] ★ ★ ☆ ☆ ☆

- **count for** 중요하다, 가치가 있다

  Mere cleverness without sound principles does not *count for* anything.

  건전한 원칙이 없는 현명함은 아무 가치가 없다.

□ **cure** [kjuər] ★ ★ ★ ☆ ☆

- **cure A of B** A(사람)의 B를 고치다

  No medicine can *cure* a man *of* discontent.

  인간의 불만을 고칠 약은 없다.

□ **cut** [kʌt] ★ ★ ★ ★ ☆

- **cut down** 깎아 내리다(=reduce), 베어 넘기다

  However much I *cut down*, I cannot make both ends meet.

  아무리 절약해도 적자가 된다.

- **cut in(into)** ~에 끼어들다

  He suddenly *cut into* our conversation.

  그는 갑자기 우리의 대화에 끼어들었다.

- **cut off** 잘라내다(=sever), 중단하다

  He was *cut off* in early youth.

  그는 젊은 나이로 죽었다.

- **cut out** 도려내다, 제거하다, 예정하다

  She *cut* a picture *out* of a newspaper.

  그녀는 신문의 사진을 도려냈다.

  He is *cut out* for an artist.

  그는 천성이 예술가로 되어 있다.

- **cut up** 찢어버리다, 혹평하다(=criticize severely)

  Her recent novel has been terribly *cut up*.

  그녀의 최근 소설은 혹독한 평을 받았다.

☐ **dare** [dɛər] ★★★☆☆

- **dare to + V** 감히 ~하다

  She *dared to* call on John the next day.

  다음 날 그녀는 감히 존에게 찾아갔다.

☐ **date** [deit] ★☆☆☆☆

- **date from** ~로 거슬러 올라가다

  His house *dates from* the 16th century.

  그의 가게는 16세기로 거슬러 올라간다.

☐ **deal** [diːl] ★★★☆☆

- **deal in** 거래하다(=buy and sell), 종사하다, 관계하다

  He *deals in* politics.

  그는 정치에 관계하고 있다.

- **deal out** 분배하다(=give)

  He is going to *deal out* cards.

  그는 카드를 나눠주려고 하고 있다.

- **deal with** 처리하다, 취급하다(=treat), 상대를 하다

  Teachers should *deal* fairly *with* all their pupils.

  선생은 생도들 전체를 공평하게 대해야 한다.

☐ **decrease** [dikríːs] ★★☆☆☆

- **decrease to** ~로 줄다, 감소하다

  The population of our city has *decreased to* 40,000.

  우리 시 인구는 4만으로 줄었다.

C
D

☐ **dedicate** [dèdikéit]　　　　　　★ ★ ☆ ☆ ☆

• dedicate A to B A를 B에 헌납하다, 헌신하다, 봉사하다

To my wife I *dedicate* this volume in token of affection and gratitude.

내 아내에게 사랑과 감사의 징표로 이 책을 바친다.

He has *dedicated* his life *to* helping the poor.

그는 불쌍한 사람들을 돕는 데 헌신했다.

☐ **deduce** [didjúːs]　　　　　　★ ★ ★ ☆ ☆

• deduce A from B B에서 A를 연역·추론하다

We should learn to *deduce* unknown truths *from* principles alt known.

우리는 이미 알고 있는 원리에서 미지의 진리를 연역하는 법을 배워야 한다.

☐ **defend** [difénd]　　　　　　★ ★ ☆ ☆ ☆

• defend ~ against(from) 막다, 지키다

Defend your country *against* all sorts of invasion.

온갖 침략에 대항하여 너의 나라를 지켜라.

• depend on(upon) ~에 달려 있다

That *depends on* your ability.

그건 네 능력에 달렸다.

☐ **deliver** [dilívər]　　　　　　★ ★ ☆ ☆ ☆

• deliver ~ from 해방하다, 구출하다

The reinforcements *delivered* the city *from* the attacker.

중원부대가 그 도시를 적으로부터 해방시켰다.

☐ **deprive** [dipráiv]　　　　　　　　　★★☆☆☆

- **deprive A of B** A(사람)에게서 B를 빼앗다(=rob A of B)
  The angry people *deprived* the king *of* all his powers.
  분노한 국민들은 왕에게서 모든 권력을 박탈하였다.

☐ **derive** [diráiv]　　　　　　　　　★☆☆☆☆

- **derive from** ~로부터 유래하다
  French and Italian *derive from* Latin.
  불어와 이태리어는 라틴어에서 유래한 것이다.

☐ **despair** [dispέər]　　　　　　　　★★★☆☆

- **despair of** ~을 절망하다
  At last I *despaired of* being rescued.
  결국 나는 구조되리라는 희망을 잃고 말았다.

☐ **deter** [ditə́:r]　　　　　　　　　★☆☆☆☆

- **deter A from B** A(사람)가 B하는 것을 제지하다
  The extreme cold *deterred* him *from* going downtown.
  극도의 추위로 그는 시내에 갈 수 없었다.

☐ **devote** [divóut]　　　　　　　　★★☆☆☆

- **devote A to B** A를 B에 바치다, 충당하다, 맡기다
  He *devotes* all his time *to* studying.
  그는 공부하는데 모든 시간을 바쳤다.

D

die [dai] ★★☆☆☆

- **die from** (상처, 부주의, 부상으로) 사망하다

  Many birds *die from* eating the poisons on fruits and seeds.

  과일이나 씨에 묻은 독약을 먹고 죽는 새가 많다.

- **die of** (병, 기아, 노쇠로) 사망하다

  He *died of* cancer(hunger, old age).

  그는 암으로(굶주림으로, 노환으로) 사망했다.

differ [dífər] ★★★☆☆

- **differ from** ~와 다르다

  I *differ from* him on this problem.

  나는 이 문제에 관해 그와 다르다.

differentiate [dìfərénʃièit] ★☆☆☆☆

- **differentiate A from B** A와 B를 구분하다

  What *differentiates* cheese *from* butter?

  치즈와 버터는 어떻게 다른가?

disagree [dìsəgríː] ★★★☆☆

- **disagree with** 일치하지 않다, 맞지 않다

  The climate *disagrees with* me.

  날씨가 내게 맞지 않는다.

discourage [diskə́ːridʒ] ★☆☆☆☆

- **discourage A from B** A(사람)가 B하는 것을 방해하다

  His friends tried to *discourage* him *from* going there.

  그의 친구들이 그가 거기 가지 못하도록 말렸다.

□ **discriminate** [diskrímənèit]   ★☆☆☆☆

- **discriminate A from B** A를 B와 식별하다

  They cannot *discriminate* liberty *from* license.

  그들은 자유와 방종을 식별할 수 없다.

□ **dismiss** [dismís]   ★★★☆☆

- **dismiss A from B** A(사람)를 B에서 해고하다

  The minister was *dismissed from* the position shortly after the meeting.

  장관은 회의 직후에 직위해제 되었다.

□ **dispense** [dispéns]   ★☆☆☆☆

- **dispense with** ~없이 지내다(=do without)

  We cannot *dispense with* a stove in this cold weather.

  이런 추위에 난로 없이 지낼 수는 없다.

□ **dissuade** [diswéid]   ★☆☆☆☆

- **dissuade ~ from** 그만두게 하다, 단념하게 하다

  I *dissuaded* him *from* marrying her.

  나는 그에게 그녀와 결혼하지 말라고 말렸다.

□ **distinguish** [distíŋgwiʃ]   ★★☆☆☆

- **distinguish A from B** A를 B와 식별하다

  Nowadays it is difficult to *distinguish* man *from* woman by dress.

  요즘엔 옷으로 남녀를 분간하기 힘들다.

D

☐ **distribute** [distríbju:t]   ★ ★ ★ ☆ ☆

- distribute ~ among 나누어주다, 배당하다, 분배하다
  The church *distributed* the alms *among* the poor.
  교회는 구호품을 빈민들에게 배급하였다.

☐ **dive** [daiv]   ★ ★ ☆ ☆ ☆

- dive into 손을 집어넣다, ~에 몰두하다
  Tom *dived into* his pockets and fished out a cent.
  탐은 호주머니에 손을 넣어 1센트를 꺼냈다.

  He has been *diving into* the history of civilization.
  그는 문명사 연구에 전념해 오고 있다.

☐ **divest** [divést]   ★ ☆ ☆ ☆ ☆

- divest ~ of 벗기다, 박탈하다(=deprive), 빼앗다
  They *divested* the aristocrats *of* their property.
  그들은 귀족들이 재산을 몰수했다.

☐ **divide** [diváid]   ★ ★ ☆ ☆ ☆

- divide ~ between 분배하다, 여럿이 나누다
  The two brothers *divided* everything *between* them.
  그 두 형제는 모든 것을 둘이서 나눠가졌다.

☐ **do** [du]   ★ ★ ★ ★ ★

- do away with ~을 없애다, 폐지하다
  This practice should be *done away with*.
  이 관습은 폐지되어야 한다.

- **do by** ~을 (좋게/나쁘게) 대하다

  He *does* well *by* his friends.

  그는 친구들에게 잘 해준다.

- **do the dishes** 설거지하다(=wash)

  Does your father *do the dishes* at your home?

  너희 아버지는 집에서 설거지를 하시니?

- **do well to** ~하는 것이 좋을 것이다(=act wisely)

  You *did well to* follow your doctor's advice.

  의사의 권고에 따른 것이 좋았다.

- **do without** ~없이 지내다(=dispense with)

  I cannot *do without* books.

  책 없이는 못 산다.

☐ **dominate** [dɑ́mənèit]　　　　★☆☆☆☆

- **dominate over** ~을 지배하다

  The strong *dominate over* the weak.

  강자는 약자를 지배한다.

☐ **dose** [dous]　　　　★☆☆☆☆

- **dose A with B** A(사람)에게 B(약물)를 투여하다

  The doctor *dosed* the girl *with* quinine.

  의사는 소녀에게 키니네를 투여하였다.

☐ **dot** [dat]　　　　★☆☆☆☆

- **dot A with B** A를 B로 점재(點在)시키다

  The wind *dotted* the pond *with* hundreds of fallen leaves.

  바람이 불어 연못 위엔 수백의 낙엽이 흩어져 덮여 있었다.

☐ **drain** [drein]   ★☆☆☆☆

- **drain A of B** A에게서 B를 소모시키다, 빼앗다

  The war *drained* the country *of* its people and money.

  전쟁으로 그 나라는 인명과 국고를 소모하였다.

☐ **draw** [drɔ:]   ★★★☆☆

- **draw in** 줄이다, 짧아지다(=get shorter)

  The days begin to *draw in* when November comes.

  11월이 오면 해가 짧아지기 시작한다.

- **draw on** ~에 기대다(=depend on)

  He *draws on* his friend's sympathy.

  친구의 동정에 기대고 있다.

- **draw out** 길어지다, 길게 끌다

  The engagement was long *drawn out*.

  약혼은 자꾸 연기되었다.

- **draw up** 끌어올리다, 차를 세우다, 다가오다

  The car *drew up* at the rear gate.

  차는 뒷문에서 정지했다.

☐ **drop** [drap]   ★★★★☆

- **drop behind** 뒤지다

  Soon he *dropped behind* others.

  곧 그는 일행보다 뒤처져버렸다.

- **drop from** 말이 불쑥 나오다

  The remark *dropped from* him.

  그 말이 그의 입에서 불쑥 튀어 나왔다.

- **drop in** 들르다

  Drop in and have some tea.

  잠깐 들러 차라도 마시렴.

352

- **drop into** ~에 빠지다

  He soon *dropped into* reveries.

  그는 곧 몽상에 빠졌다.

- **drop off** 떠나가다, 잠자리에 들다, 쇠퇴하다

  Sales of some weekly magazines are *dropping off*.

  주간지 중에는 매상이 좋지 않은 것이 있다.

- **drop out of** ~로부터 빠지다, 물러서다(=withdraw from)

  That cinemactress will some day *drop out of* public favour.

  저 여배우도 언젠가는 세상에서 잊혀질 것이다.

□ **dwell** [dwel]　　　★☆☆☆☆

- **dwell on** 곰곰이 생각하다, 상세히 설명하다

  Her mind *dwelt on* the happy days she spent with him.

  그녀는 그와의 행복했던 시절을 곰곰이 회상하였다.

  The old woman *dwelt on* her miserable life.

  그 노파는 불행했던 일생을 장황하게 늘어놓았다.

□ **ease** [iːz]　　　★☆☆☆☆

- **ease A of B** A(사람)에게서 B(물건)를 덜어주다, 빼앗다

  He *eased* me *of* the burden.

  그는 내 짐을 덜어주었다.

  I was *eased of* my wallet.

  나는 지갑을 도둑맞았다.

353

□ **emigrate** [émigrèit] ★ ☆ ☆ ☆ ☆

- **emigrate from A to B** A에서 B로 이민가다
  They *emigrated from* Korea *to* Brazil.
  그들은 한국에서 브라질로 이민을 갔다.

□ **employ** [implɔ́i] ★ ★ ☆ ☆ ☆

- **employ oneself in** ~에 종사하다
  Instead of wasting time, I *employed myself in* reading.
  허송세월 하는 대신에, 나는 독서에 열중하였다.

□ **end** [end] ★ ★ ★ ☆ ☆

- **end in** (결과적으로) ~으로 끝나다
  Our enterprise *ended in* failure.
  우리 사업은 실패로 끝났다.

- **end with** ~으로 끝맺다
  The concert *ended with* the playing of the National Anthem.
  음악회는 국가 연주로 막을 내렸다.

□ **engage** [ingéidʒ] ★ ★ ★ ★ ☆

- **engage for** ~을 보증하다
  The doctor *engaged for* my recovery.
  의사는 내 병의 쾌유를 장담하였다.

- **engage in** ~에 관계하다, 종사하다
  After finishing school, I'd like to *engage in* foreign trade.
  방과 후 나는 해외 무역에 종사한다.

- **engage oneself to + V** ~하기로 약속하다

  He *engaged himself to* pay the money by the end of the next month.

  그는 다음달 말까지 그 돈을 지불하기로 약속하였다.

- **engage to** 약혼하다

  He became *engaged to* a childhood sweetheart.

  그는 어릴 때 사랑하던 여자와 약혼하였다.

□ **enlarge** [inlάːrdʒ]　　　★☆☆☆☆

- **enlarge on** ~를 자세히 설명하다

  Let me *enlarge on* this point.

  이 점에 대해 소상히 설명드릴까 합니다.

□ **enter** [éntər]　　　★★★☆☆

E

- **enter for** (경기에) 참가하다

  He finally *entered for* the race.

  그는 마침내 경주에 참가하였다.

- **enter into** ~을 시작하다

  They *entered into* a long discussion.

  그들은 장시간의 토의에 들어갔다.

- **enter on** ~을 착수하다(=begin, start)

  He *entered on* a new business.

  그는 새 사업에 착수했다.

□ **entertain** [èntərtéin]　　　★★☆☆☆

- **entertain A with B** A(사람)를 B(사물)로 환대하다

  He *entertained* us *with* music.

  그는 우리에게 음악을 선사했다.

□ **entrust** [intrʌst]　　　★ ★ ☆ ☆ ☆

- **entrust ~ with** (남에게 임무를) 맡기다, 위임하다, 위탁하다
  He *entrusted* me *with* the matter.
  그는 그 일을 나에게 일임했다.

□ **equal** [íːkwəl]　　　★ ★ ☆ ☆ ☆

- **equal A in B** B에 있어서 A(사람)를 필적하다
  Nobody can *equal* him *in* intelligence.
  총명한 점에 있어 그를 필적할 사람이 없다.

□ **equip** [ikwíp]　　　★ ★ ☆ ☆ ☆

- **equip A with B** A에게 B를 갖추도록 하다
  He *equipped* all his children *with* a good education.
  그는 자녀 모두에게 훌륭한 교육을 받게 했다.

□ **escape** [iskéip]　　　★ ★ ☆ ☆ ☆

- **escape from** ~을 모면하다, 탈출하다
  One of the prisoners *escaped from* the prison.
  죄수 한 명이 감옥을 탈출했다.

□ **estimate** [éstəmèit]　　　★ ★ ★ ☆ ☆

- **estimate ~ at** 평가하다, 추정하다, 견적하다, 예상하다
  I *estimate* his monthly income *at* $2,000.
  나는 그의 월수입을 2,000불로 어림잡는다.

□ **exact** [igzǽkt]   ★★★☆☆

  ● exact ~ from 강요하다(=insist upon), 강제하다
    The feudal lords *exacted* taxes *from* their subjects.
    봉건 군주가 국민으로부터 세금을 착취하였다.

□ **examine** [igzǽmin]   ★★☆☆☆

  ● examine into ~을 조사·심리하다
    He *examines into* the rumor.
    그는 소문을 조사한다.

□ **exceed** [iksíːd]   ★★★☆☆

  ● exceed A by B A를 B만큼 초과하다
    20 *exceeds* 17 *by* 3.
    20은 17보다 3이 많다.

  ● exceed A in B B에 있어서 A(사람)를 능가하다
    No boy can *exceeds* him *in* cleverness.
    영리함에 있어 그보다 나은 소년은 없다.

□ **exchange** [ikstʃéindʒ]   ★★★☆☆

  ● exchange A with B A와 B를 교환하다
    Will you *exchange* seats *with* me?
    저와 자리를 바꾸시겠어요?

□ **exclude** [iksklúːd]   ★★☆☆☆

  ● exclude A from B B에서 A를 배제하다
    They *excluded* the boy *from* their group.
    그들은 소년을 그룹에서 추방했다.

□ **exempt** [igzémpt] ★★★☆☆

- **exempt A from B** A를 B에서 면제하다

  He was *exempted from* military service.

  그는 병역에서 면제되었다.

□ **exert** [igzə́:rt] ★★☆☆☆

- **exert oneself to + V** 전력을 다하다

  He *exerted himself to* win the race.

  그는 경주에서 이기려고 전력을 다했다.

□ **extract** [ikstrǽkt] ★★☆☆☆

- **extract A from B** B에서 A를 발췌하다

  He has *extracted* a great many examples *from* the grammar book.

  그는 문법책에서 많은 용례를 인용하였다.

□ **fade** [feid] ★☆☆☆☆

- **fade out** 사라지다, 시들다

  The stars were *fading out* from the sky.

  별들은 하늘에서 사라지고 있었다.

□ **fail** [feil] ★★★☆☆

- **fail in** ~에 실패하다, ~이 모자라다

  Helen *failed in* the exam.

  헬렌은 시험에 떨어졌다.

  He *fails in* patience.

  그는 인내심이 없다.

☐ **fall** [fɔːl]   ★★★★☆

● **fall away** 멀어져 가다

   It has certainly *fallen away* in public interest.

   그것은 확실히 일반사람들의 흥미에서 멀어져 갔다.

● **fall back on(upon)** ~에 의지하다

   I have nothing to *fall back on*.

   나는 의지할 것이 없다.

● **fall behind** 늦어지다

   He has *fallen behind* his age.

   그는 시대에 뒤떨어져 버렸다.

● **fall foul of** ~와 충돌하다(=collide with), 다투다

   They *fell foul of* each other.

   두 사람은 사이가 멀어졌다.

● **fall in with** ~와 일치하다(=agree with)

   I always *fall in with* his opinion.

   나는 늘 그의 의견과 일치한다.

● **fall into** 갑자기 ~하다

   He *fell into* a rage.

   그는 벌컥 화를 냈다.

● **fall out** 사이가 틀어지다, 일어나다, ~로 판명되다(=turn out)

   The enterprise *fall out* well.

   그 계획은 좋은 결과가 되었다.

● **fall out of** ~로부터 빠지다

   Many people have *fallen out of* employment in post-war Korea.

   전후의 한국에서는 많은 사람들이 실직상태에 있었다.

● **fall to** ~하기 시작하다(=begin), ~로 돌아오다

   The scheme *fell to* pieces.

   그 기획은 와해되고 말았다.

E
F

- **fall under** (분류상) ~에 해당되다

  This example *falls under* the next head.

  이 예는 분류상 다음 항목에 해당된다.

□ **fare** [fɛər]   ★☆☆☆☆

- **fare with** (일이 잘, 신통찮게) 되어가다

  How did it *fare with* him?

  그는 어떻던가?

□ **fasten** [fǽsn]   ★☆☆☆☆

- **fasten A on B** A를 B에 집중시키다

  The child *fastened* his eyes *on* the stranger.

  그 아이는 낯선 사람을 유심히 응시하였다.

□ **feed** [fi:d]   ★☆☆☆☆

- **feed on** ·을 먹고살다

  The tiger *feeds on* meat.

  호랑이는 육식을 한다.

□ **feel** [fi:l]   ★★★☆☆

- **feel no pain** 술에 만취하다

  He *felt no pain* at all.

  그는 통증을 전혀 느끼지 않았다.

- **feel one's way** 조심스레 나아가다

  He was *feeling his way* toward the accomplishment of his plan.

  그는 자신의 계획 실현을 향해 신중히 나아가고 있었다.

☐ **fence** [fens]   ★ ☆ ☆ ☆ ☆

- **fence with** (질문을) 받아넘기다
  He cleverly *fenced with* the question.
  그는 그 질문을 교묘히 받아 넘겼다.

☐ **fight** [fait]   ★ ☆ ☆ ☆ ☆

- **fight one's way** (인생에서) 활로를 개척하다
  He *fought his way* in life.
  그는 인생의 활로를 개척했다.

☐ **fill** [fil]   ★ ★ ☆ ☆ ☆

- **fill with** ~으로 가득 채우다
  Her heart was *filled with* sorrow.
  그녀의 마음은 슬픔으로 가득했다.

☐ **find** [faind]   ★ ★ ★ ★ ☆

- **find oneself** (자기가 어디에 있음을) 알다, 발견하다
  When I awoke I *found myself* in hospital.
  눈을 떠보니 병원이었다.

- **find one's way** 길을 찾다, (신문 등에) 나오다
  How did such a foolish statement *find its way* into
  print?
  어떻게 해서 이같이 우스꽝스러운 글이 인쇄물로 나왔을까?

- **find out** 찾아내다, 의문을 풀다
  I could not *find out* the riddle, however hard I tried.
  아무리 생각해 보아도 수수께끼가 풀리지 않았다.

- **cannot find it in one's heart to** 생각이 들지 않는다
  I *could not find it in my heart to* speak.
  도저히 말하고 싶은 기분이 들지 않았다.

F

finish [fíniʃ]   ★★☆☆☆

- **finish with** ~으로 끝맺다, ~와 관계를 정리하다
  I've already *finished with* him.
  나는 이미 그와 결별했다.

fit [fit]   ★☆☆☆☆

- **fit out** 장비를 갖추다
  They have *fitted out* a party for an antarctic expedition.
  그들은 남극탐험을 위한 필요품을 갖추어 왔다.

fix [fiks]   ★★★☆☆

- **fix on** ~으로 결정하다
  We *fixed on* the second plan.
  우리는 제2안으로 결정했다.

flame [fleim]   ★☆☆☆☆

- **flame with** 불꽃처럼 빛나다
  The garden *flamed with* red tulips.
  정원은 붉은 튤립으로 빛났다.

flatter [flǽtər]   ★★☆☆☆

- **flatter oneself that** ~임을 자랑으로 여기다
  She *flatters herself that* she is the most beautiful girl in the school.
  그녀는 자기가 학교에서 최고 미녀임을 자랑스럽게 여긴다.

□ **fling** [fliŋ] ★☆☆☆☆

• **fling oneself into** ~에 뛰어들다
  She *flung herself into* her mother's arms.
  그녀는 쓰러질 듯이 몸을 던져 어머니의 팔에 안겼다.

□ **flirt** [fləːrt] ★☆☆☆☆

• **flirt with** (남녀가) 연애하다
  Daisy was *flirting with* the young man.
  데이지는 그 젊은 남자와 연애하고 있었다.

□ **flock** [flak] ★☆☆☆☆

• **flock together** 떼지어 다니다
  Sheep usually *flock together*.
  양은 보통 떼지어 다닌다.

F

□ **free** [friː] ★★★☆☆

• **free A from B** A(사람)를 B로부터 해방하다
  Only you can *free* me *from* my cares.
  그대만이 나를 걱정에서 해방시킬 수 있어요.

□ **furnish** [fəˊːrniʃ] ★★☆☆☆

• **furnish A with B** A에게 B를 공급하다
  The river *furnishes* this town *with* water.
  (= The river furnishes water to this town.)
  그 강이 이 도시에 물을 공급한다.

gather [gǽðər] ★★☆☆☆

- **gather A from B** B로부터 A를 추측하다

  From his words I *gathered* that he did not know the truth.

  그의 얘기에서 나는 그가 진실을 모른다고 추측했다.

gaze [geiz] ★★☆☆☆

- **gaze at** ~을 응시하다(=stare at)

  She was *gazing at* the setting sun.

  그녀는 지는 해를 응시하고 있었다.

get [get] ★★★★★

- **get about** 돌아다니다(=move about), 퍼지다

  The invalid can now *get about*.

  환자는 이제 걸을 수 있게 되었다.

- **get along** (그럭저럭) 지내다

  How are you *getting along*?

  요즈음 어떻게 지내십니까?

  How is he *getting along* with his wife?

  그는 부인과 사이가 어떻습니까?

- **get at** 이해하다(=grasp)

  It is not easy to *get at* the thoughts of men.

  사람의 마음을 이해하는 것은 쉬운 일이 아니다.

- **get away** 떠나다(=leave), 도망치다(=run away), 출발하다

  There is no *getting away* from the facts.

  진실로부터 도망칠 수는 없다.

- **get away with** ~을 가져가다, 가지고 도망가다

  The robbers *get* clear *away with* the booty.

  도둑들은 훔친 물건을 가지고 깨끗이 도주한다.

- **get in** 도착하다, 당선되다

  What time does the train *get in*?
  열차는 몇 시에 도착합니까?

  He *got in* for Chaster.
  그는 체스터 지역에서 국회의원에 당선되었다.

- **get off** 하차하다, 형벌에서 면제되다

  It began to rain as we *got off* the bus.
  버스에서 내리자 비가 오기 시작하였다.

  He *got off* with a fine.
  그는 벌금을 내고 풀려 나왔다.

- **get on** 승차하다, ~하게 지내다, 착용하다

  He *got on* his horse.
  그는 말에 올라탔다.

  How are you *getting on*?
  어떻게 지냅니까?

  He *got* his shoes *on*.
  그는 신발을 신었다.

- **get on for** ~에 다가가다(=approach)

  He is *getting on for* seventy.
  그는 70에 가깝다.

- **get out** 꺼내다, 공표하다

  She could hardly *get ou*t a word.
  그녀는 말 한 마디도 꺼내기가 어려웠다.

- **get over** 극복하다(=overcome)

  He finally *got over* his bad habit.
  그는 마침내 나쁜 버릇을 고쳤다.

- **get through** 끝마치다, 해내다

  She's *got through* a lot of work.
  그녀는 많은 일을 해냈다.

G

- **get to do** ~하게 되다(=cause)

  How did you *get to* know him?

  어떻게 해서 그를 알게 되었습니까?

- **get under** 아래에 들다, 불을 끄게 하다, 굴복시키다

  A child *got under* a motor-car.

  아이가 자동차에 깔렸다.

- **get up** 일어나다, 일어서다, 복장을 가다듬다, 공부하다

  She was well *got up*.

  그녀는 좋은 복장을 하고 있었다.

□ **gift** [gift]   ★ ★ ☆ ☆ ☆

- **gift A with B** A에게 B를 주다

  He was *gifted* by nature *with* great talents.

  그는 선천적으로 대단한 재능을 타고났다.

□ **give** [giv]   ★ ★ ★ ★ ★

- **give away** 폭로하다, ~의 정체를 들추어내다

  Her accent *gave* her *away*.

  그녀의 사투리로 고향이 드러났다.

- **give forth** (소리나 냄새를) 내다(=emit)

  This flower *gives forth* a nice smell.

  이 꽃은 좋은 냄새를 풍긴다.

- **give in** 제출하다, 양보하다

  Give in your examination papers now.

  이제 답안지를 제출하시오.

  He has given in to me.

  그는 고집을 꺾고 내 말에 따랐다.

- **give off** 발산·방출하다

  The engine *gives off* a terrible noise.

  엔진에서 심한 소음이 난다.

- **give oneself up to** ~에 자수하다, ~에 골몰하다

  He *gave himself up to* pleasure.

  그는 쾌락에 골몰했다.

- **give one to understand that** ~라는 것을 납득시키다

  I am *given to understand that* minors are prohibited from smoking.

  미성년자는 흡연이 금지되어 있다고 알고 있습니다.

- **give or take** 약간의 차이는 있더라도

  He's 60 years old, *give or take* a year.

  한 살쯤은 틀릴지 모르겠으나 그는 예순살이다.

- **give out** 발표하다, 주장하다

  The result will be *given out* next month.

  결과는 내달에 발표될 예정이다.

- **give over** 넘겨주다, 양도하다

  She has *given over* thinking of her own beauty.

  그녀는 자신이 아름답다는 생각을 하지 않게 되었다.

- **give up** 포기·단념하다

  They did not *give up* hope.

  그들은 희망을 버리지 않았다.

G

□ **glide** [glaid]　　　　　　★☆☆☆☆

- **glide into** 차차 변하다

  Feeling of hostility *glided into* those of peculiar courtesy.

  적대감이 어느새 특별한 호감으로 변했다.

□ **glitter** [glítər]　　　　　　★☆☆☆☆

- **glitter with** ~로 번쩍이다

  The rich lady *glittered with* jewels.

  그 부유한 여인은 보석단장으로 눈부셨다.

□ **go** [gou]　　　　★ ★ ★ ★ ★

- **go about** 돌아다니다, 항간에 퍼지다, 일을 하다

  He *went about* his work in a cold way.

  그는 냉정히 일에 착수했다.

- **go by** (세월이) 흐르다, 잠깐 들르다, ~로 판단하다

  Years have *gone by*.

  세월이 흘러갔다.

  He was not in when I *went by*.

  내가 들렀을 때, 그는 나가고 없었다.

  You can't *go by* what he says.

  그가 말하는 것으로 판단할 수는 없다.

- **go in for** (시험을) 치르다, 열중하다

  The firm *goes in* exclusively *for* this class of goods.

  그 회사는 이러한 종류의 물품을 전문으로 취급하고 있다.

  He *went in for* an examination.

  그는 시험을 치렀다.

- **go into** ~에 들어가다, 조사하다(=inquire)

  There is no need to *go into* detail.

  상세히 살필 필요는 없다.

- **go off** (잘, 잘못) 되어가다(=be carried off), 발포하다

  The meeting *went off* quite successfully.

  회합은 매우 성공적이었다.

  The bullet failed to *go off*.

  탄알은 불발에 그쳤다.

- **go on** 계속해서 ~하다, 지내다

  Let's *go on* to the next lesson.

  다음 과로 넘어갑시다.

  How is the work *going on*?

  그 일은 어떻게 되고 있습니까?

- **go out** 외출하다, (유행이) 쇠퇴하다, 파업하다, (애정을) 쏟다

  When will you *go out*?

  언제 외출할 거니?

  The fashion for miniskirts has *gone out*.

  미니스커트 유행은 이미 한물갔다.

  They *went out* for higher wages.

  그들은 임금인상을 위해 파업에 들어갔다.

  His heart *went out* to the beautiful girl.

  그의 마음은 그 예쁜 소녀에게 빠졌다.

- **go over** 주의 깊게 조사하다

  Let's *go over* the facts again.

  진상을 다시 정밀조사 하자.

- **go round(around)** 순회하다

  The moon is always *going (a)round* the earth.

  달은 항상 지구를 돌고 있다.

- **go so far as to + V** ~까지노 하다

  She *went so far as to* permit me to dine with her.

  그녀는 식사를 함께 하는 것까지도 나에게 허락해 주었다.

- **go through** 빠져버리다, 경험하다(=suffer)

  I had to *go through* with it as my duty.

  나는 의무로서 그것을 관철하지 않으면 안 되었다.

- **go together** 어울리다, 애인 사이이다

  This tie and your dress *go* well *together*.

  이 넥타이와 당신 옷은 매우 잘 어울립니다.

  They have *gone together* for two years.

  그들은 애인으로서 2년간 지내왔다.

- **go to near** ~에 가까이 되다

  He *went to near* bankruptcy.

  그는 거의 파산할 것 같았다.

G

- **go up** 오르다(=climb), 폭발하다(=explode)

  A roar of laughter *went up*.

  와 하고 웃음소리가 일어났다.

- **go with** 동행하다, 조화를 이루다, ~와 같은 의견이다

  I'd like to *go with* you.

  동행하고 싶습니다만.

  This new curtain *goes* well *with* my room.

  이 새 커튼은 내 방과 잘 어울린다.

  That doesn't *go with* my view.

  그것은 내 의견과 맞지 않는다.

- **go without** ~없이 지내다(=dispense with)

  He cannot *go without* wine even a day.

  그는 포도주 없이 하루도 못산다.

- **it goes without saying that** ~라고 하는 것은 말할 나위 없다

  It goes without saying that they lived happy ever after.

  그 후 두 사람이 행복하게 지냈다는 것은 말할 필요도 없다.

□ **greet** [griːt]　　　　★ ☆ ☆ ☆ ☆

- **greet A with B** A(사람)를 B로 환영하다

  She *greeted* me *with* a smile.

  그녀는 나를 미소로 환영하였다.

□ **grow** [grou]　　　　★ ★ ★ ★ ☆

- **grow into** ~이 되다(=become)

  The two races *grew* together *into* one.

  두 민족이 융합하여 하나가 되었다.

- **grow on** ~으로 심해지다

  The habit of keeping early hours *grew upon* me.

  일찍 자고 일찍 일어나는 습관이 내게 붙었다.

- **grow out of** ~으로 벗어나다, ~에는 너무나 크게 되다

  All arts *grow out of* necessity.

  모든 예술은 필요에서 생긴다.

- **grow up** 성장하다, 성인으로 되다 cf. grownup 어른

  She has *grown up* to be a beautiful woman.

  그녀는 아름다운 여성으로 성장했다.

□ **guess** [ges]　　　　　　　　★★★☆☆

- **guess at** 짐작·추측하다

  I *guessed at* the length of the bridge, but could not hit upon it.

  그 다리의 길이를 짐작 했지만, 적중시키지는 못했다.

□ **hammer** [hǽmər]　　　　　　　★☆☆☆☆

- **hammer A into B** B를 A에게 주입시키다

  They *hammered* the bad ideas *into* his head.

  그들은 그에게 그릇된 생각을 주입시켰다.

□ **happen** [hǽpən]　　　　　　　★★★☆☆

- **happen to + V** 우연히 ~하다

  I *happened to* have no money with me.

  (= It happened that I had no money with me.)

  알고 보니 내게 돈이 하나도 없었다.

□ **harmonize** [há:rmənàiz]　　　　★☆☆☆☆

- **harmonize A with B** A를 B와 조화시키다

  You'd better *harmonize* your wishes *with* your abilities.

  제 능력에 맞는 꿈을 가져라.

G
H

371

harp [ha:rp]   ★ ☆ ☆ ☆ ☆

- **harp on** 같은 말을 되풀이하다

  Why do you keep *harping on* the same subject?

  어째서 너는 밤낮 같은 이야기만 하고 있니?

have [hæv]   ★ ★ ★ ★ ★

- **have an eye for** ~에 대한 안목이 있다

  He *has an eye for* the picturesque.

  그는 아름다움을 볼 줄 아는 안목이 있다.

- **have it** 이기다, 주장하다, 말하다

  The yeses *have it*.

  찬성자가 과반수이다.

- **Rumor has it that~.** 소문에 의하면, ~라고들 한다.
- **As Kant has it, ~.** 칸트가 말한 바와 같이
- **have on** 몸에 지니고 있다

  Not a few Koreans *have* spectacles *on*.

  한국 사람 중에 안경을 쓴 사람이 적지 않다.

- **have one's own way** 마음내로 하나

  You cannot *have your own way* in everything.

  만사를 마음대로 할 수는 없다.

- **have only to + V** ~하기만 하면 된다

  You *have only to* keep silent.

  너는 그저 잠자코 있으면 돼.

- **have something(a great deal, much, little, nothing) to do with**

  어느 정도(상당히, 매우, 별다른, 전혀) 관계가 있다(없다)

  We *have nothing to do with* your work.

  우리는 네 일과 무관하다.

☐ **hear** [hiər]   ★ ★ ★ ★ ☆

- **hear about** ~에 관하여 듣다

  I have *heard about* your accident.
  나는 네 사고 소식을 들었다.

- **hear from** ~로부터 소식을 듣다(=get news from)

  I have *heard* nothing *from* him for nearly half a year.
  난 거의 반년 동안 그의 소식을 듣지 못했다.

- **hear of** ~의 소식을 듣다

  I'm very glad to *hear of* your success.
  네 성공을 들으니 매우 기쁘다.

- **hear say** 남이 말하는 것을 듣다 cf. hearsay 소문

  I have *heard say* that it is so.
  나는 그렇다고 남이 얘기하는 것을 들었다.

- **make oneself heard** (자기 목소리를) 들려주다

  I tried hard to *make myself heard* over the
  telephone.
  전화로 이 쪽이 말하는 것을 알아듣게 하려 했으나, 되지 않았다.

☐ **help** [help]   ★ ★ ★ ★ ☆

- **help oneself to** ~을 마음대로 들다

  Please *help yourself to* the salad.
  샐러드를 마음껏 드세요.

- **help A with B** A(사람)가 B(사물)하는 것을 돕다

  He *helped* me *with* my homework.
  그가 내 숙제를 도와줬다.

☐ **hide** [haid]   ★ ★ ☆ ☆ ☆

- **hide oneself** 숨다

  The child *hid himself* behind the curtain.
  아이가 커튼 뒤에 숨었다.

☐ **hinder** [híndər]   ★★☆☆☆

- **hinder A from B** A가 B하는 것을 방해하다
  Rain *hindered* us *from* completing the work.
  우천으로 그 일을 완성하지 못했다.

  Heavy traffic *hindered* me *from* getting here earlier.
  나는 혼잡한 교통 때문에 이곳에 일찍 올 수가 없었다.

☐ **hit** [hit]   ★★★★☆

- **hit on** 갑자기 떠오르다
  At last he *hit on* a good idea.
  마침내 그는 좋은 생각이 떠올랐다.

☐ **hold** [hould]   ★★★★☆

- **hold back** 제지하다, 주춤하다
  He *hold back* rising anger.
  그는 화가 나는 것을 억제했다.

- **hold on** 계속하다(=continue), 기다리다(=wait)
  He *held on* his way.
  그는 자기 방식을 지속했다.

  Hold on, I'll call him to the telephone.
  기다리세요. 그에게 전화를 받도록 하겠습니다.

- **hold oneself** 거동하다(=behave)
  She *holds herself* like a queen.
  그녀는 여왕처럼 행동하고 있다.

- **hold out** 끝까지 버티다
  They *held out* against the enemy attacks for a month.
  그들은 한 달 동안 적의 공격을 견뎠다.

- **hold to** ~을 고수하다

  He *held to* his opinion to the last.
  그는 자기 의견을 끝까지 고수했다.

- **hold up** 정지를 명하다(=stop), 보여주다(=show)

  The vehicles were *held up* in the street.
  승용차들은 거리에서 정지당했다.

  She *held* it *up* for admiration.
  그녀는 이것 보라는 듯이 그것을 내보였다.

- **hold water** (설명 등이) 조리에 맞다

  His arguments do not *hold water*.
  그의 주장은 조리에 맞지 않는다.

☐ **identify** [aidéntəfài] ★★★☆☆

- **identify oneself with** ~와 함께 하다

  He *identified himself with* the party.
  그는 그 당과 함께 하였다.

- **identify A with B** A와 B를 동일시하다

  They *identified* him *with* God.
  사람들은 그를 신으로 여겼다.

☐ **illustrate** [íləstrèit] ★☆☆☆☆

- **illustrate A with B** B를 들어 A를 설명하다

  He *illustrated* the new theory *with* a lot of examples.
  그는 새 이론을 많은 예를 들어 설명했다.

☐ **impose** [impóuz] ★★☆☆☆

- **impose A on B** B에게 A를 부과하다, 강요하다

  They *imposed* a tax of 100 dollars *on* me.
  그들은 나에게 100달러의 세금을 부과하였다.

impute [impjúːt]　　　　　★☆☆☆☆

- **impute ~ to** ~의 탓으로 돌리다, 전가하다, 뒤집어씌우다

  They *imputed* the accident *to* the driver's carelessness.

  그들은 사고를 운전사의 부주의로 생각했다.

incline [inkláin]　　　　　★★☆☆☆

- **incline to** ~하는 경향이 있다

  You *incline to* luxury.

  너는 사치하는 경향이 있다.

induce [indjúːs]　　　　　★★☆☆☆

- **induce A to + V** A가 ~하게끔 권유하다

  You cannot *induce* me *to* buy a car.

  나에게 자동차를 사게 하려고 해도 헛일이다.

indulge [indʌldʒ]　　　　　★☆☆☆☆

- **indulge in** ~에 빠지다

  He seldom *indulged* himself *in* such idle thoughts.

  그는 좀처럼 그런 부질없는 생각에 잠기는 일이 없었다.

infer [infə́ːr]　　　　　★★☆☆☆

- **infer A from B** B로부터 A를 추론하다

  He *inferred* the fact *from* the evidence he had gathered.

  그는 자신이 수집한 증거로 그 사실을 추론하였다.

□ **inform** [infɔ́ːrm]   ★★★☆☆

- **inform against** 밀고·고발하다

  One thief *informed against* the others.

  도둑 하나가 다른 패거리를 밀고하였다.

- **inform A of B** A(사람)에게 B(사물)를 알려주다

  I *informed* her *of* my departure.

  나는 그녀에게 내가 떠남을 알려주었다.

- **inform A with B** A에게 B를 불어넣다, 채우다

  God *informed* their hearts *with* pity.

  신은 그들에게 동정심을 심어주었다.

□ **inherit** [inhérit]   ★☆☆☆☆

- **inherit A from B** B로부터 A를 상속받다

  He *inherited* a large fortune *from* his father.

  그는 부친에게서 많은 재산을 상속받았다.

□ **inquire** [inkwáiər]   ★★☆☆☆

- **inquire after** ~의 안부를 묻다(=ask after)

  He *inquired after* your health.

  그가 네 건강을 물었다.

- **inquire into** ~을 조사하다

  We must *inquire into* the matter.

  우리는 그 문제를 조사해야 한다.

- **inquire of** 질문·문의하다

  She *inquired of* the soldier about the battle.

  그녀는 병사에게 전투에 관해 질문했다.

I

377

□ **insist** [insíst] ★ ★ ★ ☆ ☆

- **insist on** 주장하다

  Shylock still *insisted on* having a pound of
  Antonio's flesh.

  샤일록은 안토니오의 살점 1파운드를 가지겠다고 끝까지 우겼다.

□ **jar** [dʒɑːr] ★ ☆ ☆ ☆ ☆

- **jar with** ~와 어긋나다, 조화되지 않다

  His view always *jar with* mine.

  그의 견해는 늘 내 것과 다르다.

□ **job** [dʒab] ★ ★ ☆ ☆ ☆

- **job A into B** (직권을 이용하여) A를 B에 앉히다

  He *jobbed* his friend *into* the post.

  그는 직권으로 친구를 그 자리에 앉혔다.

□ **jump** [dʒʌmp] ★ ★ ☆ ☆ ☆

- **jump on(upon)** 맹렬히 꾸짖다

  He often *jumps on* his men for the slightest fault.

  그는 종종 부하 직원의 사소한 잘못만 보아도 호되게 꾸짖는다.

- **jump with** 일치하다(=agree with)

  That *jumps with* the spirit of the age.

  그것은 시대정신과 부합된다.

□ **keep** [kiːp] ★ ★ ★ ★ ★

- **keep at** ~를 계속해서 하다

  They *kept at* him for payment.

  그들은 돈을 지불하기 위해 그를 따라갔다.

378

- **keep away** 가까이 하지 않게 하다, 가까이 하지 않다

  Keep the matches *away* from the children.

  성냥을 아이들 가까이에 두지 마라.

  Keep away from the water's edge.

  물가에 가지 마라.

- **keep back** 제압하다, 감추다(=hide)

  I will *keep back* nothing from you.

  나는 당신에게 아무 것도 숨기지 않습니다.

- **keep down** 억제하다, 진압하다

  She could not *keep down* her excitement.

  그녀는 흥분을 억누를 수 없었다.

- **keep A from B** A에 B 시키지 않는다

  He *kept* me *from* knowing the truth.

  그는 나에게 진상을 알려주지 않았다.

- **keep house** 살림을 꾸려나가다

  My sister *keeps house* for me.

  내 여동생이 가사를 돌봐주고 있다.

- **keep off** 달라붙지 못하게 하다

  We carry an umbrella with us to *keep off* the rain.

  우리는 비를 막기 위해 우산을 가지고 있다.

- **keep on** 계속해서 ~하다

  He *kept on* smoking all the time.

  그는 늘 계속해서 흡연했다.

- **keep one's promise** 약속을 지키다

  You must *keep your promise*.

  너는 약속을 지켜야 한다.

- **keep out** 배척하다, 억제하다

  We should *keep* children *out* of mischief.

  애들이 장난치지 못하도록 해야 한다.

- **keep to** ~을 지키다, ~을 끝내 지키다, 죽이다

  Keep to the right.
  우측통행.

  She *keeps to* bed.
  그녀는 죽을 자리에 누워 있다.

- **keep under** 억제하다(=restrain)

  He tried hard to *keep under* his temper.
  울화통을 터뜨리지 않으려고 무척 애를 썼다.

- **keep up** 유지하다, 굽히지 않다

  Woman as she is, she *keeps up* a large household.
  가냘픈 여자이지만 커다란 살림을 꾸려나가고 있다.

□ **kick** [kik]   ★ ☆ ☆ ☆ ☆

- **kick against** ~에 반대하다

  They *kicked against* the company's measure.
  그들은 회사의 조치에 대해 불평을 해댔다.

- **kick out** 해고하다, 퇴학시키다

  He was *kicked out* of the university.
  그는 대학에서 쫓겨났다.

□ **kill** [kil]   ★ ★ ☆ ☆ ☆

- **kill oneself** 자살하다(=commit suicide)

  She *killed herself* in despair.
  그녀는 절망 끝에 자살하고 말았다.

- **kill time** 소일하다

  The old man *killed time* by reading magazines.
  노인은 잡지를 읽으며 시간을 보냈다.

☐ **kindle** [kíndl] ★☆☆☆☆

- **kindle with** ~로 빛나다

  Her eyes *kindled with* curiosity.

  그녀의 눈은 호기심으로 빛났다.

☐ **kiss** [kis] ★★☆☆☆

- **kiss A on B** A의 B에 입맞추다

  He *kissed* her *on* the lips.

  그는 그녀의 입술에 키스했다.

☐ **knock** [nak] ★★★☆☆

- **knock against** ~와 부딪치다

  The wave *knocked against* the rocks.

  파도가 바위에 부딪쳤다.

- **knock off** 일을 그만두다(=cease working)

  Let's *knock off* for the day.

  오늘은 이제 그만 하자.

- **knock out** 녹아웃시키다(=knock down)

  He was *knocked out* in the 4th round of the final fight.

  그는 최종전 4라운드에서 KO패 당했다.

☐ **know** [nou] ★★★★★

- **know better than to + V** ~하지 않을 정도의 분별이 있다

  I *know better than to* quarrel.

  말다툼할 정도로 내가 바보는 아니다.

- **know A by heart** 암기하다(=learn by heart)

  I *know* the poem *by heart*.

  나는 그 시를 외우고 있다.

K

- **know A from B** A와 B를 구분하다

  We must *know* right *from* wrong.

  우리는 잘못과 옳은 것을 구분할 수 있어야 한다.

- **for all I know** 내가 아는 한도 내에서는

  He may be very rich *for all I know*.

  그는 아마도 큰 부자일 것이다.

- **know of** ~에 관한 일을 알고 있다

  I *know of* him, but I do not know him.

  그에 관해서는 알고 있으나, 만나 본 적은 없다.

- **know what's what** 세상물정을 알다

  He *knows what's what*.

  그는 알 것은 다 아는 사람이다.

- **God(Heaven) knows~** 맹세코 ~이다, 신만이 안다

  God knows that it is true.

  그것은 신에 맹세코 사실이다.

  God know where he fled.(= Nobody knows~.)

  그가 어디로 달아났는지 아무도 모른다.

☐ **label** [léibəl]   ★ ☆ ☆ ☆ ☆

- **label A as B** A를 B로 분류하다, 칭하다

  They *labeled* him *as* a demagogue.

  사람들은 그를 선동정치가로 불렀다.

☐ **labor** [léibər]   ★ ★ ☆ ☆ ☆

- **labor under** ~으로 괴로워하다

  She *labored under* a persistent headache.

  그녀는 고질적인 두통으로 고생하였다.

lace [leis] ★☆☆☆☆

• **lace A with B** A에 B를 수놓다

I have a handkerchief *laced with* a green string.

나는 푸른 실로 수놓은 손수건을 한 장 가지고 있다.

lack [læk] ★★☆☆☆

• **lack for** 부족하다

They *lacked for* nothing.

그들은 무엇 하나 부족한 것이 없었다.

lag [læg] ★☆☆☆☆

• **lag behind** 뒤쳐지다

The tall boy *lagged behind* in the race.

그 키 큰 소년은 달리기에서 뒤쳐졌다.

last [læst] ★☆☆☆☆

• **last out** 끝까지 지탱하다

Our food will not *last out* the voyage.

이 식량으로는 항해가 끝날 때까지 못 가겠다.

laugh [læf] ★★☆☆☆

• **laugh at** 조소·냉소하다

Nobody likes to be *laughed at*.

비웃음을 받고 싶은 사람은 아무도 없다.

• **laugh over** ~을 읽으면서(생각하면서) 웃다

I *laughed over* the letter.

나는 그 편지를 읽으면서 웃었다.

L

383

□ **lay** [lei]   ★ ★ ★ ★ ☆

- **lay aside** 저축하다

  She *laid aside* much money for her old age.
  그녀는 노년을 위해 많은 돈을 저축해 두었다.

- **lay by** 저장하다(=save)

  He *lays by* a certain sum of his salary every month.
  매달 봉급의 약간을 저축한다.

- **lay down one's life** 자신을 희생하다

  He is willing to *lay down his life* for his country.
  그는 조국을 위해서라면 기꺼이 자신을 희생할 각오가 되어 있다.

- **lay off** 그만두다, 해고시키다(=dismiss)

  Lay off teasing.
  놀리지 마라.

  The company *laid off* several workers.
  그 회사는 몇 명의 근로자들을 해고시켰다.

- **lay A on B** A를 B에 두다, 부과하다

  He *lays* hope *on* his second son.
  그는 둘째 아들에게 희망을 걸고 있었다.

- **lay on** ~을 마련하다

  We decided to *lay on* a concert for children.
  우리는 어린이를 위한 콘서트를 준비하기로 했다.

- **lay oneself out for(to + V)** ~하려고 애쓰다

  She *laid herself out for* making her guests comfortable.
  그녀는 손님들을 편하게 해주려고 애썼다.

- **lay out** 전개하다, 설계하다, 돈을 사용하다

  A glorious sight was *laid out* before our eyes.
  우리 눈앞에 영광스러운 광경이 펼쳐졌다.

  He *laid out* the garden.
  그가 정원을 설계하였다.

We must *lay out* our money carefully.
돈은 신중히 써야 한다.

- **lay stress on** ~에 강조를 두다

He *laid stress on* the need for attending the meeting.
그는 모임 참석의 필요성을 역설하였다.

- **lay up** 저축하다(=save), 쉬게 하다

She is *laid up* with illness.
그녀는 병으로 누워 있다.

- **lay A with B** A를 B로 덮다

The wind *laid* the garden *with* leaves.
바람이 불어 뜰이 낙엽으로 덮였다.

☐ **lead** [li:d]   ★☆☆☆☆

- **lead up to** ~로 유도하다, 결국 ~하게 되다

What is she *leading up to*?
그녀의 속셈은 무엇일까?

Their hot discussion *led up to* a quarrel.
그들의 격렬한 논쟁은 결국 싸움이 되고 말았다.

☐ **lean** [li:n]   ★☆☆☆☆

- **lean on** ~에 의지하다, 기대다(=depend on)

He never *lean on* his teacher for advice.
그는 그의 선생에게 조언을 구하는 일이 결코 없다.

☐ **learn** [lə:rn]   ★★★☆☆

- **learn A by heart** A를 암기하다(=know A by heart)

I have *learned* the poem *by heart*.
나는 그 시를 암기했다.

□ leave [liːv] ★★★☆☆

- **leave A behind** A를 남겨두고 가다
  He *left* a great name *behind* him.
  그는 명성을 남기고 세상을 떠났다.

- **leave A cold(cool)** ~에게 아무런 감흥도 일으키지 않다
  The news *left* me *cold*.
  그 소식을 들었어도 나는 아무렇지도 않았다.

- **leave off** 그만두다(=stop)
  He has *left off* the work.
  그는 일을 그만두었다.

- **leave out** 생략하다, 잊다(=omit)
  See that no one is *left out* at the party.
  파티에 한 분도 빠짐 없도록 주의하라.

- **leave over** 뒤에 남기다, 이월하다
  Debt is to be *left over* to the next account.
  채무는 후기로 이월할 것.

- **leave A to B** A를 B에 맡기다, 일임시키다
  I'll *leave* the decision *to* you.
  나는 너에게 결정을 맡기겠다.

□ lecture [léktʃər] ★★☆☆☆

- **lecture on** ~을 강의하다
  He *lectured on* chemistry to that class.
  그는 그 학급에 화학을 강의했다.

□ lend [lend] ★★★☆☆

- **lend itself to** ~에 소용이 되다, ~에 맞다
  This encyclopedia *lends itself to* children.
  이 백과사전은 어린이들에게 맞는다.

- **lend oneself to** ~에 골몰하다

  You should not *lend yourself to* such a transaction.

  그런 거래에 골몰해서는 안 된다.

□ **lengthen** [léŋkθən]   ★☆☆☆☆

- **lengthen into** 늘어나서 ~이 되다

  Summer *lengthen into* autumn.

  여름이 가고 가을이 된다.

□ **let** [let]   ★★★★☆

- **let alone** ~은 물론이고(=besides, not to mention)

  I cannot afford time, *let alone* the expenses.

  나는 시간적인 여유가 없다, 쓸 돈이 없는 것은 물론이고.

- **let fall** 무심코 지껄이다

  He *let fall* words about it.

  그는 거기에 관해 무심코 말했다.

- **let on** 비밀을 누설하다, 밀고하다

  He didn't *let on* that he had seen her.

  그는 그녀를 본 일을 누설하지 않았다.

- **let oneself go** 자제력을 잃다

  The stout man *let himself go* and ate the pie up.

  그 비대한 사람은 자제력을 잃고 파이를 다 먹어치웠다.

□ **lie** [lai]   ★★★★☆

- **lie at anchor** 정박하고 있다

  The ship is *lying at anchor* in the bay.

  배는 만 내에 정박하고 있다.

- **lie at one's door** (책임 따위가) ~에 있다

  The blame must *lie at his door*.

  죄는 그에게 있음이 틀림없다.

- **lie back** 뒤로 기대다

  She *lay back* in the arm chair.

  그녀는 안락의자에 등을 기댔다.

- **lie down under** 달게 ~을 받다

  He *lay down under* an insult.

  그는 모욕을 달게 받았다.

- **lie in** ~에 있다, 달려 있다(=consist in)

  The trouble *lies in* the engine.

  고장난 곳은 엔진이다.

  It *lies in* your effort whether you will succeed or not.

  네가 성공할지 여부는 너의 노력에 달렸다.

- **lie in wait for** ~를 잠복하여 기다리다

  Highwaymen were *lying in wait for* the merchant.

  노상강도들은 그 상인을 잠복하여 기다리고 있었다.

- **lie with** ~의 일(임무)이다

  It *lies with* us to decide the matter.

  그걸 결정하는 것은 우리 일이다.

☐ **limit** [límit]　　　　　　　　★★☆☆☆

- **limit A to B** A를 B로 제한하다

  We *limited* our expense *to* 20 dollars.

  우리는 지출을 20달러로 제한했다.

☐ **line** [lain]　　　　　　　　★★★☆☆

- **line up** 정렬하다

  The soldiers *lined up* for inspection.

  군인들은 사열을 받기 위해 일렬로 정렬하였다.

listen [lísn] ★★★☆☆

• **listen to** 경청하다, 따르다

You'd better always *listen to* reason.

언제나 도리를 따르는 게 좋다.

live [liv] ★★★★★

• **live again** (상상 속에서) 또다시 경험하다

When I read my past diary I feel as if I were *living* the old days *again*.

과거의 일기를 읽으면 옛 일을 눈앞에 보듯 상기한다.

• **live by** ~을 업으로 먹고 산다

He *lives by* teaching English.

그는 영어 선생님으로 살아간다.

• **live down** (과거의 오명 따위를) 세월의 흐름에 따라 씻다

He has *lived down* the scandal.

그는 옛날의 추문을 깨끗이 씻었다.

• **live in** ~에 살다

He *lives in* an apartment.

그는 아파트에서 살고 있다.

• **live off** ~에 의해 살다

Farmers *live off* the land.

농사꾼은 땅으로 산다.

• **live on** ~을 먹고 산다

The Korean *live* largely *on* rice.

한국사람들은 대부분 쌀을 주식으로 한다.

• **live through** ~동안 목숨을 유지하다

He will not be able to *live through* this winter.

그는 올 겨울을 나기 어려울 것이다.

- **live up to** ~을 따라 살다
  Do you *live up to* your principle?
  너는 네 원칙에 따라 사니?

- **where one lives** 급소에
  The word goes right *where I live*.
  그 말은 정확히 내 급소를 찌르는 것이다.

☐ **load** [loud]　　　　　　　　　★☆☆☆☆

- **load A with B** A에 B를 적재하다
  They *loaded* the ship *with* coal.
  그들은 배에 석탄을 실었다.

☐ **long** [lɔːŋ]　　　　　　　　　★☆☆☆☆

- **long for** 갈망하다(=eager for)
  She *longed for* you to write her a letter.
  그녀는 네가 자기에게 편지 써주길 갈망한다.

☐ **look** [luk]　　　　　　　　　★★★★★

- **look about** ~을 경계하다
  He *looked about* to see what had happened.
  그는 무슨 일인가 하고 사방을 둘러 보았다.

- **look after** ~을 돌보다
  He *looked after* the baby.
  그는 아기를 돌봤다.

- **look at** ~을 바라보다
  The hotel is not much to *look at*.
  그 여관은 별로 보잘것이 없다.

- **look back** 뒤돌아보다, 회고하다

  Since that day, he has never looked back.

  그날 이후, 그는 결코 주저하는 법이 없었다.

- **look down on(upon)** 업신여기다(=despise)

  Do not look down upon the poor.

  가난한 이를 업신여기지 마라.

- **look for** ~을 구하다, 기다리다, 기대하다

  She looked in her bag for the key of the house.

  그녀는 집열쇠를 찾으려고 가방을 뒤졌다.

  I'll look for you about five o'clock.

  5시경에 기다리고 있겠습니다.

- **look forward to ~ing** 기대하다(=anticipate)

  I'm looking forward to seeing you.

  나는 당신을 만나길 고대합니다.

- **look into** ~을 연구하다(=inspect)

  The police promised to look into the matter.

  경찰은 그 사건을 조사하겠다고 약속하였다.

- **look on** 방관하다

  You all play and I'll look on.

  너희들 모두가 해 봐, 나는 구경이나 할 테니.

- **look on A as B** A를 B로 간주하다(=regard A as B)

  We look on him as an imposter.

  우리는 그를 협잡꾼으로 보고 있다.

- **look out** 주의하다, 조심하다

  We must look out for the wet paint.

  새로 칠한 페인트를 조심해야 한다.

- **look over** 검토하다, 훑어보다

  Please look over the paper before you submit it.

  제출하기 전에 서류를 검토해 보시오.

- **look through** 간파하다

  He can *look through* any of your cheap tricks.

  그는 너의 값싼 계략 따위는 곧 간파한다.

- **look to** ~에 주의하다

  Look to your tools.

  연장을 잘 챙겨라.

- **look up** 올려보다, 찾다, 상향으로 되다

  The prices are *looking up*.

  물가가 오르고 있다.

- **look up to** 존경하다(=respect)

  They all *looked up to* him as their leader.

  그들은 모두 그를 지도자로서 우러러보았다.

☐ **lord** [lɔːrd]   ★☆☆☆☆

- **lord it over** 좌지우지하다(=king(queen) it over)

  Sam seems to *lord it over* his wife.

  샘은 자기 처에게 군림하는가 보다.

☐ **lose** [luːz]   ★★★★☆

- **lose oneself** 길을 잃다

  He *lost himself* in the woods.

  그는 숲에서 길을 잃었다.

- **lose (one's) face** 체면을 잃다

  Nobody wishes to *lose his face*.

  아무도 체면을 잃고 싶지는 않다.

- **lose oneself in** ~에 열중하다, 정신없이 ~하다

  He *lost himself in* astonishment.

  그는 놀라서 멍청해졌다.

- **lose (one's) mind** 미치다(=become insane)

  She *lost her mind* when she heard of her son's death.

  그녀가 아들의 사망소식을 들었을 때 제정신이 아니었다.

- **lose (one's) temper** 화를 내다

  He *lose his temper* at times.

  그는 때때로 화를 내곤 한다.

- **be lost upon** ~에 소용없다(=fail to impress)

  This lesson has not *been lost upon* him.

  이 쓰라린 경험은 그에게 약이 되었다.

- **be lost to** ~을 느끼지 않다(=be insensible to)

  The art *was lost to* the world forever.

  그 예술은 이 세상에서 영원히 사라져 버렸다.

- **give up for lost** 글렀다고 체념하다

  He was *given up for lost*.

  그는 글렀다고 체념하고 있었다.

□ **love** [lʌv] ★★☆☆☆

- **love for A to + V** A가 ~하는 것을 기뻐하다

  She will *love for* you *to* come with her.

  그녀는 네가 그녀와 함께 가는 것을 기뻐할 것이다.

□ **major** [méidʒər] ★★★☆☆

- **major in** ~을 전공하다

  He *majored in* economics at college.

  그는 대학에서 경제학을 전공했다.

☐ make [meik] ★★★★★

- **make at** ~을 향해 나아가다, 덤벼들다

  The dog *made* straight *at* him with a roar.

  그 개는 으르렁거리며 곧장 그에게 덤벼들었다.

- **make away** 급히 떠나다(=hasten away)

  He quickly *made away*.

  그는 재빨리 떠나갔다.

- **make away with** ~을 파기하다, 다 써버리다

  He *made away with* all his fortune.

  그는 재산을 전부 날렸다.

- **make believe** ~인 척하다(=pretend)

  The boys *made believe* that they were explorers in the South Pole.

  소년들은 남극 탐험대 놀이를 했다.

- **make for** ~쪽으로 나아가다, ~에 도움이 되다

  Seeing a light, I *made for* it.

  빛을 보고, 나는 그쪽을 향해 나아갔다.

  His proposal *made for* world peace.

  그의 제안은 세계평화에 기여하였다.

- **make A from B** B를 이용하여 A를 만들다

  American cider is *made from* apples.

  미국식 사이다는 사과로 만들어진다.

  We can *make* chemical fibers *from* petroleum.

  석유로 화학섬유를 만들 수 있다.

- **make A into B** A로 B를 만들다, A를 B가 되게 하다

  Nylon is *made into* shirts, stockings and others.

  나일론으로 셔츠, 양말 등을 만든다.

- **make it** 해내다, 성공하다

  You'll *make it* if you hurry.

  서둘러 하면 해낼 수 있을 거야.

- **make A of B** B를 이용하여 A를 만들다

  The house was *made of* stone(wood).

  그 집은 석조(목조) 가옥이다.

- **make out** 기안하다, 이해(납득)하다, ~처럼 행동하다,

  He *made out* the list of the members.

  그는 회원 명부를 작성하였다.

  I can't *make out* what he wants.

  나는 그가 원하는 게 뭔지 도무지 모르겠다.

  He *made out* that he was a friend of mine.

  그는 마치 자기가 내 친구인 양 행동하였다.

  His store is *making out* very well.

  그의 상점은 장사가 잘 되고 있다.

- **make over** 양도·이양하다

  The king *made over* the kingdom to his son.

  왕은 아들에게 왕국을 물려주었다.

- **make up** 꾸미다, 지어내다, 화장하다, 변상하다

  The story is *made up*.

  그 이야기는 지어낸 것이다.

  The actor *made up* for the part of Hamlet.

  그 배우는 햄릿 역으로 분장했다.

  We must *make* the loss *up* next month.

  다음 달에는 그 손실을 변상하여야 한다.

- **make up one's mind** 결심하다(=decide)

  I *made up my mind* to keep a diary.

  나는 일기를 쓰기로 결심했다.

☐ **man** [mæn]   ★ ☆ ☆ ☆ ☆

- **man oneself** 격려하다

  He *manned himself* for the ordeal.

  그는 시련을 이겨내기 위해 용기를 냈다.

manage [mǽnidʒ] ★★★☆☆

- **manage to + V** 그럭저럭 ~해내다

  He *managed to* get what he wanted.

  그는 자신이 원하던 것을 용케 수중에 넣을 수 있었다.

marry [mǽri] ★★☆☆☆

- **marry into** ~로 시집(장가)가다

  She *married into* a rich family.

  그녀는 부잣집으로 시집갔다.

match [mætʃ] ★★★☆☆

- **match A against B** A를 B와 경쟁시키다

  Match your strength *against* John's.

  존과 경쟁해 봐라.

- **match A with B** A를 B와 결혼시키다

  He *matched* his daughter *with* his friend's son.

  그는 친구 아들과 사기 딸을 결혼시켰다.

measure [méʒər] ★★☆☆☆

- **measure A by B** A를 B로 평가하다

  A man's character can be *measured by* the types of men with whom he associates.

  사람의 성격은 그가 교제하고 있는 부류의 유형으로 판단할 수 있다.

meditate [médətèit] ★★☆☆☆

- **meditate on** ~을 깊이 생각하다

  He *meditated on* the meaning of life.

  그는 인생의 의미를 깊이 생각했다.

□ **mistake** [mistéik]　　　　　　　　★ ★ ★ ☆ ☆

• **mistake A for B** A를 B로 오인하다

I *mistook* a visitor *for* the postman.
나는 손님을 우체부로 착각했다.

□ **name** [neim]　　　　　　　　　　★ ★ ☆ ☆ ☆

• **name after** ~의 이름을 따서 명명하다

England was *named after* the Angles.
잉글랜드는 앵글로 족의 이름을 따서 명명되었다.

□ **negotiate** [nigóuʃièit]　　　　　　★ ★ ★ ☆ ☆

• **negotiate with** ~와 협상하다

They *negotiated with* their employer about their wages.
그들은 고용주와 임금협상을 했다.

□ **nerve** [nəːrv]　　　　　　　　　　★ ☆ ☆ ☆ ☆

• **nerve oneself** 어려움에 맞서 기력을 내다

They *nerved themselves* for the new attempt.
그들은 용기 백배하여 새로운 시도에 나섰다.

□ **noise** [nɔiz]　　　　　　　　　　★ ★ ☆ ☆ ☆

• **noise about(abroad)** 퍼뜨리다

It is *noised about* that the taxi fares will be raised.
택시 요금이 인상되리라는 소문이 자자하다.

□ **nose** [nouz] ★☆☆☆☆

- **nose into** ~에 파고들다, 간섭하다
  Don't *nose into* another's affair.
  남의 일에 참견 말라.

□ **number** [nʌ́mbər] ★★☆☆☆

- **number A among B** A를 B의 일부로 보다
  Mary *numbered* John *among* her friends.
  메리는 존을 자기 친구 중의 한 사람으로 쳤다.

□ **object** [άbdʒikt] ★★★☆☆

- **object to** ~에 반대하다
  I'll not *object to* your plan.
  네 계획에 반대하지 않을게.

□ **oblige** [əbláidʒ] ★★★☆☆

- **oblige A to + V** A로 하여금 억지로 ~하게 하다
  The laws *oblige* us *to* pay taxes.
  우리는 법률에 의해 세금을 물어야만 한다.

- **oblige with** ~에 호의를 보이다, 청을 들어주다
  Can you *oblige with* a song?
  노래 한 곡 들려주시겠습니까?

□ **observe** [əbzə́:rv] ★★★☆☆

- **observe on** 소견을 말하다, 강평하다
  No one has ever *observed on* this phenomenon.
  여태껏 그 누구도 이 현상에 대해 의견을 개진하진 않았다.

□ occur [əkə́ːr] ★★★☆☆

- **occur to** 문득 떠오르다

  Then a good idea *occurred to* me.

  그때 좋은 생각이 떠올랐다.

□ offer [ɔ́ːfər] ★★☆☆☆

- **offer oneself** (기회 등이) 나타나다

  A good chance *offered itself*.

  좋은 기회가 왔다.

□ omit [oumít] ★★★☆☆

- **omit A from B** B에서 A를 생략하다

  He *omitted* an item *from* the list.

  그는 목록에서 한 가지를 뺐다.

□ operate [ápərèit] ★★★☆☆

- **operate on** ~에 작용하다, 수술하다

  Our physical conditions *operate* strongly *on* our mental state.

  우리의 신체적인 조건은 정신상태에 커다란 작용을 한다.

  The surgeon *operated on* the wounded soldier.

  그 외과의사는 부상병을 수술하였다.

□ oppose [əpóuz] ★★★★☆

- **oppose A to B** A를 B에 대립시키다

  He *opposed* himself *to* the scheme.

  그는 그 계획에 반대하였다.

□ **order** [ɔ́:rdər]   ★ ★ ★ ☆ ☆

- order A from B A를 B에 주문하다

  I *ordered* the book *from* the publishers.
  나는 출판사에 그 책을 주문했다.

□ **orient** [ɔ́:riənt]   ★ ☆ ☆ ☆ ☆

- orient A to B A를 B에 적응시키다, 방향지우다

  It is necessary to help the freshmen to *orient*
  themselves *to* college life.
  신입생들이 대학생활에 적응할 수 있게끔 도와주는 일이 필요하다.

□ **originate** [ərídʒənèit]   ★ ☆ ☆ ☆ ☆

- originate from ~에서 발생하다, 나오다, 시작하다

  The quarrel *originated from* a misunderstanding.
  싸움은 오해에서 일어났다.

□ **overflow** [òuvərflóu]   ★ ★ ☆ ☆ ☆

- overflow with ~이 넘쳐나다

  The market *overflows with* goods.
  시장에 상품이 넘친다.

□ **overlap** [ouˈvərlæ̀ˌp]   ★ ★ ☆ ☆ ☆

- overlap with ~와 겹치다

  His vacation *overlaps with* mine.
  그의 휴가는 내 것과 겹친다.

☐ **owe** [ou]　　　　　　　　　　　　★ ☆ ☆ ☆ ☆

- **owe A to B** A를 B에게 빚지다

  I *owe* 10 dollars *to* him. (= I owe him 10 dollars.)
  그에게 10달러를 빚지고 있다.

☐ **own** [oun]　　　　　　　　　　　　★ ★ ☆ ☆ ☆

- **own to** 인정하다, 자백하다

  I *own to* a great many faults.
  나에게 많은 결점이 있음을 인정한다.

☐ **pace** [peis]　　　　　　　　　　　★ ★ ☆ ☆ ☆

- **pace up and down** 이리저리 왔다갔다하다

  He was *pacing up and down* considering how to settle the problem.
  그는 문제를 어떻게 결말지을까 생각하면서 왔다갔다하였다.

☐ **parallel** [pǽrəlèl]　　　　　　　　★ ☆ ☆ ☆ ☆

- **parallel A in B** B라는 점에서 A를 닮다, 필적하다

  The war in Vietnam *paralleled* the China Incident *in* many points.
  베트남 전쟁은 많은 점에서 중국사변과 흡사했다.

  Nobody can *parallel* her *in* cooking.
  요리에 관한 한 그녀에게 필적할 사람은 없다.

☐ **participate** [pɑːrtísəpèit]　　　　★ ★ ★ ☆ ☆

- **participate in** ~에 참여하다, 함께 하다(=take part in)

  The teacher *participated in* the children's games.
  교사는 어린이 놀이에 참여했다.

401

□ **pay** [pei]　　　　　　　　　　　　★ ★ ★ ☆ ☆

- **pay attention to** ~에 유의하다
  She didn't *pay attention to* my advice.
  그녀는 내 충고에 주의를 기울이지 않았다.

- **pay one's respect to** 존경을 표하다
  He always *pay his respect to* his teachers.
  그는 늘 선생님들을 존경한다.

- **pay one's (own) way** 빚지지 않고 살아가다
  He *paid his way* through college.
  그는 고학으로 대학까지 마쳤다.

□ **perform** [pərfɔ́:rm]　　　　　　　　★ ☆ ☆ ☆ ☆

- **perform on** (악기를) 연주하다
  He *performed on* the piano.
  그는 피아노를 연주했다.

□ **permit** [pərmít]　　　　　　　　　★ ★ ☆ ☆ ☆

- **permit of** ~의 여지가 있다
  The words *permit of* no doubt.
  그 말에는 의심의 여지가 없다.

□ **persist** [pərsíst]　　　　　　　　★ ★ ★ ☆ ☆

- **persist in** 고집하다(=insist on)
  He *persist in* his opinion.
  그는 자기주장을 고집했다.

□ **persuade** [pərswéid]　　　★★☆☆☆

• **persuade A of B** A(사람)에게 B(사물)를 납득시키다

I could not *persuade* him *of* my honesty.
그에게 나의 정직성을 납득시킬 수가 없었다.

□ **pertain** [pərtéin]　　　★☆☆☆☆

• **pertain to** ~에 속하다, 어울리다

They own the house and the land *pertaining to* it.
그들은 집과 거기에 딸린 토지를 소유하고 있다.

□ **phone** [foun]　　　★★☆☆☆

• **phone to** ~에 전화하다

Please *phone to* the police station.
경찰서에 전화하세요.

□ **pine** [pain]　　　★☆☆☆☆

• **pine for** 그리워하다, 갈망하다

They were *pining for* their homes and families.
그들은 집과 가족을 그리워했다.

□ **play** [plei]　　　★★★★☆

• **play at** ~를 하고 놀다

He *plays at* cards for stakes.
그는 카드로 내기를 걸었다.

• **play fair** 공정한 승부를 가리다, 공명정대하게 행동하다

We should *play fair* in anything.
무슨 일이나 공명정대하게 해야 한다.

P

403

- **play on(upon)** ~을 이용하다, 편승하다, ~을 연주하다
  You should not *play upon* their ignorance.
  그들의 무지에 편승해서는 안 된다.

- **be played out** 지칠 대로 지치다(=be exhausted)
  Owing to a long examination we *are played out*.
  오랜 시험 때문에 우리는 지칠 대로 지쳤다.

- **play with** ~를 노리개로 삼다, 노닥거리다
  Children are fond of *playing with* fire.
  애들은 불장난을 좋아한다.

☐ **plunge** [plʌndʒ]　　　　　　　　★ ☆ ☆ ☆ ☆

- **plunge into** ~에 갑자기 빠지다, ~하기 시작하다
  We must prevent our country from *plunging into* war by any means.
  어떻게든 조국이 전쟁에 처하는 것을 피해야 한다.

☐ **point** [pɔint]　　　　　　　　★ ★ ★ ☆ ☆

- **point out** 지적하다
  I *pointed out* his mistakes.
  나는 그의 실수를 지적했다.

☐ **prepare** [pripέər]　　　　　　　　★ ★ ★ ☆ ☆

- **prepare for** 준비하다
  They had to *prepare for* death.
  그들은 죽음을 각오해야만 했다.

□ **prepossess** [prìːpəzés]   ★☆☆☆☆

• **prepossess A with B** A가 B를 선입관으로 가지게 하다
He is *prepossessed with* a queer idea.
그는 묘한 편견을 가지고 있다.

□ **prevent** [privént]   ★★★☆☆

• **prevent A from B** A가 B를 못하게 하다, 방해하다
Business *prevent* him *from* going out.
사업으로 그는 외출할 수 없었다.

□ **prohibit** [prouhíbi]   ★★☆☆☆

• **prohibit A from B** A가 B하는 것을 금지하다
The doctor *prohibits* me *from* smoking.
의사는 나에게 끽연을 금했다.

The law *prohibits* ships *from* approaching this
island.
이 섬에 배가 접근하는 것은 법으로 금지된다.

□ **promise** [prάmis]   ★★★☆☆

• **promise oneself** 즐겁게 기대하다
I *promised myself* a trip to the mountain with them.
나는 그들과 함께 산에 가는 기대를 걸고 기다렸다.

□ **promote** [prəmóut]   ★☆☆☆☆

• **promote ~ to** 승진시키다, 진급시키다(=advance)
He *promoted* Tom *to* a manager.
그는 톰을 지배인으로 승진시켰다.

□ **protect** [prətékt]　　　　　　　　　★ ★ ☆ ☆ ☆

- **protect A from B** A를 B로부터 보호하다
  Protect your eyes *from* the sun.
  태양으로부터 네 눈을 보호해라.

□ **protest** [próutest]　　　　　　　　★ ★ ☆ ☆ ☆

- **protest against** 항의하다, 이의를 제기하다
  The demonstrators *protested against* the continuation of the war.
  시위자들은 전쟁을 계속하는 것에 항의하였다.

□ **provide** [prəváid]　　　　　　　　★ ★ ★ ☆ ☆

- **provide A with B** A에게 B를 제공하다
  Bees *provide* us *with* honey.
  벌은 우리에게 꿀을 준다.

□ **put** [put]　　　　　　　　　　　　★ ★ ★ ★ ★

- **put aside** (일시적으로) 중단하다, 저축하다
  I *put* the work *aside* and watched television.
  나는 일을 중단하고 TV를 봤다.

  She has *put aside* a lot of money.
  그녀는 많은 돈을 모았다.

- **put away** 버리다
  He *put away* all prejudices.
  그는 모든 편견을 버렸다.

- **put back** 도로 갖다놓다, 정체(후퇴)시키다
  Put the dictionary *back* on the shelf when you're through.
  다 봤으면 사전을 서가에 되돌려 놓아라.

Such a long rain *put back* the ripening of the grain.

몹시 긴 우천으로 곡식의 결실이 늦어졌다.

- **put by** 저축하다(=save)

Put by something for a rainy day.

어려울 때를 대비하여 저축을 해라.

- **put down** 내려놓다, 저장하다, 억누르다, ~라고 생각하다

Please *put* me *down* at Oxford Circus.

옥스퍼드 광장에서 나를 내려주시오.

She *put down* vegetables in salt.

그녀는 야채를 소금에 절여 저장하였다.

The revolt was soon *put down*.

반란은 즉시 진압되었다.

She *put* Tom *down* as a fool.

그녀는 톰을 바보로 생각했다.

He *put* the mistake *down* to me.

그는 그 잘못이 내 탓이라고 했다.

- **put forth** (움 따위가) 트다

In spring plants *put forth* buds and leaves.

봄이 되면 식물은 싹이나 잎이 튼다.

- **put in** 넣다, 참견하다, 제출하다, 실행하다

She *put* her head *in* at the window and looked around.

그녀는 창문으로 얼굴을 내밀고 둘러 보았다.

He always *puts* a word *in* for her.

그는 항상 그녀를 위해 한 마디 거들어 준다.

We finally *put in* a plea.

마침내 우리는 탄원서를 제출하였다.

He *put* a new plan *in* practice.

그는 새로운 계획을 실행하였다.

P

- **put off** 연기하다(=postpone), 제거하다

  We had to *put off* the meeting because of the storm.
  폭풍우 때문에 모임을 연기해야 했다.

  You must *put off* childish fears.
  너는 그 어린애 같은 공포심을 없애야 한다.

- **put on** ~을 입다, ~인 체하다

  She likes to *put on* ordinary clothes.
  그녀는 평상복 입기를 즐긴다.

  His innocent air is all *put on*.
  그가 천진난만하게 보이는 것은 속임수에 불과하다.

- **put out** (불을) 끄다(=extinguish), 내밀다

  The firemen soon *put out* the fire.
  소방대원은 불을 곧 진압했다.

  I *put* my tongue *out* for the doctor.
  나는 의사에게 혀를 내밀어 보였다.

- **put through** 관철하다, 성취하다, 전화를 잇다

  He *put through* the plan with success.
  순조롭게 그 계획을 실행했다.

- **put together** 한데 모으다

  They *put* their heads *together*.
  그들은 머리를 맞대고 상의했다.

- **put up** 걸다, 게양하다, (양산을) 받치다

  Put up your hand when you want to ask me a question.
  내게 질문하고 싶을 때는 손을 들어라.

- **put up at** ~에 묵다(=stay)

  They *put up at* a hotel by the lake that night.
  그들은 그날 밤 호반의 호텔에 묵었다.

- **put up with** 참다(=endure, tolerate)

  I had to *put up with* a great many inconveniences.
  나는 큰 수많은 불편을 참아야 했다.

408

- **be (hard) put to it** (무척) 딱하다

  He used to *be* well off, but now *hard put to it*.

  그는 유복했으나, 지금은 무척 딱하다.

☐ **puzzle** [pʌzl]   ★☆☆☆☆

- **puzzle out** 생각해내다, 알아맞히다

  I succeed in *puzzling out* the mystery of the case.

  나는 곰곰이 생각하여 그 사건의 수수께끼를 풀 수 있었다.

☐ **qualify** [kwάləfài]   ★☆☆☆☆

- **qualify for** ~의 자격을 얻다

  He has not yet *qualified for* the race.

  그는 아직 경주에 참가할 자격을 얻지 못했다.

- **qualify A with B** A를 B로 진정시키다, 순하게 하다

  He *qualified* spirits *with* water.

  그는 물을 타서 술을 순하게 하였다.

☐ **quarrel** [kwɔ́:rəl]   ★☆☆☆☆

- **quarrel with** ~와 다투다

  They *quarreled with* each other over a trifling matter.

  그들은 시시콜콜한 문제를 놓고 서로 다투었다.

☐ **quote** [kwout]   ★★☆☆☆

- **quote A from B** A를 B에서 인용하다

  He *quoted* a phrase *from* Shakespeare.

  그는 셰익스피어의 작품에서 한 구절을 인용했다.

P
Q

□ **radiate** [réidièit]   ★ ☆ ☆ ☆ ☆

• **radiate from** ~로부터 방출되다
Light and heat *radiate from* the sun.
빛과 열이 태양에서 방출된다.

□ **rain** [rein]   ★ ☆ ☆ ☆ ☆

• **rain itself out** 비가 그치다
It has *rained itself out.*
비가 그쳤다.

□ **reach** [ri:tʃ]   ★ ★ ☆ ☆ ☆

• **reach to** ~에까지 미치다
His land *reaches to* the road over there.
그의 땅은 저기 도로까지 걸쳐 있다.

□ **react** [riǽkt]   ★ ★ ☆ ☆ ☆

• **react on** ~에 반응하다
Nitrous oxide *reacts on* this metal.
일산화질소는 이 금속에 반응을 보인다.

□ **read** [ri:d]   ★ ★ ★ ☆ ☆

• **read for** ~를 위해 연구하다
He is *reading for* a degree.
그는 학위를 따려고 공부하고 있다.

• **read A out of B** A(사람)를 B에서 제명하다
They *read* him *out of* the party.
그들은 그를 당에서 제명시켰다.

□ **reconcile** [rékənsàil]   ★☆☆☆☆

• **reconcile A to B** A를 B로 만족하게 하다

I was *reconciled to* living in the country.
나는 시골생활에 만족하게 되었다.

• **reconcile A with B** A와 B를 화해·조화·일치시키다

What he said could not be *reconciled with* the facts of the case.
그가 말한 사실은 사건의 진실과 일치할 수가 없었다.

□ **recover** [rikʌ́vər]   ★☆☆☆☆

• **recover from** ~로부터 회복하다

She is *recovering from* a severe illness.
그녀는 심한 질병에서 회복하고 있다.

□ **recruit** [rikrúːt]   ★☆☆☆☆

• **recruit A from B** B로부터 A를 모집하다

The new party was largely *recruited from* the labor classes.
신당의 당원은 노동자 계급에서 상당수가 모집되었다.

R

□ **reduce** [ridjúːs]   ★★☆☆☆

• **reduce A to B** A를 B로 줄이다, 분해하다

We have *reduced* our expenditure almost *to* nothing.
우리는 경비를 줄여 거의 제로로 만들었다.

Let's *reduce* this compound *to* its elements.
이 화합물을 원소로 분해해 보자.

□ **refer** [rifə́ːr] ★★☆☆☆

- refer A to B A를 B에 참조시키다, 맡기다, 있다고 보다

  The teacher usually *refers* us *to* the dictionary.
  선생님은 대개 우리더러 사전을 찾아보게 합니다.

  They decided to *refer* the problem *to* the committee.
  그들은 그 문제를 위원회에 일임하기로 하였다.

  The soldiers *referred* the defeat *to* poor training.
  병사들은 패배 원인을 훈련부족 때문이라고 봤다.

□ **reflect** [riflèkt] ★☆☆☆☆

- reflect on 영향을 미치다, 심사숙고하다, 비난하다

  Your rudeness only *reflect on* yourself.
  너의 무례함은 네 자신의 체면만 손상할 뿐이다.

  Reflect on what I have said to you.
  내가 말한 것을 잘 생각해 보아라.

  She *reflected on* my conduct.
  그녀는 내 행동을 비난하였다.

□ **refrain** [rifrèin] ★☆☆☆☆

- refrain from ~을 그만두다, 삼가다

  I could not *refrain from* laughter.
  나는 웃음을 참을 수 없었다.

□ **regard** [rigáːrd] ★★★☆☆

- regard A as B A를 B로 간주하다

  We *regard* him *as* one of the best players.
  우리는 그를 최고의 선수로 생각한다.

412

☐ **rejoice** [ridʒɔ́is]　　　　　　　　★☆☆☆☆

• **rejoice in** ~을 향유하다

He *rejoices in* good health.

그는 좋은 컨디션을 유지하고 있다.

☐ **relate** [rilèit]　　　　　　　　★★★☆☆

• **relate A to B** 친족관계이다, ~에게 말하다, ~와 관련이 있다

She is closely *related to* me.

그녀는 나와 가까운 친척관계이다.

Tom *related to* his parents some amusing stories about his classmates.

탐은 자기 반 친구들에 관한 재미난 이야기를 부모님에게 들려드렸다.

She won't notice anything but what *relates to* herself.

그녀는 자신에게 직접 관계가 되는 것 이외에는 어떤 것에도 주의를 기울이지 않을 것이다.

• **relate A with B** A와 B를 관계시키다

We cannot *relate* these results *with* any particular cause.

이러한 결과를 어떤 특정한 원인에만 결부시켜 생각할 수는 없다.

☐ **release** [rilí:s]　　　　　　　　★☆☆☆☆

• **release A from B** A에게 B를 면제해주다

I'll *release* you *from* your obligation.

내가 네 책임을 면제해주겠다.

☐ **relieve** [rilíːv]   ★ ★ ☆ ☆ ☆

- **relieve A from B** A를 B에서 구하다
  Death *relieved* him *from* the pain.
  죽음이 그를 고통에서 구해주었다.

- **relieve A of B** A에게서 B를 없애 주다
  A cup of coffee *relieved* me *of* a headache.
  커피를 한 잔 했더니 두통이 사라졌다.

☐ **remove** [rimúːv]   ★ ☆ ☆ ☆ ☆

- **remove A from B** A를 B에서 옮기다
  He *removed* the piano *from* the drawing room.
  그는 화실에서 피아노를 가져 나왔다.

☐ **rent** [rent]   ★ ★ ☆ ☆ ☆

- **rent A from B** A를 B에게서 임대하다
  They *rent* a house *from* Mr. Smith.
  그들은 스미스 씨에게 집을 임대한다.

- **rent A to B** A를 B에게 임대하다
  He *rented* the house *to* us at 600 dollars a year.
  그는 우리에게 그 집을 1년에 6백 달러로 임대했다.

☐ **repent** [ripènt]   ★ ☆ ☆ ☆ ☆

- **repent of** ~을 후회하다
  She soon *repented of* her hasty marriage.
  그녀는 곧 서두른 결혼을 후회했다.

□ **replace** [riplèis] ★★☆☆☆

- **replace A with B** A를 B로 교체하다

They have *replaced* their sedan *with* a new one.
그들은 승용차를 신형으로 교체했다.

□ **reside** [rizáid] ★☆☆☆☆

- **reside in** ~에 있다, 존재하다

Her charm *resides in* her attitude of reserve.
그녀의 매력은 겸양한 태도에 있다.

□ **resign** [rizáin] ★★☆☆☆

- **resign oneself to** 단념하다, 포기하다, 물러나다

He *resigned himself to* fate.
그는 운명이라고 단념했다.

□ **resolve** [rizálv] ★★☆☆☆

- **resolve into** ~로 분해하다, 변하다

Does water *resolve into* oxygen and hydrogen?
물이 산소와 수소로 변하나요?

- **resolve on** 결심하다(=decide)

They *resolved on* going back the same way.
그들은 같은 길로 돌아가려고 결심했다.

□ **resort** [rizɔ́ːrt] ★☆☆☆☆

- **resort to** (자주) 가다, 의지(호소)하다

Many people *resort to* the beach in summer.
여름에 그 해안을 찾는 사람들이 많다.

R

Don't *resort to* force.
폭력에 호소하지 말라.

☐ **restore** [rist ɔ́:r]　　　　　　　　★ ☆ ☆ ☆ ☆

- **restore A to B** A를 B의 상태로 복귀·회복시키다
  The treatment *restored* the child *to* health.
  치료는 아이를 건강하게 회복시켰다.

  They *restored* him *to* his old position.
  그들은 그를 복직시켰다.

☐ **restrain** [ristréin]　　　　　　　★ ★ ☆ ☆ ☆

- **restrain ~ from** 제지하다, 방해하다, 억제하다, 속박하다
  Nothing can *restrain* the boy *from* mischief.
  아무것도 그 소년이 장난하는 것을 막지 못했다.

☐ **result** [riz ʌ lt]　　　　　　　　★ ★ ★ ★ ★

- **result from** ~의 결과로 일어나다
  Disease often *results from* poverty.
  질병은 흔히 빈곤에서 일어난다.

- **result in** ~로 귀착되다, 끝나다
  The plan *resulted in* failure.
  계획은 실패로 끝났다.

☐ **rub** [r ʌ b]　　　　　　　　　　★ ★ ☆ ☆ ☆

- **rub ~ against(on, over)** 비비다, 문지르다
  She *rubbed* her glove *against* something.
  그녀는 장갑으로 뭔가를 비볐다.

run [rʌn] ★★★★★

• **run about** 뛰어다니다

Children should not be allowed to *run about* the streets.

어린이는 도로를 뛰어다니면 안 된다.

• **run across** ~을 횡단하다, 우연히 만나다

I saw a man *running across* the street.

남자가 도로를 가로질러 뛰는 걸 봤다.

I *ran across* him on the way home.

집에 오는 길에 우연히 그를 만났다.

• **run away with** ~을 가지고 달아나다, 다 써버리다

The servant *ran away with* the pearls.

하인이 진주를 가지고 달아났다.

Heavy drinking *run away with* your money.

과음하다 보면 돈을 다 쓰게 된다.

You must not *run away with* the idea that the exam will be easy.

시험이 쉬울 것이라고 속단해서는 안 된다.

• **run down** 깔다, 쇠퇴하다, 멎다(=stop), 시골에 가다

An old man was *run down* and killed by a truck.

노인이 트럭에 깔려 죽었다.

• **run for** 입후보하다

He will *run for* Parliament.

그는 의회에 입후보할 것이다.

• **run into** ~와 충돌하다, ~에 이르다

The two cars *ran into* each other.

차 두 대가 서로 충돌했다.

The book will soon *run into* ten editions.

그 책은 곧 10판을 거듭하게 될 것이다.

R

- **run out of** ~이 떨어지다

  We have *run out of* sugar.

  설탕이 떨어졌다.

- **run over** (차가) 치다

  The old man was *run over* and immediately was taken to hospital.

  그 노인은 차에 치여 곧 병원으로 후송되었다.

- **run through** 대강 보다, 찌르다, 지우다, 다 써버리다

  The actor *ran through* the script.

  그 배우는 대본을 대강 보았다.

- **run up** (가격이) 급등하다

  Prices have *run up* remarkably.

  가격이 엄청나게 올랐다.

- **run up to** ~에 이르다(=amount to)

  His debts had *run up to* more than a hundred dollars.

  그의 부채는 100달러 이상으로 늘어났다.

□ **salt** [sɔːlt]   ★ ☆ ☆ ☆ ☆

- **salt away** 저장하다, 간수하다

  Because of depression I shall have to *salt away* most of my shares.

  불경기이므로 나는 증권의 대부분을 보유해 두어야만 될 것 같다.

□ **save** [seiv]   ★ ★ ☆ ☆ ☆

- **save A for B** B를 위해 A를 저축하다

  He is *saving* money *for* his old age.

  그는 노년에 대비하여 돈을 저축하고 있다.

- **save A from B** A를 B에서 구하다

  He *saved* her *from* being drowned.

  그는 물에 빠진 그녀를 구해줬다.

418

☐ **say** [sei] ★ ★ ★ ★ ★

• **say one's say** 하고 싶은 말을 하다

Say your say.

그래, 네가 하고픈 말을 해봐.

• **as much as to say** ~라고 말하는 듯이(=as if saying)

She shrugged her shoulders *as much as to say* "How stupid!"

"바보같이!"라고 말하는 듯이 그녀는 어깨를 으쓱해 보였다.

• **It goes without saying** ~는 말할 나위도 없다

It goes without saying all is not gold that glitters.

반짝거린다고 모두 다 금이 아니라는 것은 말할 필요도 없다.

• **not to say** ~라고는 말할 수 없지만

She is very clever, *not to say* cunning.

그녀는 교활하다고는 말할 수 없지만, 무척 영리하다.

• **that is to say** 즉, 바꿔 말하면

Father went to see his sister, *that is to say*, my aunt.

아버지는 자신의 누이동생, 즉 나의 고모를 만나러 갔다.

• **so to say** 말하자면(=so to speak)

He is, *so to say*, a great big baby.

그는 말하자면 커다란 아이다

• **let us say** 이를테면

Anyone, *let us say* a child, could do it.

누구나, 이를테면 어린애라도 할 수 있을 것이다.

• **to say nothing of** ~는 물론이려니와

She can speak French, *to say nothing of* English.

그녀는 영어는 물론이려니와, 불어도 말할 수 있다.

• **to say the least of it** 줄잡아 말한다 해도

He is in possession of ten million won, *to say the least of it*.

적게 잡아 말한다 해도, 그는 천만 원은 가지고 있다.

S

☐ school [sku:l]　　　★ ☆ ☆ ☆ ☆

- **school A to B** A에게 B를 가르치다

  School yourself *to* patience.

  참을성을 길러라.

☐ scold [skould]　　　★ ★ ☆ ☆ ☆

- **scold A for B** B를 이유로 A를 꾸짖다

  He *scolded* his son *for* being out until late.

  그는 늦게까지 밖에 있었다는 이유로 아들을 꾸짖었다.

☐ season [síːzn]　　　★ ★ ☆ ☆ ☆

- **season A to B** A를 B에 적응시키다

  The soldiers were not yet *seasoned to* the rigorous climate.

  군인들은 아직까지 혹독한 기후에 적응되어 있지 않았다.

- **season A with B** B로 A의 맛을 더하다

  He *seasoned* the beef *with* ginger.

  그는 쇠고기에 생강을 넣어 풍미를 더했다.

☐ see [si:]　　　★ ★ ★ ★ ★

- **see about** ~를 고려하다, 조사하다, ~의 조치를 하다

  I'll *see about* it.

  그것을 어떻게 해 봅시다.

- **see after** ~을 돌보다(=look after, attend on)

  I'll *see after* your children.

  내가 네 아이들을 봐주겠다.

- **see into** ~을 조사하다

  Let's *see into* the cause of the trouble.

  문제의 원인을 알아보자.

- **see off** 전송하다

  I saw her *off* at the door.
  그녀를 현관까지 배웅했다.

- **see out** 끝까지 보다, 현관까지 바래다주다

  We *saw* the play *out*.
  연극을 끝까지 보았다.

- **see over** 살피다, 둘러보다

  He *saw over* the plantation several times a week.
  일주일에 몇 차례 농장을 둘러보았다.

- **seeing that** ~인 것을 보면, ~이므로(=since)

  Seeing that newspapermen come to see him one after another, he may be appointed minister.
  신문 기자가 계속 그에게 몰려오는 것을 보면, 장관에 임명될지도 모른다.

- **see through** ~을 간파하다, ~을 도와서 극복케 하다

  He is able to *see through* a person.
  그는 사람 됨됨이를 꿰뚫어 볼 줄 안다.

  I'll see you *through*.
  내가 계속 너의 힘이 되어 주마.

- **see to** ~에 유의하다, 처리하다

  I'll see to the patient.
  내가 그 환자를 처리하겠다.

- **see to it that** 틀림없이 ~하도록 하다

  I'll see to it that the parcel will reach him by the end of this month.
  이 달 말까지 소포가 그에게 틀림없이 도착하도록 하겠다.

□ **segregate** [sègrigéit]   ★☆☆☆☆

- **segregate A from B** A를 B로부터 격리하다

  They *segregated* sick children *from* the rest of the group.
  그들은 병든 아이들을 나머지 아이들로부터 격리시켰다.

S

☐ **send** [send]　　　　　　　　　　★ ★ ★ ★ ★

● **send away** 떠나보내다, 해고하다(=dismiss)

We *sent away* boats to the rescue.
우리들은 구조를 위해 보트를 떠나보냈다.

● **send for** ~를 부르러 보내다

You should *send for* the baggage without delay.
당장 그 짐을 가져오게 해야 한다.

She was *sent for* down.
그녀는 아래층으로 내려오라는 부름을 받았다.

● **send forth** 내다, 말하다(=emit)

Trees *sending forth* twigs and branches make cool shade.
가지를 펴고 있는 나무들은 신선한 나무 그늘을 만든다.

● **send in** 제출하다(=present)

Send in your paper.
답안지를 내시오.

● **send off** 발송하다, 전송하다(=see off)

Please *send off* this luggage at once.
이 화물을 곧 내어 달라.

● **send out** 내다(=despatch), 발하다(=emit)

Flowers *sent out* fragrance.
꽃은 향기를 발산한다.

● **send round** 돌리다

After service was over, a hat was *sent round*.
예배가 끝나면, 모자가 돌려졌다.

● **send up** 올리다(=raise), 제출하다(=present)

The Government prohibited to *send up* prices.
정부는 가격인상을 금지시켰다.

□ **sentence** [séntəns]　　　　　★ ☆ ☆ ☆ ☆

● **sentence A to B** A에게 B를 선고하다

He was *sentenced to* death.

그는 사형선고를 받았다.

□ **set** [set]　　　　　★ ★ ★ ★ ★

● **set about** ~하기 시작하다(=start)

He *set about* his work.

그는 일에 착수했다.

● **set apart** 따로 떼어놓다(=reserve)

She *sets apart* some of her salary for her wedding.

그녀는 결혼을 위해 월급의 일부를 떼어놓는다.

● **set aside** 제거하다, 저축하다(=save)

Set aside some money for the future.

장래에 대비해서 돈을 약간 남겨둬라.

● **set down A as B** A를 B로 규정·생각하다

I *set* him *down as* a professional boxer.

나는 그를 프로복서라고 생각한다.

● **set forth** 발표하다

The theory has been *set forth* in his recent book.

그 이론은 그의 최근 저서에 발표되어 있다.

● **set in** 시작하다(=begin)

An atomic bomb was *set in* over Hiroshima.

원자폭탄이 히로시마의 상공에서 폭발했다.

● **set out** 착수하다

He *set out* to educate the public.

그는 대중 교육에 손을 대었다.

● **set up** 세우다, 시작하다, 주장하다, 뽐내다

He *set up* for a great scholar.

그는 대학자로 뽐내고 있다.

S

423

□ share [ʃɛər] ★★☆☆☆

• **share A with B** A를 B와 공유하다

I *shared* a room *with* my brother.

나는 동생과 방을 같이 쓴다.

□ shelter [ʃéltər] ★☆☆☆☆

• **shelter A from B** A를 B에서 보호하다

The wall *shelters* the house *from* the north wind.

벽이 가옥을 북풍으로부터 지켜준다.

□ show [ʃou] ★★★★★

• **show off** 과시하다

This swimsuit will *show off* your figure.

이 수영복은 당신의 몸매를 돋보이게 할 것이다.

• **show oneself** 임석하다, 나타나다

The queen *showed herself* on the balcony.

여왕은 발코니에 모습을 드러냈다.

• **show up** 대조적으로 눈에 띄다

Her hair *showed up* against the sky.

그녀의 머리는 하늘과 대비되어 눈에 띄었다.

□ shrink [ʃriŋk] ★☆☆☆☆

• **shrink from** ~을 꺼리다

She *shrinks from* meeting people.

그녀는 사람들과 대면을 꺼린다.

□ **side** [said]　　　　　　　　　　　★☆☆☆☆

- side with ~의 편을 들다(↔ side against)

  He always *sides with* the strongest party.

  그는 늘 강자 편을 든다.

□ **sit** [sit]　　　　　　　　　　　　★☆☆☆☆

- sit up 자지 않고 ~하다

  He *sat up* at work all night.

  그는 밤새도록 일을 하였다.

□ **speak** [spiːk]　　　　　　　　　　★★★★★

- speak for ~을 변호하다

  I am *speaking for* the neighbors who are not here.

  나는 여기 부재중인 이웃사람들을 변호하고 있다.

- speak of ~에 관해서 말하다

  Speak of the devil, and he's sure to come.

  호랑이도 제 말을 하면 온다.

- strictly speaking 엄밀히 말하면

  Strictly speaking, she is ten years and seven months old.

  엄밀히 말하면 그녀는 열 살하고 7개월이다.

- speak to ~에게 말을 걸다, ~을 확증하다

  I'll *speak to* you about that matter.

  그 문제에 관해 말해주겠다.

  I can *speak to* his having been here.

  나는 그가 그 장소에 있었음을 확증할 수 있다.

- speak well of ~을 칭찬하다(↔speak ill of)

  Everybody *speaks well of* him.

  모두가 그를 칭찬한다.

S

- **to speak of** (부정구문으로) 말할 가치가 있는, 중요한
  That's nothing *to speak of*.
  언급할 만한 것이 없다.

□ **specialize** [spéʃəlàiz]   ★☆☆☆☆

- **specialize in** ~을 전공하다(=major in)
  What did you *specialize in* at college?
  대학에서 뭘 전공했지?

□ **speed** [spi:d]   ★★☆☆☆

- **speed up** 속도를 늘리다, 빨라지다
  Everything is getting *speeded up*.
  만사가 달라지고 있다.

□ **split** [split]   ★☆☆☆☆

- **split A into B** A를 B로 분해하다
  They *split* a compound *into* its elements.
  그들은 화합물을 원소로 분해하였다.

□ **sport** [spɔ:rt]   ★☆☆☆☆

- **sport with** ~을 가지고 놀다
  The kitten is *sporting with* a ball.
  고양이가 공을 갖고 놀고 있다.

□ **square** [skwɛər]   ★☆☆☆☆

- **square with** ~와 일치하다
  His statement does not *square with* the facts.
  그의 발언은 사실과 일치하지 않는다.

☐ **stain** [stein] ★☆☆☆☆

- **stain A with B** A를 B로 더럽히다

He *stained* the family honor *with* a scandal.

그는 추문을 일으켜 가문의 명예를 더럽혔다.

☐ **stand** [stænd] ★★★★☆

- **stand a chance(show)** 기회가 있다, 유망하다

He doesn't *stand a chance* of winning the prize.

그는 상을 수상할 가망이 없다.

- **stand alone** 고립되다, 견줄 만한 사람이 없다

He *stood alone* among his colleagues.

그의 동료 가운데에는 그와 어깨를 나란히 할 수 있는 사람이 없었다.

- **stand by** 방관하다, ~을 돕다

I can't *stand by* and see them ill-treated.

나는 그들이 푸대접받고 있는 것을 가만히 보고만 있을 수 없다.

He always *stood by* his friends in difficult time.

그는 친구들이 어려울 때면 항상 도왔다.

- **stand for** ~을 나타내다, ~에 입후보하다, ~을 참고 견디다

"U.N." *stands for* the United Nations.

U.N.은 국제연합을 나타낸다.

Mr. White has *stood for* Parliament.

화이트 씨는 국회의원에 입후보하고 있다.

I can't *stand for* his rude behavior.

나는 그의 무례한 행동을 참을 수 없다.

- **stand on one's feet** 자립하다

He tried to *stand on his feet*.

그는 자립하려고 노력했다.

- **stand out** 두드러지다

The tall man *stand out* in the crowd.

키 큰 남자는 군중 속에서 두드러져 보인다.

- **stand to** ~을 고집하다(=stick to)

  It *stands to* reason that the firm should dismiss a dishonest clerk.

  회사가 불성실한 점원을 해고하는 것은 당연하다.

- **stand up against(for)** ~에 반항하다(호응하다)

  They *stood up against* the tyrant.

  그들은 폭군에게 반항했다.

□ **stay** [stei]   ★☆☆☆☆

- **stay up** 자지 않고 있다

  My mother *stayed up* until I got back.

  모친은 내가 돌아올 때까지 자지 않고 기다리셨다.

□ **stick** [stik]   ★★☆☆☆

- **stick to** ~을 고수하다, 지속하다

  Our discussion *stuck to* one topic.

  우리 토론은 한 가지 주제를 고수했다.

  He *sticks to* any task until he finishes it.

  그는 어떤 업무를 종료시킬 때까지 지속한다.

□ **stop** [stap]   ★★★★☆

- **stop over** 도중 하차하다

  With this ticket you may *stop over* at any intermediate station.

  이 차표로는 어느 역에나 도중 하차가 가능합니다.

- **stop at nothing** 아무 일에나 망설이지 않는다

  Once he has made up his mind, he *stops at nothing*.

  한번 이렇다 마음먹으면, 척척 해낸다.

428

☐ **strike** [straik]　　★ ★ ★ ☆ ☆

- **strike off** 떨어뜨리다, 삭제하다, 인쇄하다

  His head was *struck off*.

  그는 목을 잘리었다.

- **strike out** 시작하다, 삭제하다, 휘두르다

  They *struck out* for the shore.

  그들은 해안을 향해 헤엄치기 시작했다.

- **strike up** ~하기 시작하다(=begin)

  The band *struck up* as the Prince entered.

  황태자가 입장함과 동시에 악대는 주악을 연주하기 시작했다.

☐ **strip** [strip]　　★ ☆ ☆ ☆ ☆

- **strip ~ of** (남에게서) 빼앗다, 강탈하다

  A thief *stripped* her fingers *of* the rings.

  도둑이 그녀의 손가락에서 반지를 빼 갔다.

☐ **submit** [səbmít]　　★ ★ ☆ ☆ ☆

- **submit to** 제출하다, 복종하다(=yield to)

  The motion was *submitted to* the city council.

  그 동의안은 시의회에 제출되었다.

☐ **subordinate** [səbɔ́ːrdənət]　　★ ☆ ☆ ☆ ☆

- **subordinate A to B** A를 B의 하위에 두다

  He *subordinates* work *to* pleasure.

  그는 업무를 오락보다 하위에 둔다.

S

subscribe [səbskráib] ★ ★ ☆ ☆ ☆

- **subscribe to** ~을 신청하다, 동의하다

  I have *subscribed to* the new magazine.
  나는 새 잡지를 구독신청 했다.

  I cannot *subscribe to* that opinion.
  나는 그 의견에 동의할 수 없다.

succeed [səksíːd] ★ ★ ☆ ☆ ☆

- **succeed to** ~을 계승하다

  His only son *succeeded to* all his wealth.
  그의 유일한 아들은 전 재산을 상속받았다.

summer [sʌmər] ★ ☆ ☆ ☆ ☆

- **summer at(in)** ~에서 여름을 보내다

  They *summer at* the seashore in Switzerland.
  그들은 스위스에 있는 해변에서 여름을 보냈다.

supercede [súːpərsiːd] ★ ☆ ☆ ☆ ☆

- **supercede A by B** A를 B로 교체하다

  We must *supercede* old machines *by* new ones.
  우리는 낡은 기계를 새것으로 바꿔야 한다.

sympathize [símpəθàiz] ★ ★ ☆ ☆ ☆

- **sympathize with** ~에 동정하다, 공감하다, 찬성하다

  The poet *sympathized with* the spirit of nature.
  시인은 자연의 영기에 감응하였다.

□ **tail** [teil]   ★ ★ ☆ ☆ ☆

- **tail after** ~의 뒤를 따르다

  Many boys and girls *tailed after* the circus procession.
  수많은 소년소녀들이 서커스 행렬을 뒤따랐다.

□ **take** [teik]   ★ ★ ★ ★ ★

- **take after** ~을 닮다

  Henry *takes after* his mother.
  헨리는 모친을 닮았다.

- **take apart** 분해하다(=disassemble)

  The child *took* the clock *apart*.
  아이는 시계를 분해했다.

- **take a turn for the better** 호전되다

  After the depression, he *took a turn for the better*.
  침체기 후 그는 호전되었다.

- **take away** 치우다

  Please *take away* these pencils.
  이 연필들을 치우세요.

- **take away one's breath** 깜짝 놀라게 하다

  The unexpected gift *took away my breath*.
  뜻밖의 선물로 나는 깜짝 놀랐다.

- **take care of** ~을 돌보다(=care for)

  She always *takes care of* the children.
  그녀는 늘 그 아이들을 돌본다.

- **take charge of** ~을 맡다

  He *took charge of* the business.
  그는 사업을 떠맡았다.

- **take down a peg** 콧대를 꺾다

  The mistakes *took* her *down a peg*.
  그 실수로 그녀의 코가 납작해졌다.

S
T

- **take A for B** A를 B로 착각하다

  He *took* me *for* an American.
  그는 나를 미국인으로 착각했다.

- **take in** 숙박시키다, 구경하다, 이해하다, 속이다

  Can you *take* me *in* for a few days?
  나를 며칠 묵게 해줄 수 있니?

  While in New York, he *took in* the World's Fair.
  뉴욕에 머무는 동안 그는 세계박람회를 구경했다.

  Give me time to *take in* the whole situation.
  사태전반을 파악하게끔 시간을 좀 주시오.

  She told the lie so well that I was easily *taken in*.
  그녀가 어찌나 거짓말을 잘했던지, 난 쉽게 속아넘어갔다.

- **take A into account** ~을 고려하다

  We must *take* it *into account*.
  우리는 그것을 고려해야 한다.

- **take off** 벗다, 공제하다, 폐지하다, 이륙하다

  He *took off* his hat.
  그는 모자를 벗었다.

  He *took* ten percent *off* the price.
  그는 정가에서 1할을 공제하였다.

  Two express trains will be *taken off* next month.
  내달부터 두 대의 급행열차가 없어진다.

  Four airplanes *took off* at the same time.
  비행기 네 대가 동시에 이륙했다.

- **take on** 고용하다, 맡다, ~를 지니다, 태우다, 인기를 얻다

  We are going to *take on* some additional workers.
  추가로 몇 명 더 일꾼을 고용할 예정이다.

  He *took on* extra work.
  그는 과외의 일을 맡았다.

  He *takes on* an Irish accent.
  그에게는 아일랜드식 말투가 있다.

The bus *took on* some tourists at the next stop.

버스는 다음 정류장에서 수명의 관광객을 태웠다.

His theory has *taken on* among the young scholars.

그의 학설은 소장파 학자들 사이에서 인기를 얻고 있다.

- **take one's part** ~의 편을 들다

He *took my part* in a quarrel.

그는 싸움에서 내 편을 들었다.

- **take out** 데리고 나가다, 제거하다, ~을 따다

He *took* me *out* to dinner.

그는 저녁 식사에 나를 데리고 나갔다.

She *took out* the ink stains from the blouse.

그녀는 블라우스에 묻은 잉크 자국을 제거하였다.

He *took out* a doctorate.

그는 박사학위를 땄다.

- **take over** 데려다 주다, 인수하다

He *took* me *over* to the city in his car.

그는 자기 차로 나를 시까지 데려다 주었다.

The building was *taken over* by the army.

그 건물은 군대가 접수하였다.

- **take pains** 애쓰다

He *takes* great *pains* in educating his children.

그는 자녀들을 교육시키느라 큰 고생을 했다.

- **take part in** 참가하다(=participate in)

He didn't *take part in* the meeting.

그는 모임에 참석하지 않았다.

- **take sick** 병이 들다(=become ill)

She *took sick* last week.

그녀는 지난주 병을 앓았다.

- **take the floor** 발언권을 가지다

The chairman gave me permission to *take the floor*.

의장은 내게 발언권을 허락했다.

T

- **take to** ~에 몰두하다, ~을 좋아하게 되다

  He *took to* writing after he retired from the college.
  그는 대학에서 은퇴한 후 저술에 몰두했다.

  The children *took to* each other.
  아이들은 서로가 마음에 들었다.

- **take together** 통틀어서 생각하다

  Taken together, there cannot be more than a dozen.
  통틀어서 한 타스 이상 될 리 없다.

- **take turns** 교대로 ~하다

  The children *took turns* jumping rope in the yard.
  아이들은 마당에서 교대로 줄넘기를 하였다.

- **take up** 채택하다, 정하다, 흡수하다

  A sponge will *take up* water.
  해면은 물을 빨아들인다.

□ **tease** [tiːz]   ★ ☆ ☆ ☆ ☆

- **tease A for B** A에게 B를 조르다

  My wife always *teases* me *for* new dresses.
  아내는 새 옷을 사달라고 늘 내게 조른다.

□ **tell** [tel]   ★ ★ ★ ★ ☆

- **tell of** ~에 관해서 얘기하다

  Can you *tell* me *of* a good doctor in the neighborhood?
  이 근방에서 잘 보는 의사 선생님을 아십니까?

- **tell the world** 공언·단언하다

  I can *tell the world* it's true.
  그게 진실이라고 난 단언할 수 있다.

☐ **testify** [téstəfài]　　　　　　　　★☆☆☆☆

• **testify to** ~의 증거가 되다

The excellence of Shakespeare's plays *testifies to* his genius.

셰익스피어 연극의 우수성은 그의 천재성을 증명한다.

☐ **thank** [θæŋk]　　　　　　　　★★☆☆☆

• **thank ~ for** 감사하다, 사의를 표하다

I *thank* you *for* your assistance.

당신의 도움에 감사드립니다.

☐ **think** [θiŋk]　　　　　　　　★★★★☆

• **think aloud** 독백하다, 중얼거리다

He is in the habit of *thinking aloud* it.

그는 소리를 내면서 생각하는 버릇이 있다.

• **think better of** 다시 생각하다

Now I *think better of* you.

너를 다시 봤어.

• **think fit(proper, good, right) to + V**
~하는 게 적절하다고 생각하다

I didn't *think fit to* do what he suggested.

그가 제안한 일을 하는 것이 적절하다고 생각하지 않는다.

• **think nothing of** ~을 아무렇지 않게 여기다

She seems to *think nothing of* lying.

그녀는 거짓말하는 것을 아무렇지 않게 여기는 것 같다.

• **think of** ~에 관해서 생각하다

She is *thinking* too highly *of* herself.

그녀는 지나치게 자만하고 있다.

T

- **think out** 생각해 내다, 생각해 내고야 말다

  She *thought* the matter *out*.

  그녀는 그 문제를 생각해 내고야 말았다.

- **think over** 숙고하다

  I must *think* the matter *over* before giving my answer.

  내가 대답하기 전에 문제를 숙고해야 한다.

□ **tie** [tai]　　　　　　　　　　★☆☆☆☆

- **tie the hands of** ~의 자유를 빼앗다

  The martial law *tied the hands of* the people.

  계엄령으로 국민의 자유가 송두리째 빼앗겼다.

□ **thrill** [θril]　　　　　　　　★★☆☆☆

- **thrill at** ~을 보고·듣고 오싹하다, 기쁨으로 떨리다, 감격하다

  We *thrilled at* the good news.

  우리는 희소식에 감격했다.

□ **trace** [treis]　　　　　　　　★★☆☆☆

- **trace back to** ~의 기원(원인)을 …까지 거슬러 올라가다

  Her dislike for mathematics *traces back to* experiences in her girlhood.

  그녀가 수학을 싫어하는 것은 소녀시절의 경험에서 비롯된다.

□ **treat** [tri:t]　　　　　　　　★★★☆☆

- **treat ~ to** 한턱내다, 대접하다, 향응하다

  He *treated* me *to* a bottle of beer.

  그는 나에게 맥주를 한턱냈다.

□ **triumph** [tráiəmf]　　　　　　　★☆☆☆☆

• **triumph over** ~을 이기다

They *triumphed over* the Egyptians.

그들은 이집트인을 꺾었다.

□ **trouble** [trʌbl]　　　　　　　★★★★☆

• **trouble oneself about** ~을 걱정하다

She doesn't *trouble herself about* her household.

그녀는 집안 살림을 걱정하지 않는다.

• **trouble ~ with** 괴롭히다, 난처하게 하다, 걱정시키다

The child *troubles* his mother *with* embarrassing questions.

그 애는 난처한 질문으로 그의 어머니를 괴롭혔다.

□ **try** [trai]　　　　　　　★★★★★

• **try on** 한 번 입어보다, ~을 속이다

I can't really see how this dress suits me until I *try* it *on*.

가봉해서 입어 보기 전에는 이 옷이 내게 맞는지 잘 모르겠어요.

It's no good *trying* it *on* with me.

그런 수작으로 나를 속이려 해도 소용없어.

• **try out** 시험해 보다

This project is apparently good but we must *try* it *out*.

이 계획은 좋을 듯이 보이지만, 시험을 해 보아야만 한다.

T

□ **turn** [tə:rn]   ★ ★ ★ ★ ★

- **turn against** ~을 적대시하다, 거역하다

  He *turned against* his motherland.
  그는 조국을 배신했다.

- **turn away from** 얼굴을 ~에서 돌리다

  She *turned away from* them in embarrassment.
  그녀는 당황하여 그들에게서 얼굴을 돌렸다.

- **turn back** 발길을 돌리다(=return)

  Because of the deep snow we had to *turn back*.
  깊은 눈길 때문에 우리는 발길을 돌려야 했다.

- **turn down** 거절하다(=reject)

  She *turned down* every suitor.
  그녀는 모든 구혼자에게 퇴짜를 놓았다.

- **turn into** ~로 변하다, ~로 바꾸다

  It looks as if it would *turn into* rain.
  아무래도 비가 올 것 같은 느낌이야.

- **turn off** 끄다(↔ turn on)

  She *turned off* the television.
  그녀는 TV를 껐다.

- **turn on** 켜다, ~을 공격하다

  He *turned* the lights *on*.
  그는 등을 켰다.

  The dog suddenly *turned on* the owner.
  그 개는 갑자기 주인에게 덤벼들었다.

- **turn one's back** 무시하다(=ignore)

  She *turned her back* on him when he asked for help.
  그가 도움을 청했을 때 그녀는 이를 무시하였다.

- **turn out** 쫓겨나다, 생산하다, ~임이 판명되다

  If you don't pay rent, you'll be *turned out* into the street.
  집세를 내지 않으면 당신은 거리로 쫓겨날 것이다.

The factory *turns out* thirty thousand cars a year.
그 공장은 연간 3만 대의 차량을 만들어 낸다.

The plan *turned out* to have had no effect.
그 계획은 어떤 효과도 가져올 수 없었음이 판명되었다.

• **turn over** 뒤집다, 숙고하다
The waves *turned* our boat *over*.
파도가 우리 배를 뒤집어 버렸다.

Let me *turn* the matter *over* for a few days.
그 문제를 숙고할 수 있게끔 며칠간 시간을 주시오.

• **turn over a new leaf** 개심하여 생활을 일신하다
He has *turned over a new leaf* since he was
released from prison.
교도소에서 석방되고부터 그는 새 사람이 되었다.

• **turn the tables** 정세를 일변시키다
The tables have been turned in favor of our side.
정세는 일변하여 우리쪽이 유리하게 되었다.

• **turn to** 찾아보다
He always *turns to* a dictionary for guidance.
그는 지도를 위해 늘 사전을 찾아본다.

• **turn to A for B** A에 B를 청하다
I *turn to* literature *for* consolation.
나는 문학에서 위안을 구한다.

• **turn up** 나타나다(=show up, appear)
She *turned up* an hour later.
그녀는 한 시간 후에 나타났다.

T U

☐ **umpire** [ʌmpaiər] ★☆☆☆☆

• **umpire between** ~사이를 중재하다
Mr. Smith was asked to *umpire between* the two
parties.
스미스 씨는 양측의 중재역할을 의뢰 받았다.

□ **unfold** [ʌnfóuld] ★☆☆☆☆

- **unfold A to B** A를 B에게 표명하다, 털어놓다
  He *unfolded* his plans *to* her.
  그는 그녀에게 자기 계획을 털어놓았다.

□ **unite** [juːnáit] ★★☆☆☆

- **unite ~ with** (성질, 재능 따위를) 함께 지니다, 겸비하다
  He *unites*[combines] ability *with* courage.
  그는 재능과 용기를 겸비하고 있다.

□ **up** [ʌp] ★★★☆☆

- **up and + V** 갑자기 ~하다
  The fool *upped and* died.
  바보가 갑자기 죽었다.

  He *upped and* married a show girl.
  그는 갑자기 여배우와 결혼했다.

□ **use** [juːs] ★★★☆☆

- **use up** 다 써버리다, 지치다
  The soldiers had *used up* all their supplies.
  병사들은 보급품을 전부 소비했다.

  He was pretty well *used up* by walking.
  그는 걸어 다녀서 상당히 지쳤다.

□ **vaccinate** [vǽksənèit] ★☆☆☆☆

- **vaccinate A against B** A에게 B에 대한 예방주사를 놓다
  He is *vaccinated against* typhus.
  그는 티푸스 예방주사를 맞았다.

440

□ **vary** [véəri]   ★☆☆☆☆

• **vary with** ~에 따라 다르다

The prices *vary with* the size.

값은 크기에 따라 다르다.

□ **venture** [véntʃər]   ★☆☆☆☆

• **venture on** 위험을 무릅쓰고 ~하다

He *ventured on* an ambitious project.

그는 야심찬 계획을 위험을 무릅쓰고 시도했다.

□ **verge** [vəːrdʒ]   ★★☆☆☆

• **verge on** ~에 인접하다, 거의 ~이 되려 하다

The path *verges on* the edge of a precipice.

그 길은 벼랑 가장자리에 인접해 있다.

He is *verging on* ruin.

그는 거의 파멸상태에 있다.

□ **visit** [vízit]   ★★☆☆☆

• **visit with** ~와 이야기(잡담)하다

He *visited with* his friend over the phone.

그는 전화로 친구와 잡담하였다.

□ **vote** [vout]   ★★★☆☆

• **vote for** 찬성투표를 하다(↔ vote against)

He *voted for* the measure.

그는 그 의안에 찬성투표를 하였다.

□ **wage** [weidʒ] ★☆☆☆☆

- **wage A against B** B에 맞서 A를 수행하다

  The physicians have *waged* war *against* cancer.

  의사들은 암과 전쟁을 치렀다.

□ **wait** [weit] ★★★☆☆

- **wait on** 시중들다(=attend on)

  He *waits on* his wife hand and foot.

  그는 하나부터 열까지 아내를 돌봐준다.

□ **warn** [wɔːrn] ★★☆☆☆

- **warn ~ of** 경고하다, 조심시키다

  The teacher *warned* the boy *of* coming late to school.

  선생님은 그 소년에게 지각하지 말라고 경고했다.

□ **wash** [waʃ] ★☆☆☆☆

- **wash one's hands** 화장실 가다

  Where can I *wash my hands*?

  화장실은 어디죠?

□ **wear** [wɛər] ★★☆☆☆

- **wear down** 극복하다, 버티다

  They *wore down* the enemy's resistance.

  그들은 적의 저항을 견뎠다.

□ **weary** [wíəri]　　　　　　　　　　★☆☆☆☆

- **weary of** ~에 싫증나다, 피로하다, 싫어지다

  Weary of living all alone.

  혼자 사는 것이 싫어진다.

□ **wink** [wiŋk]　　　　　　　　　　★☆☆☆☆

W

- **wink at** ~에 눈짓하다, 눈감아 주다(=overlook)

  The girl *winked at* him.

  그녀는 그에게 윙크했다.

  He *winked at* her faults.

  그는 그녀의 잘못을 눈감아 주었다.

□ **withdraw** [wiðdrɔ́ː]　　　　　　　★★☆☆☆

- **withdraw from** ~에서 철수하다

  The American Army *withdrew from* the Korean peninsula finally.

  미군은 마침내 한반도에서 철수했다.

□ **work** [wəːrk]　　　　　　　　　　★★★★☆

- **work on** ~에 작용하다, 착수하다(=act on)

  It *works on* the curiosity of children.

  그것은 아이들의 호기심을 불러일으킨다.

- **work out** 만들어 내다, 풀다(=accomplish)

  You should *work out* the problem of life by yourself.

  인생문제는 자기 스스로 해결해 나가지 않으면 안 된다.

- **work up** 점차로 만들어 내다, 흥분시키다

  Things were *worked up* to a climax.

  사태는 점차로 절정에 다가가고 있다.

443

☐ **wrestle** [résl] ★ ☆ ☆ ☆ ☆

- **wrestle with** ~와 고투하다

  They had to *wrestle with* a difficult problem.

  그들은 난제와 씨름해야 했다.

☐ **yield** [ji:ld] ★ ★ ★ ★ ☆

- **yield to** 굴복하다, 따르다

  I will never *yield to* such a demand.

  그런 요구에 결코 굴복하지 않겠다.

  His disease will not *yield to* any cure.

  그의 병은 어떤 치료를 해도 낫지 않을 것이다.